McGRAW-HILL SERIES IN SPEECH

Clarence T. Simon, *Consulting Editor*

Basic Voice Training for Speech

McGraw-Hill Series in Speech

CLARENCE T. SIMON, *Consulting Editor*

ARMSTRONG AND BRANDES · The Oral Interpretation of Literature

BAIRD · American Public Addresses

BAIRD · Argumentation, Discussion, and Debate

BAIRD · Discussion: Principles and Types

BAIRD AND KNOWER · Essentials of General Speech

BAIRD AND KNOWER · General Speech

BLACK AND MOORE · Speech: Code, Meaning, and Communication

CARRELL AND TIFFANY · Phonetics

HAHN, LOMAS, HARGIS, AND VANDRAEGEN · Basic Voice Training for Speech

KAPLAN · Anatomy and Physiology of Speech

KRUGER · Modern Debate

LONEY · Briefing and Conference Techniques

OGILVIE · Speech in the Elementary School

POWERS · Fundamentals of Speech

VAN DUSEN · Training the Voice for Speech

Basic Voice Training for Speech

ELISE HAHN   CHARLES W. LOMAS

DONALD E. HARGIS   DANIEL VANDRAEGEN

University of California at Los Angeles

SECOND EDITION

McGRAW-HILL BOOK COMPANY, INC.

New York   Toronto   London

1957

BASIC VOICE TRAINING FOR SPEECH

IX
25505

Preface

The revised edition of *Basic Voice Training for Speech* retains the same focus which characterized the first edition. It is student centered; it integrates theory with practice; it stresses the importance of listening as a prime factor in personal improvement; it contends that basic voice training is equally important to students interested in public speaking, interpretation, acting, or speech correction. In fact, the revision has been designed to intensify the emphasis of the first edition on these basic concepts. Most of the chapters have been extensively rewritten in terms of our experience with the book and on the advice of others who have used it. We have tried to sharpen passages which have seemed difficult for students to comprehend, and to add to exercises which have proved effective in practice. The integration of theory with practice has been carried a step further than in the first edition. Information on the physics of sound, formerly in the chapter "How Sound Is Produced in Speech," has been transferred to the appropriate sections of chapters on breathing, tone production, and resonation. The chapter on integration of vocal skills has been moved to the end of the book in order to include articulation as one of the skills to be developed.

A considerable number of new selections for practice have been added, many of them from recent authors, while those we found most useful in the first edition have been retained. As in the first edition, we have made no effort to present a comprehensive anthology of reading selections, but have tried to present some material which we believe will help students at each step in the development of their vocal skills. Frequent references in the text suggest selections in the Appendix which may prove useful at the point of reference.

We have drawn upon comments by scores of persons in preparing the revision. Naturally, members of the speech staff at the University of California at Los Angeles have contributed the most since we were able to discuss problems with them in person. Because it is impossible to thank all of those who have contributed to our thinking, this general acknowledgement must suffice.

Elise Hahn
Charles W. Lomas
Donald E. Hargis
Daniel Vandraegen

Contents

1

Critical Listening and Self-analysis

But if you mouth it, as many of your players do, I had as lief the town-crier spoke my lines.—SHAKESPEARE

To Shakespeare's Hamlet, the town crier was the personification of unintelligent, indifferent, and meaningless speech. The monotony of his voice and its lack of clear and understandable articulation were symbols of his indifference to his material and his disinterest in his hearers. But we do not need to be town criers—or players—to have "town-crier" voices.

Listen to the students around you. You may find, for instance, that one student has attracted your interest. You know that he is an athlete and, by his general manner and appearance, you judge him to be sure of himself and successful in whatever he undertakes. Yet as he starts to talk, your opinion of him changes. Instead of a deep and resonant voice coming from his big frame, you hear a high-pitched, thin tone. Moreover, his words come tumbling out at a rapid rate that makes them difficult to understand, because many small syllables and words are omitted.

Again, you may think that you want to make friends with the girl who sits next to you in class, but you lose interest when you talk together. What she has to say may have no bearing on your reaction to her, but how she says it is not attractive. From her whining nasal voice, you conclude that she is complaining and self-centered. You may find that you make a broad generalization about her entire personality on the basis of her speech alone.

When you become better acquainted with both of these students, you may realize that they have compensating personality traits. You may gradually discount your first criticism and even forget that you made it as you get used to their manner of speaking. However, there are many occasions when you do not take the time to establish a sympathetic relationship with others; your initial judgment, right or wrong, is allowed to stand.

As you listen to a person in the college classroom or in business and social situations, you are inclined to accept him and attend to his ideas if he is pleasant to hear and easy to understand. If his speech habits interfere with his communication or cause you to feel uncomfortable in any way, you may reject his ideas, overlook his assets, and react negatively to his personality.

Many of the specific judgments you make about a speaker are on a sound basis. For instance, speech can give you clues to the speaker's early environment: his education, race, and socioeconomic level. From his voice you may detect how a speaker feels about himself: assured, uncertain, proud, self-effacing. In the same way you may know how he feels toward others: friendly, defensive, sympathetic, aggressive, indifferent. Moreover, at the moment of speaking he may be displaying or hiding his emotions about the subject under discussion; you judge him on this, too.

But you yourself are judged by other people, and by the same standards you apply to them. You may have acquired considerable skill in the use of your voice through the process of unconscious imitation and of trial and error. Yet you may be aware that you sometimes have a "town-crier" voice —that you are not always equally effective in communicating your ideas and feelings to others. Many an average speaker will say, "I can argue with a friend. Why can't I convince a *group* of people that I believe in what I am saying?"; or, "I sound interested and enthusiastic when I talk at home. Why can't I always sound that way?"; or again, "I'm sure I can read aloud with meaning or act a scene when I am alone. Why can't I make an audience respond to me?"; or in still another situation, "My voice sounds strong and vital when I practice my speeches. What happens to it when I deliver my speech to the class?"

Of course, there may be many answers. The influence of your emotions may distort your speech; habits of speech which served you well in one situation may not be adapted to a new occasion; you may be using a pattern of speech appropriate to an earlier level of growth but no longer suitable to your age and education.

If you wish to improve your communication, you must know what your present speaking skills are, how you can vary them to suit specific purposes and situations, and what faults or emotional obstacles stand in the way of your further development as a speaker. These suggestions may sound reasonable as you read them, but there are serious barriers to undertaking this analysis.

BARRIERS TO OBJECTIVE ANALYSIS

Resistance to Change

As a small child, when you first started to talk, you listened and watched intently as the people around you spoke together. By imitating, you learned new words, more complex structuring of the language, communicative gestures and facial expressions, and ways of changing pitch, loudness, and timing to express meanings. When your speech seemed to meet the demands of your particular life situation, the acquisition of new skills began to slow down. You now had vocal habits which suited your needs; at seven or eight, these habits of communication—because of constant repetition and relative effectiveness—were becoming more and more fixed.

As you progressed into new life situations, you gradually added new speech skills, usually in imitation of people whom you admired. At the present time, your manner of speaking represents a very complex structure of habits.

Any indication that even one of the habits in this complex structure may need changing is likely to produce an emotional response. You may, for instance, believe that you cannot look at your listeners because this will make you forget your ideas. You feel that you cannot slow down because you will then sound dull. You may argue against modifying your wide and abrupt inflections because you believe that they contribute to your animation, or, on the other hand, you may feel that slight variations in pitch and loudness sound affected. In your conclusions about your own speech, you will link certain of your habits with some of your skills in communication. You will be unable at first to divorce the poor and ineffective behaviors from those which are highly effective. You may unconsciously believe that speech is only "good" or "poor" rather than a complex of habits, some of which are skilled and some inadequate. Believing this, you may be unaware of the fact that individual aspects of your speech can be isolated, analyzed, practiced consciously, improved, and then incorporated as new habits into your daily communication.

You may resist an analysis of your speech for emotional reasons. Because any criticism of your voice strikes too closely to your concept of yourself, you may be defensive even when helpful suggestions are given. If someone tells you that the tone of your voice sounds strident, you bristle: "If you don't like it, don't listen." Or you may rationalize: "I was tired at the time. I didn't like the people. I didn't feel like talking anyway." In this way, you protect yourself from both criticism and improvement. You think of your speech, quite correctly, as an intimate part of your personality. Criticism shakes not only your belief in yourself as a speaker, but your faith in yourself as an effective individual. If you can find no way of nullifying the criticism, you may, as a last resort, turn on the critic with the irrelevant remark, "You're not so good yourself." Consequently, you may never really have analyzed your skills and shortcomings as a speaker. You would much rather have your faith in yourself unshaken.

Failure to Listen Critically

Throughout your schooling, your attention has been directed toward the examination of content: What did the story say? What was the man's idea? What event did the play depict? Both style of writing and delivery in speaking have been neglected.

In a particular listening situation, you may have failed to grasp the speaker's idea. You then concluded that the idea itself was valueless, was poorly defined and organized, or finally, that the manner of delivering the idea was ineffective. Your judgment will frequently stop here. You do not ask: Why was the delivery ineffective? Could everyone hear and understand what was said? Was the speaker's voice pleasant and conducive to rapt attention? Was it flexible enough to convey shades of meaning to you? These critical questions were not formulated; you said only that his speech was poor.

Often, if the reputation of the speaker is good, or you are predisposed to like a person because mutual friends have influenced you, you may dispense with all critical judgment. In certain listening situations, such as a lecture in a classroom or a sermon in church, you may hear only fragments of the talk, adopting actual habits of inattentiveness.

All those factors which prevent or minimize listening, or which condition you to accept ideas unquestioningly, build up poor listening habits. The analysis of your own speech and that of the people around you may seem difficult. You are accustomed to listen only for content; now you are asked to attend to both content and delivery.

LEARNING TO LISTEN

You will not acquire an ability to analyze speaking habits by listening passively. Like any other skill, listening ability can be developed only by constant attention and practice. Every minute of hearing others speak can be made a conscious part of your drill in listening. You will hear many types of speakers around you: professors lecturing to their classes, preachers, political speakers, radio announcers, workmen, bus drivers, and actors—and you can eavesdrop without a pang of conscience in bus, store, or cafeteria. Some of the speakers you hear will have better speech than your own; some will have poorer. You can profit from listening critically to both.

But it is not enough simply to hear different voices and to watch different speakers. You must have a method of analyzing their speech behaviors.

Consider for a moment some of the voices you may have heard during your last week end at home. On Saturday afternoon, your small brother burst into the room and excitedly described how his team won the ball game on a home run in the last inning with two men out and the count three and two. He spoke rapidly in a high-pitched, shrill voice that rang throughout the house. In fact, you tried to calm him down so that you could understand him better. Yet if he had entered quietly and given a sedate and exact description of those tense moments, would you have given him so much attention?

On Sunday morning you went to church with your family. The preacher read from the Bible in a clear, strong voice. His rate was slow, but he varied it to bring out the meaning of the words. You were impressed as he read, "And God said, 'Let there be light.' And there was light." That afternoon you returned to the campus just in time to sit in on a "bull session." As usual, everyone wanted to talk at once, and the louder, shriller voices dominated the argument, but you were unconvinced—perhaps even hostile. In the evening you took your girl to the beach, and a different quality of voice proved effective.

Assuming that each of these speakers had something interesting and worthwhile to say, and that he organized his ideas and chose his words well, the effectiveness of his speech was determined in large part by his vocal skills. Your problem is now to analyze the function of voice in the entire communicative act, ascertaining what aspects contributed to the speaker's effectiveness and what interfered with his communication. The basic aspects to which you will attend will be the speaker's loudness, his timing, his pitch, his tone quality, and the distinctness of his articulation.

1. *Loudness.* Was the level of the speaker's loudness adequate to the conditions of listening? Was it appropriate to the idea he wished to convey and to the mood of the listeners? Did he vary it to communicate his changing attitudes toward his ideas and to emphasize important words?

2. *Timing.* Did the speaker talk so rapidly that he could not be understood readily, or so slowly that he sounded dull? Did the rate suit the listen-

ing situation—the size of the room, the number of listeners, and the acoustic conditions? Was the timing appropriate to the idea and the mood? Were some words spoken slowly, for emphasis, or faster, to indicate movement or excitement? Did the phrasing of the material show clearly the relationships between ideas, and did the use of pauses emphasize important points and permit the audience to think and respond? Were the pauses too long and too frequent?

3. *Pitch.* Was the pitch too high or too low for the age, sex, and body build of the speaker? Was it varied in such a way as to select and emphasize the important ideas? Did the pitch changes reflect the feelings inherent in what was said?

4. *Quality.* Was the voice pleasant to listen to, or did it sound strained? Was it full and resonant? Was it harsh, nasal, hoarse, or strident? Were there vocal qualities which made you resent the speaker rather than accept his ideas? Did the tone quality reflect the speaker's emotions?

5. *Distinctness of articulation.* Did the speaker run his words together, distorting or omitting some of the sounds? On the other hand, did he over-articulate, breaking up phrases and losing the natural smoothness of the flow of language? Were his vowel and consonant sounds acceptable in production? Did you recognize them easily, or were they different from those used by the best speakers in your community?

It is unlikely that you will bother to analyze any of these elements in your tête-à-tête at the beach, and we have no wish to spoil your evening. But in retrospect, you may discover that part of your satisfaction or lack of enjoyment in a social situation may lie in your unconscious reaction to the voices of those around you. Similarly, in the more formal speaking occasion, you may willingly accept or sharply reject the speaker or reader because of his habits of communication.

As you begin to analyze voices in all possible situations, you will perceive more and more how the skilled speaker adjusts his loudness, timing, pitch, tone quality, and distinctness of articulation to meet the needs of the speaking environment, to suit the type of material and the kind of audience, to reflect his emotions, and to enhance his purposes in speaking. You may realize that a speaker is effective in all aspects of delivery but one, or perhaps believe that if he improved one thing, his whole speech could then develop in a more satisfactory fashion. You may suddenly want to suggest to him, "Slow down. Pick up speed here. Give us some pauses. Speak more loudly. Drop the pitch." Then you realize that he, like you, would resent such a bombardment of criticism. But you discover now that your awareness of speaking habits has increased greatly. You are ready to assess your own skills and faults.

A PLAN FOR IMPROVEMENT

The material of this book will be of value to you only to the extent that you use it to plan a systematic program of improvement of your voice. To examine your own speech habits, you will need to understand the functioning of the physical mechanisms which produce speech. Then too, you cannot acquire new vocal habits unless you have a definite desire to do so. Moreover, there must be a clear concept of the specific improvement you wish to make, and a continual check on your progress in relation to both your starting point and your goal.

Understand the Mechanism Which Produces Speech

Your speech mechanism differs from those of the persons around you. However, the general processes of speech production are basically the same for everyone. You need to understand these processes.

You may ask, "Why is it necessary to study the physiological backgrounds of speech? Isn't it perfectly possible to acquire a good voice without knowing how it is produced? Haven't there been hundreds of actors and public speakers—even teachers of speech—who didn't understand the mechanism, or who may even have had incorrect ideas about it?"

The answer is obvious. It is certainly possible. But as we acquire more and more knowledge about how voice is produced, this haphazard approach to voice training makes less and less sense. Without some knowledge of vocal physiology your chances of making improvements on your own initiative are severely limited; you may find yourself only imitating your instructor without any idea of the reason for the exercises he suggests; your ability to hear and define your own defects will be circumscribed. The intelligent approach is to know what the mechanism is, how it operates, and how to detect and change the improper use of it. This book, therefore, gives basic information on breathing, phonation, resonation, and articulation.

Develop Habits of Self-analysis

As we have noted in the preceding pages, the first step in your improvement should be the development of habits of self-analysis. But this is not a preliminary process, to be practiced at the beginning of the course and straightway forgotten. Self-examination, to be effective, must be continuous during the learning period. Throughout the book, as new problems are discussed, specific directions are given for self-analysis and listening. You must use these as they are presented, but you must also recheck yourself constantly on suggestions offered earlier. In this way you can fix the habit of listening to yourself and avoid dropping back into old habits when you have completed a semester of concentrated drill and study.

Distinguish Practice from Performance

It is difficult to establish new vocal skills in actual performance. To be effective, good vocal usage must be habitual, and in performance you must be free to direct your attention to communication rather than to the mechanical details of voice production. If you must constantly plan each step in vocalization, you cannot speak naturally, nor can you produce a voice which is free of strain and tension. The purpose of practice periods is to provide time when you can make mistakes and correct them without the social consequences of failure in performance. At the same time, we should note that appearances before the speech class are still within the practice framework. Public performances of plays or readings, public speeches, business interviews, and important social occasions should be classed as performances. Your aim should be to establish habits that will operate without effort in these situations.

Establish Automatic Control

Perhaps you can recall your first experiences in driving a car. All your attention was directed to the manipulation of the mechanical devices which kept the machine running. Probably you were tense, using more muscles and expending more nervous energy than were needed. After some experience, however, you began to relax unneeded muscles; your control over the car became a matter of automatic reflexes rather than of conscious thought, and you became a better driver in the process.

In the same way, you should learn the new motor skills involved in improving your use of the vocal mechanism. You may improve your control over new habits by learning them so thoroughly that you do not need to think about them. Thus, control becomes a matter of less attention to detail rather than more. Control need not involve tension; if good habits are thoroughly learned, you will find yourself using less physical activity than you did under your previous faulty habits of voice production.

Practice Continuously

While you are attempting to develop new vocal habits, you should, if possible, avoid public-performance situations. These often compel you to revert to your old habits. But in every other speaking situation where social pressures do not prohibit, you should practice the new skills you are seeking to establish. For example, you may tell your friends and family what you are trying to accomplish and ask them to listen to your voice in conversation, calling attention to your errors. With a little experimentation, you will find that you can practice vocal drills in time you now waste. You can practice breathing exercises while walking, phonation exercises in your shower, and articulation exercises while driving to school. So far as possible, once you have determined the nature of your new habit, you should avoid falling back into your old way of speaking in any situation whatsoever.

Concentrate on One Problem at a Time

If you have many vocal problems, do not try to remedy them all at once. With the help of your instructor determine what is most important, then concentrate on that problem, moving on to others as you begin to make substantial progress. At the same time, remember your ultimate goal—better communication in speech. Each skill you learn is a step toward that end.

SUMMARY

In the plan of this book, critical listening and self-analysis are constant tools for improvement. They are the means by which you may overcome your inertia and compel yourself to take positive steps to improve your voice. As you read the book, you should take advantage of the materials dealing with self-analysis, and apply your findings to the development of new skills.

Exercises to Improve Listening and Self-analysis

1. Listen to a public speaker talking to an audience of one hundred or more. Are his vocal habits appropriate to the situation in which he is speaking? Can he be heard without effort on your part? Do his words and phrases reach you clearly so that you can understand them easily? Is his voice pleasant to listen to? Is his voice responsive to shades of meaning in his material? As far as you are able, at this point in your training as a listener, analyze the factors which influence the answers you have given to these questions.

2. Make the same type of analysis for as many of the following situations as you are able to observe: (*a*) the actors in a play you attend; (*b*) a friend or a member of your family conversing with you in a casual situation; (*c*) a person you overhear in casual conversation on a bus, at a party, or in a

public place; (*d*) a group of children at play; (*e*) a professor lecturing in a classroom.

3. In the Columbia album *I Can Hear It Now*, Volumes I and II, listen to the voices of Will Rogers, Huey Long, Adolf Hitler, Joseph Stalin, Fiorello La Guardia, Alfred E. Smith, Franklin D. Roosevelt, Winston Churchill, Harry Truman, Thomas Dewey, Arthur Godfrey, and radio announcer Herbert Morrison describing the burning of the Hindenburg. As far as you are able to do so from the recordings, analyze these voices according to the standards set forth in Exercise 1. Some of these voices have marked faults. Are there compensating factors in the voices themselves, or would you have to know more about the speech situation and the personality of the speakers to discover why audiences were attracted to these men?

4. Make a record of your voice, preferably on one side of a disk record which you can play on your own phonograph. Part of the record should consist of reading and part of informal or extemporaneous speaking. Your instructor will help you to select suitable material. Listen to the record as if it were the voice of another person, and analyze it in the same way you did the voices in the previous exercises.

5. Keeping in mind the factors you noted in analyzing your voice recording, listen to your voice as you read aloud, as you converse with a friend, as you talk informally before the class. Can you hear the same problems?

2

Why You Speak as You Do

There is no index of the character so sure as the voice.—TANCRED

In the preceding chapter, you were urged to listen to yourself and answer the question, "What is my speech like?" To gain greater insight into your present habits, you must now come to some conclusions on the question, "Why do I speak as I do?" It may be difficult for you to answer this until you know something about the factors which influence speech development: the effects of past and present physical conditions, environment, and emotional adjustment. Then as you become conscious of these influences on the speech habits of other people, you may be ready to make a calm and objective study of the same factors in your own background as they have affected your voice.

Begin by eavesdropping on a family argument. John had decided to "talk it out" with his father. The time had come when he had to follow his own ambitions instead of the career which his father had selected for him.

As they got up from the table, John began cautiously, "Mr. Stone was saying business was good. He has a nice place there." His tone was guardedly casual.

"How do you happen to be so interested?" his father asked sharply.

"Who said I was so interested?" John asked defensively, as if to protect himself.

"You've heard he's looking for a new man, haven't you?" the older man bristled.

"Well, what if he is? I've got a right to consider my *own* future, haven't I?" All the uncertainty of John's position was marked by the high pitch and the rush of his words.

The father's voice was ominously quiet. "All I want is an explanation."

So John explained, described, and grew enthusiastic about the position open to him, trying to make the older man see his point and share his feelings.

Since this is not a story, you will never know what happened. It is only an example of the many voice changes which take place quickly in a single, brief situation. The personal relationship of the two men was quite evident, and the emotions present in the immediate situation could be judged by the tone of the voices alone, even without words. You might also have been able to tell some things about their physical and environmental backgrounds by careful observation of the men as they talked, but you probably would have needed more information than can be obtained from a single incident if you were to make a valid judgment of those influences which affect loudness, timing, pitch, quality, and articulation.

Thus, in this chapter we shall examine four factors in the speaker's background and experience which may affect his production of voice: (1) his physical structure and function, (2) his environment, both past and present, (3) his personal adjustment to his environment, and (4) the influences operating in the immediate situation. All these factors are interrelated and modify one another.

THE INFLUENCE OF PHYSICAL STRUCTURE
AND FUNCTION UPON SPEECH

To understand the influence of physical structure on your own voice, you need a quick and simplified overview of the entire vocal process.

The act of speaking employs many structures and functions of the body which were originally designed for biological purposes. There is actually no speech mechanism per se, although the term is a convenient one. The structures used in breathing, holding the breath, swallowing, chewing, and sucking have all been borrowed and somewhat modified in action so that they produce vocal tone and articulate speech. Speech is therefore called an *overlaid function*.

The vital biological needs often take precedence over speaking. Even the most garrulous gossip must stop long enough to swallow her food. The athlete finishing his race cannot speak until he stops gasping for breath. The small boy finds that he does not talk clearly when his mouth is full of bread and jam. You need to understand the concept of overlaid function to comprehend the operation of the total vocal process and to be aware of the ways in which basic functions may interfere with speaking.

As you initiate speech, the first mechanism you borrow is the breathing apparatus. The physical structures of lungs, diaphragm, ribs, and the muscles which elevate and lower the rib cage in breathing must all be functioning efficiently to give strength and steadiness to the exhalation you need for adequate voice.

As the exhaled breath stream passes out through the larynx, it vibrates the vocal folds. These folds are located in the larynx directly behind the Adam's apple; they act as a valve which can open and close with a great variety of adjustments. These folds, however, like the breathing mechanism, serve more basic functions. They protect the tube below them which goes down to the lungs; they close during swallowing or separate explosively to expel foreign matter in a cough. Their closure can trap air in the lungs so that the ribs are supported firmly while you push and pull with vigor. In the production of voice, the two inner edges of the folds come together under tension and the breath expelled from the lungs sets them into vibration. The rate and extent of this vibration affects the loudness and pitch of the tone heard by the listener.

The sound waves started by this vibration are amplified and resonated as they move up and out through the throat, mouth, and nose. In the mouth, you make amazingly fine adjustments of the jaw, lips, tongue, and soft palate, imposing a pattern of articulated sounds on the exhaled breath stream. We have been taught to interpret these sound patterns as words. These structures serving the overlaid functions of resonation and articulation are intended primarily for breathing, chewing, sucking, and swallowing.

The remarkable coordination in timing and spatial relationships of all of these movements is governed by the higher centers in the brain. Only man is capable of adapting into a complex, communicative system these muscular activities which primarily serve biological needs. Not everyone makes complete and adequate adjustments of these processes, and speech problems arise through the interference of basic functions with the selective movements necessary to skilled speaking.

As you examine your own physical structures used in speech, you will find that they are different in size and shape from those of any other individual. Consequently, your voice, though produced in the same general way as any other person's, is unique. The man next to you in class may have a powerful, deep voice. No forced lowering of your pitch is going to give you his low, resonant tone, because you may happen to have a smaller larynx and a different-sized throat and mouth. You can, however, with your particular structures, improve resonance and responsive quality at your normal pitch level, and you may develop a flexibility in usage that makes your voice more pleasant to listen to than his.

Note how the structures of the vocal mechanism can vary. Within your own class, notice differences in the size and shape of jaw, the arrangement of teeth, the development of mouth and lips, the size of larynx, and the construction of rib cage. You will not be able to see the tongue, the soft palate, and the vocal folds themselves, but after you have observed other differences, you can understand that these also may vary extensively from person to person.

These differences in the relative size and shape of structures will affect the manner in which you produce sounds, but while you may be vocalizing or articulating in a way technically different from that of your neighbor, the audible results may be good. Even pronounced differences in structure need not cause speech defects. The moving parts of the speech mechanism can make a wide variety of adjustments.

However, structural deviations may sometimes be related to poor habits of voice production. One girl will lisp because her teeth protrude; another cannot be heard because of her small mouth opening; a man may mumble because he has not learned to move his rather thick lips with agility. Sometimes the existence of former deviations in structure may have set up habits which continue even after the change in structure has been made. One girl in a speech class still held her upper lip down stiffly as if trying to hide an ugly protrusion of her teeth, although the teeth had been straightened years before.

If illness caused a prolonged state of lassitude when you were very young, you felt no inclination to use your voice in experimental vocal play and jargon, which were the necessary preparations for speech, and thus you were delayed in speaking. A student reported that, because of illness, he had not learned to talk until he was three. Because of this delay, his articulation and voice were infantile for several years after he entered school. The concern of his parents, the criticism of his teachers, and the ridicule of the children had convinced him that his speech would be habitually poor. Even at twenty, he was still painfully self-conscious of his speech, with the result that his voice was uncertain, weak, and monotonous.

Hearing loss will also affect your acquisition of speech. If as a child you did not hear accurately the high-frequency sounds of s, f, and th, you could not imitate these readily. Similarly, if you did not hear pitch and loudness differences with ease, you may have acquired a monotony of melody and loudness in your speech.

You are aware, of course, that your present physical condition influences your voice. If you are fatigued or debilitated after a recent illness, the muscles of your body do not respond quickly. Speech production is a muscular process; when the body is run down, you cannot expect the high degree of responsiveness and fine muscular coordination necessary for good voice.

To understand the way you now use your voice, you need to consider both your past and your present physical condition. Your present vocal habits may be the result of early structural deviations or of the presence of illness when you were first learning to speak. Your voice will also be affected by existing structural differences and by the present state of your health.

THE INFLUENCE OF ENVIRONMENT UPON VOICE

Home Influences

As an infant you produced an amazing variety of vocal sounds. You gradually modified and combined these into speech by imitating those around you, by trial and error, by self-imitation, and by the repetition of approved responses. Because of these processes of imitation and experimentation, members of a close family group often have the same habits of inflection, rate, or articulation and pronunciation. Young children unconsciously copy vocal patterns of parents, brothers, and sisters. Although there may be likenesses of structure among family members, these similarities in speech production are more likely to result from a common environment.

Sometimes imitation may set up habits which are not acceptable in college life. A young man whose birth into a family of four girls had once probably caused a pleasant stir discovered that his way of speaking was ridiculed. Although his voice was low-pitched and his general behavior masculine, he had a preciseness of articulation and a reserved "niceness" of manner which suggested that all five women in his family had served as models for his unconscious habits.

Sometimes imitations may be deliberate, or if not consciously pursued, may indicate an individual's need for appreciation. A girl, tall and slow moving, had attempted to copy the animated voice of her small, excitable mother. Her present speech was hesitant, with hurried broken phrases and much stridency of tone. Similarly, a boy had forced his pitch down so low, in imitation of the powerful tones of his admired lawyer-father, that he developed a chronic hoarseness. Both of these students had copied voices whose production was not suited to their particular physical structure and function.

The influence of the home upon your speech depends also upon the emotional environment provided for you as you grew up. If you competed strongly with brothers and sisters, or even with your parents, in an attempt to assert yourself, the type of speech you now habitually use may reflect the outcome of that competition. Again, the family relationships may have involved strict discipline, or extremely protective attitudes on the part of your parents, or the insecurity of confusing and little-understood conflicts in the home. Negative feeling states stirred up by interfamily relationships were reflected in physical tensions and behaviors which in turn caused you to speak in a certain way. Even though your living situation has now changed in adult life, some of your speaking habits may relate to those early emotions of aggression or submissiveness, of insecurity, of extreme dependence or independence, or of self-consciousness. Have you noticed that you now attempt to dominate a situation by the loudness, fast rate, and aggressive tone of your voice? Or do you find yourself talking in a cautious, overly restrained way, as if you expected criticism and strong opposition? Habits of using whining or strident qualities, of hurling the words out as fast as possible, or of abruptly starting a statement in a loud, high tone may once have served a purpose; they have outlasted the conditions which created them.

Poor speech models may have been introduced into the home environment. Someone may have been brought into the home to care for you, and you modeled your speech after hers. Your parents may have come from a foreign country; perhaps they lisped or stuttered or slurred their articulation. It was only when you went out from the family group that you noticed that the models you had for imitation when you learned to talk were different from those of other people whom you met. These factors are beyond your control. Fortunately, you can change your speaking habits and find models with more effective speech.

If you were that fortunate child who was brought up in a secure and happy family, who heard those close to you talking freely and effectively, you probably have great facility in speaking. You have profited by learning your good speaking habits in your home environment.

The Influence of Friends and Associates

Your relationships with friends and associates influence your speech. When you wish to be a part of a group, you tend to speak like that group. This applies not only to the use of the latest expressions, but to rate, inflection, voice quality, and pronunciations. Among small children, even good vocal habits learned at home may yield to the social pressures of the speech spoken by playmates in the local district.

Many servicemen during the war became acutely conscious of the differences between their local dialects and the speech of other men in their units. The desire to conform was often great enough to make them change their Brooklyn, Ozark, or Pennsylvania Dutch dialects in the direction of more acceptable General American.

The child or adolescent may model his behavior on that of some hero of the moment. He may first copy the voice of the television cowboy or gangster, later that of the movie star, and still later the manner of an older boy in school or of some man whom he admires. You have probably imitated certain aspects of the speech of other people because you admired them. If these traits contribute to effective speech, the tendency is good. These self-selected patterns have influenced the speech of all of us. Only when they are extremely different from the speech of others, when they do not fit the appearance and general character of the speaker, do they become faults which attract attention to themselves. The chubby little girl with the breathily sensual voice of her favorite movie star had better move back again into the world of everyday existence and speak in a way which matches her personality.

The Influence of the School

The school is another major influence. Here you may have learned negative attitudes toward speech. If a nagging teacher insisted upon pedantic articulation and precise pronunciation, if good speech was unrealistically associated with formal presentation of dull book reports, uninspired debates, and routine oral reading, it is not surprising if you resent efforts by others to improve your speech.

If, on the other hand, you have gone through a school system where the emphasis was placed upon oral communication as a tool for learning, where talking was fun because it gave you individual satisfaction in group activity, you will probably be well ahead of your college speech classes in poise and fluency.

The Influence of the Locality

The general region in which you grew up and learned to talk may influence your speech strongly. There are noticeable differences in American speech from one area to another. Sometimes these regional characteristics may be highly localized and strongly manifested, while in other instances they may be broadly distributed and only faintly suggested. Residence in several of these areas may further complicate your general speech pattern.

The culture and behavior backgrounds of a particular race or national group may also affect your speech. Within the city of Detroit, for instance, there is a section populated by Polish people. Here the customs and the language of their native land are kept alive. A student teacher showed her foreign background in the articulation, inflection, and rhythm pattern of her speech, although neither she nor her parents had ever been to Poland. Many such sections exist within large cities. A man may not wish to change his speech while he still lives in such a locality. One student made his home in a section of a large Eastern city where the majority of the people were immigrants or children of immigrants. Like other residents, he said "dis" and "dat." When his teacher tried to show him how the tongue tip is held for the TH sound, he said, "Well, I *can* put my tongue between my teeth and say 'them,' but if I do, somebody in my neighborhood will clip me on the jaw and I'll bite my tongue off."

The individuals just described speak a dialect, but so do you. Contrary to popular notion, a dialect is not necessarily a broken, substandard form of speech. It may also be highly cultivated and refined. The speech of "upper-class" London and of "lower-class" Cockney are both dialects. The same is true of "upper-class" Boston and "lower-class" East Side New York. In this larger sense, a dialect is defined as any form of a given language actually in use as a mode of communication; it is distinguishable in differences in vocabulary, pronunciation, rhythm, melody, and the like, from another form of that same language. For our purposes in training, particular attention will be directed toward the aspects of pronunciation, rhythm, and speech melody.

Broadly speaking, there are three widely spoken American dialects: Eastern, Southern, and General. Each of these dialects has marked differences within itself. In the United States, if you have traveled in the South, you will recognize that differences exist between the speech patterns of Richmond, Virginia, and those of Charleston, South Carolina, or Dallas, Texas. The speech of the educated New Yorker is unlike that of the Bostonian, and neither is quite like that of the resident of the Maine coast. Less marked but nevertheless perceptible differences exist among speech patterns in Indiana, Iowa, and Nebraska. In cosmopolitan areas like New York City and Los Angeles, where those born elsewhere frequently outnumber the natives, the dialects of all areas, including those derived from the influences of foreign languages, are mingled in confusion.

Because these differences exist, your most acceptable standard in articulation is the pronunciation used by the educated people in the broad region in which you live. For the majority of Americans, this dialect is the one we call General American, but Southerners and Easterners should retain the characteristics of their own dialects. This does not mean using all the local peculiarities of the speech in your immediate area however. Speech which is acceptable to educated people in any one of the three major areas will not be displeasing to discriminating listeners in either of the other regions.

THE INFLUENCE OF PERSONAL ADJUSTMENT ON SPEECH

You have met a man who talks too loudly with an exaggerated heartiness that deceives no one, or an effusive girl who praises everything with indiscriminate gushiness. Or you may know an aggressive student whose voice sounds as if he had to prove his simplest statement with continual argument. Again, you may recognize an inhibited person whose colorless speech is used as a barrier so that outsiders cannot intrude, by means of conversation, on his private world. Finally, you may encounter a defensive individual, endlessly explaining his actions in an apologetic tone. You will see all of these people in your classes. Their more exaggerated prototypes are common outside the university where the battle to exist may have aggravated these habits of response.

Such people as these have unconsciously evaluated themselves in a particular way. One may have failed to adjust to a physical difference; perhaps he wanted to be handsome and admired and has not yet realized that a person with a big nose or a too thin body can nevertheless be appreciated and accepted. The problems of personal adjustment posed by such physical differences are so intense that at least two great playwrights have made them dominant themes in their dramas. Rostand and Shakespeare have made Cyrano's nose and Richard III's hump the central factors in plays of great emotional power. In productions of these plays, the voices of the chief characters reflect their bitterness toward their physical abnormalities.

A man's evaluation of himself in relation to his environment and to his appearance may stand in the way of easy communication with others. He sometimes becomes too anxious to please, or aggressively hostile, or easily defeated. He may be so hypercritical of his own behavior and so analytical of his successes and failures that he has little time left to be interested in others. Instead of responding to his companions' ideas, he is hounding himself with such questions as: "Do I look funny?" "Do they think I'm not as good as they are?" "Will they know I am uncertain of myself?"

What do these evaluations of his body, his environment, and his relations with others have to do with a man's voice? These factors shape his personality. Whatever affects personality affects speech, since language behavior and personal adjustment are closely allied and interact.

Listen for signs of exaggerated response, inhibition, hostility, and defensiveness in the voices of those around you. You hear these in the quality of the voice, the rate, the pitch changes, the variations in loudness, or in inhibited or exaggerated articulation. Listen also for the highly acceptable vocal indications of friendliness and interest in others, of animation, assurance, and belief in oneself.

The increased observation of the relationship between a speaker's personal adjustment and his speech skills will lead you to examine yourself more closely. Do you perceive that the way you speak is related to aspects of your personality?

Courses in personal adjustment and mental hygiene will give you a more comprehensive knowledge of yourself, but for the time being analyze your speech and relate it to the influences of physical structure, environment, and personal adjustment. If you come to a place in your thinking where you conclude that your voice is dull and unresponsive because poor personal adjustment is contributing to poor voice usage, you will have obtained some insight into both your speech habits and your social relationships and will then be ready to move out of this type of habitual response into behavior which will be more satisfactory to you.

INFLUENCES IN THE IMMEDIATE SITUATION

Emotional Response

In any speaking situation, even the most casual, you have a purpose in using language. Closely tied up with this purpose are accompanying attitudes toward the situation, the idea discussed, your listener, and yourself as a speaker. Attitudes are emotional in nature and will be apparent to you in physical changes and feeling states. You enjoy a situation: that enjoyment is evident in muscle tonus, in the undisturbed activity of the life-maintaining processes, in what you may call the "aliveness" of the whole body. You re sent a situation: the muscles of the extremities tighten; your breath and heart rates increase; you feel the tension within the body as if certain processes had been interrupted.

Speech is, of course, a muscular activity. As the whole body reacts during the emotion, breathing is affected, muscles in the larynx and the vocal-fold region may tighten, and changes occur in throat and mouth. When you lose control over yourself during a powerful emotion, you can no longer coordinate the movements for speech. The muscles may contract so strongly that voice cannot be produced for a moment; their sudden release results in a spurt of uncoordinated activity. If you are angry or frightened, you may feel unable to make a sound; when your voice comes, it may be a sudden shout or a high-pitched, tremulous tone. Loudness, timing, pitch, quality, and articulation are all affected. Your voice sounds unpleasant. If you continue to talk in the disturbed situation, your rate may increase so much that your mouth is unable to form the complex movements required in articulation; you slur and omit syllables.

Needless to say, you do not speak often with such a violent display of emotion. Every feeling state, however, produces some of these changes in speech. The variations in tension and relaxation within the body inevitably affect the operation of the structures used in speaking. Your listeners are adept at reading the resulting changes in the voice.

A moderate amount of emotional stress is an aid to a speaker. The best speakers and actors are never completely at ease when they go before an audience. Cicero recorded his opinion that "the better the orator, the more profoundly is he frightened by the difficulty of speaking." Similar views have been expressed by such speakers as William Jennings Bryan, George Arliss, and Booker T. Washington. In fact, it is a universal experience of speakers and actors that they are seldom at their best unless they are emotionally stimulated before they speak.

There is a simple, physiological explanation for this. When you are confronted with circumstances which are unusual, or which challenge your normal faculties of response, your body reacts with a safety mechanism to give you additional energy. Your success as a speaker, either on the platform or with a group of friends, depends upon how well you can channel this extra energy into useful activity. If you can turn it into meaningful gestures and strength and vitality of voice, you will be vastly more effective than if you had not been emotionally aroused. If you do not find an outlet for this extra energy, it will be expended upon purposeless and distracting activity. Your effectiveness will be lessened and you will feel uncomfortable before your listeners.

In examining your own speech habits, criticize yourself on your ability to channel emotional responses in such a way that they contribute to the effectiveness of your speaking.

Adaptations to the Occasion

Because you have been talking since childhood, you automatically make some changes in your delivery as the occasion varies. You need now to examine your speech to see if these adaptations exist and are effective.

Note your present habits of adapting. In informal conversation with a single person you may lower your voice and tend to mumble your words. Have you caught yourself speaking in the same way to a group? If the room is large and there are quite a number to hear you, do you increase your loudness, slow down, and articulate more distinctly? In the formal situation, are you more careful in the selection of words and in their pronunciation than you are in casual talk?

All aspects of voice should be adjusted to suit the occasion. When you examine your speech, analyze what changes are the automatic products of the moment.

SUMMARY

Good speech is accepted and valued by our society. From early childhood, social pressures for continuous improvement have been exerted upon you in the home, in school, by movies, radio, and television, in business and professional life. You have been taught to associate speech skills with the successful, attractive man or woman.

With such pressures, why are not all of us near-perfect? The answer to that question lies in the fact that influences of physical structures, environment, and personal adjustment often prevent acquisition of skills.

The desire for social acceptance and approval is a basic motivation for all of us. With some, the connection between speech skill and advancement in a profession or business may constitute a very real drive. With others, ambition to use speech creatively in artistic expression for radio, television, and stage may be an incentive for improvement.

Ask yourself why you wish to improve. Develop habits of listening critically to others. Define your own skills and faults. Analyze the backgrounds of your speech habits. In this way, you will create a desire for an understanding of how the speech mechanism works and how the various processes involved in voice production may be made more efficient and more effective.

Exercises for Analysis

1. Write an analysis of the voice of a person whom you overhear or whom you do not know well. Attempt to describe personality traits which may be related to his voice habits.

2. Write an analysis of your own voice. Base this on three questions. (*a*) *What is my voice like?* Refer back to the suggestions made in Chapter 1. Seek comments from other people to contribute to the answer. Listen to the recording made of your voice. (*b*) *Why do I speak as I do?* You should present your answer freely, since this information will be confidential and read only by your instructor. You will benefit by setting the ideas down in full so that you can examine them objectively. (*c*) *How may I improve?* The material here may be sketchy, since you may not yet have a clear idea of the skills possible to you. You may add to this at a later date.

Take your time on this analysis. Return to the preliminary notes, check them, and add more. A hurried effort made the night before the assignment is due may fulfill requirements but will rarely contribute to your understanding of yourself.

3. Analyze the impression a stranger may have of your personality after listening to you on one of the following occasions: a dinner, a business interview, a conversation with an old friend, the presentation of a speech.

3

Breathing for Speech

*This being of mine, whatever it really is, consists of a little flesh, a
little breath, and the part which governs.*—MARCUS AURELIUS

As the swimmer climbs out of the pool after the race, he says to a friend, "I
could—have won—if Jack—Smith—hadn't been—in such good—shape."
You can see his ribs move in and out and his breastbone up and down as he
struggles to speak. His friend leans closer to hear him. The strenuous physical exercise has created a demand for increased oxygen and a need for faster
elimination of the waste products in the blood stream. The uncontrolled nature of his breathing activity has prevented steady tone, hampered adequate
loudness, and disturbed his general rate and phrasing. To a lesser degree,
breathing also influences the pitch of the voice, its quality, and the distinctness of articulation. Voice production is a continuous process, and any type
of activity which interferes with controlled breathing must of necessity influence tone production, resonation, and articulation, each of which is a
modification of the basic breath stream. A weak and unsteady tone cannot
be resonated adequately or formed into good vowel sounds. Disturbed rate
and rhythm patterns resulting from improper breathing inevitably interfere
with good articulation.

Ineffective breathing for speech may result from violent activity like that
of the swimmer, but other causes are even more common and certainly more
damaging to ordinary communicative speech. If a speaker is lacking in general energy and physical responsiveness, his tone will be weak and unsteady,
and he will tend to gasp for breath in the middle of phrases, thus obscuring
his meaning. On the other hand, a beginning speaker may be overstimulated
by his first experience before an audience. There may be signs of breathlessness as if he had been running to class. An uncontrolled fear reaction pre-

pares his body to meet an emergency. As a result, he may pant like a swimmer as he struggles futilely for steady tone, adequate loudness, and meaningful timing of what he wants to say.

In order to learn to use breathing for the best voice production, you need to know something of the structure of the breathing mechanism and to become aware of the conditions which disrupt its normal function. When you understand these factors, you will be able to practice intelligently to attain the best breathing habits for speech.

STRUCTURE AND FUNCTION OF THE BREATHING MECHANISM

THE STRUCTURE

The bony structure of the thorax or chest, sometimes called the *rib cage,* is made up of the backbone; the sternum, or breastbone; and the twelve

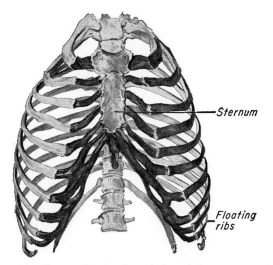

Fig. 1. The rib cage, showing frontal view of the sternum and ribs

pairs of ribs. All the ribs are attached to the backbone. The six upper pairs are joined in front by cartilage to the sternum; each of the next four pairs is attached to the rib above by cartilage. Only the two lower pairs, called the *floating ribs,* have no direct frontal connection with the other ribs, and can therefore move more freely than those above. The type of attachment of the ribs to the backbone makes movement possible so that the rib cage is not a rigid structure. The sternum can be raised and the whole thorax lifted so that the depth of the chest is increased from front to back. The lower ribs can move outward and upward so that the size of the chest cavity increases from side to side. In forced, heavy breathing, both of these expansions permit a deep inhalation.

Within this thoracic cavity are the two large, conical-shaped lungs; the heart; blood vessels; the esophagus, or passageway to the stomach; and the trachea, bronchi, and bronchial tubes, which carry the air into and out of the lungs. The cavity is a completely walled chamber; muscles fill the spaces between the ribs, and the diaphragm forms the entire floor of the cavity, separating the chest from the abdominal region. The lungs and chest wall are normally always in contact. The apex of each lung rests just above the collarbone, while the base touches the diaphragm.

The air enters the respiratory mechanism through the mouth and nose, passes down the throat between the vocal folds and into the trachea, or windpipe. The trachea consists of a four- to five-inch tube held open by horseshoe-shaped, incomplete rings of cartilage; its back wall is of muscle. In the chest cavity this tube divides into two bronchi, which in turn branch in the lungs into smaller and smaller tubes. The whole structure resembles an upside-down branching tree, with the trachea as the trunk.

Functioning of the Structure in Inhalation

The powerful diaphragmatic muscle is the chief muscle of inhalation. In its position of rest, the diaphragm is shaped like an inverted bowl. It consists of a central tendon, elliptical in shape, from which the muscles radiate outward to the inner wall of the thorax and connect to the tip of the sternum, the six lower ribs, and the backbone. When these muscles contract, the diaphragm descends and becomes flatter, pressing against the abdominal viscera or internal organs. Since the backbone and the pelvic structure restrict backward and downward movement of the viscera, the abdominal wall now bulges slightly under the pressure.

The action of the muscles between the ribs also increases the size of the chest cavity. If the upper part of the rib cage is fixed in position, the contraction of these muscles, the external intercostals, can elevate the ribs. Because of the bowed shape of the ribs, their movement is outward as well as upward as the muscles contract.

There are several other series of muscles which can elevate or depress the ribs. Some lie across the back of the thorax, some at the neck or upper chest. These need not be named in detail.

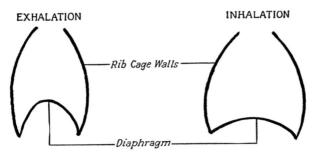

Fig. 2. Diagram showing the changes in size and shape of the thoracic cavity during breathing (front view)

The action of the rib cage is sometimes compared to that of a bellows. As the handles of the bellows are pulled apart, the space within is increased and a partial vacuum created. To equalize the pressure between the outside and the inside, the air rushes into the small opening at the top and fills the bellows. In a similar way, as the bony structure of the rib cage moves out, the air, because of the atmospheric pressure outside the body, rushes into this enlarged cavity. The lungs are not active in any way in "drawing in" the air. They are merely reservoirs for air which are acted upon by the changes in size and shape of the thorax.

Let us now follow through the process of inhalation: the muscles of the diaphragm contract and the diaphragm descends, pressing against the viscera below; the upper chest is fixed and the ribs move slightly upward and outward; if the breath is deep, the breastbone moves forward and upward. As the thoracic cavity is increased in size vertically and horizontally, the air pressure within is lowered, and the air from outside pours in to equalize the pressure.

Functioning of the Structure in Exhalation

If you are not speaking but are only breathing quietly, the relaxation of the muscles of inhalation is sufficient to force the air out. The abdominal viscera have been under pressure; in their elastic recoil these organs press against the diaphragm, which relaxes and ascends quickly. Because of the weight of the rib cage, when the muscles relax, the ribs descend. In breathing for life, the inhalation is active, the exhalation passive.

Let us suppose that you are going to use the exhaled breath to set the vocal folds into vibration. You must now control the exhalation so that you can use it efficiently for long phrases, if necessary, with accompanying changes in pitch, in loudness, and in resonance for the subtle expression of your desired meaning.

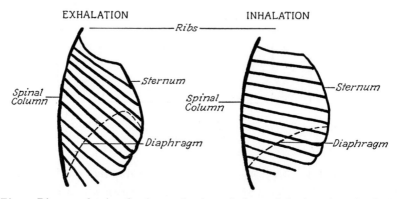

Fig. 3. Diagram showing the changes in size and shape of the thoracic cavity during breathing (from the right side)

The muscles which actively control exhalation are situated in the abdominal region. Four powerful, flat layers of muscles form the front wall of the abdomen; three of these are attached to the lower margin of the thorax. When they contract, they will pull the lower ribs down, in cooperation with muscles within the interior walls of the rib cage, and will press against the abdomen. This pressure forces the viscera up against the diaphragm. In life breathing, the diaphragm would now relax and the breath would pour out. In breathing for speech, however, a balance must be achieved between the controlled relaxation of the diaphragm and rib muscles and the firm pressure exerted by the abdominal muscles. The breath can move steadily upward under pressure, past the vocal folds, because the ribs press steadily inward against the lungs and because the diaphragm relaxes gradually under the pressure of the viscera below it.

BIOLOGICAL FUNCTION

The main function of breathing is the maintenance of life. Oxygen is supplied to the blood via the lungs on inhalation; the gaseous waste product of the blood, the carbon dioxide, is carried away on exhalation. The respiratory center in the medulla at the base of the brain automatically controls the inhalation-exhalation cycle. If you are exercising, the oxygen or fuel for physical exertion is used rapidly and the waste products in the blood increase. The rate of breathing and the amount of air taken in are increased to meet the bodily needs. If you are in an emotional state, the body gets ready to meet the emergency, and since oxygen is needed in greater amount for the impending action, the breath is taken in more quickly.

Under quiet conditions, your breathing for life is rhythmical, with the inhalation and the exhalation approximately equal in duration. You use little of the total or "vital" capacity of the lungs because your breathing is shallow and frequent.

When you speak, this process is modified. The breath is now the source of energy which sets the tensed vocal folds into vibration to produce vocal sound. To make this vibration efficient and steady, you must control the breath stream being exhaled.

FUNCTION OF BREATHING IN SPEAKING

The Modification of Life Breathing for Voice Production

The production of voice modifies breathing for life in the following ways:

1. In breathing for life, the inhalation is active, the exhalation passive; for speech, both are active processes. The exhalation is firm, steady, and controlled.

2. In breathing for life, the time cycles of inhalation-exhalation tend to be equal. For speech, the inhalation is quick and the duration of the exhalation is governed by the idea to be expressed.

3. Breathing for life, when you are quiet, is shallow. Breathing for speech is sometimes deeper, depending, of course, upon your immediate need for a long phrase or for increased general loudness. A word of caution should be given here. Deep breathing does not necessarily improve voice. The habitual taking of a deep breath before speaking can cause excessive tension, since it keeps the rib cage unnaturally distended over too long a period. If you mistakenly try to set up habits of deep breathing, you can spoil the rhythm of your whole speech and adversely affect the quality of your voice.

Types of Breathing for Voice Production

There are several different types of breathing, any of which you may be using habitually. You may have developed certain breathing habits merely by chance, or you may have acquired them because of differences in your body structure or because some "authority" has advocated a method as beneficial. Of the various types of breathing, only the first one to be discussed below is consistently associated with poor vocal quality.

1. *Clavicular breathing.* The speaker elevates the shoulders and collarbones

(clavicles) every time he inhales. The action is tiring because it involves the unnecessary lifting of the entire thoracic structure rather than merely expanding the sides of the rib cage as in other types of breathing. It is inefficient because the expansion possible by this action is less than for any other type. It impairs the pitch and quality of the voice because it compels the contraction of the muscles of the neck adjacent to the vocal folds. As the shoulders and clavicles are lowered during exhalation, a sustained flow of breath can be developed only by holding the tension in these muscles. This tension spreads to the larynx itself, and high pitch and harshness may result. On the other hand, if the muscles are relaxed suddenly, breath is exhaled all at once, and it is difficult to sustain tone on long phrases, or to get enough pressure for adequate loudness.

2. *Upper-thoracic breathing.* The speaker raises the sternum on inhalation and often pulls the lower ribs in. Occasionally, a man will learn this habit in physical training which requires the raising of the entire chest structure. If the individual is muscular and large in build, this may not affect his control over breathing for speech. If he is small, he may have the same difficulties as the man with clavicular breathing.

3. *Medial breathing.* The speaker moves the lower ribs outward and slightly upward, increasing the dimensions of the whole lower part of the rib cage. There is, however, little movement in the abdominal region. If the movement of the ribs is steady and strong, he probably has good control over breathing.

4. *Diaphragmatic-abdominal breathing.* To the expansion of the lower rib cage on inhalation, the speaker adds the pronounced downward movement of the diaphragm, which causes the bulge of the abdominal wall in the center of the body just below the ribs. On exhalation, the pressure produced by the contraction of the abdominal muscles is balanced by the gradual relaxation of diaphragmatic and rib muscles. This process and its similarity to natural breathing for life have already been described. You can analyze the actions involved if you lie down, become relaxed, and perceive the gentle rise and fall of the mid-region of the body below the ribs. Speech which changes the normal life process as little as possible will show ease in production of voice. The parts of the chest which are not actually needed in voice production can remain relaxed. If the activity for breath control is centered in this mid-region, the speaker can also learn to relax the muscles of the neck and larynx and so improve the quality of his voice.

The type of breathing you use is also related to your habits of posture. If your posture is stooped, you are actually preventing the diaphragmatic-abdominal activity, since the position crowds that region. If you lean on the lectern as you speak, you pull the whole structure of the chest upward and forward and thus tend to use upper-thoracic breathing. A slumped, one-sided posture with the body thrown out of line will distort the position of your muscles and make abdominal control difficult.

It is evident, then, that effective breathing for speech requires freedom from tension and full control over the exhalation process. Generally this is best achieved by some combination of medial and diaphragmatic-abdominal control over the breath stream. It is almost never achieved when breathing is primarily dependent on movement of the shoulders and clavicles.

ANALYSIS OF BREATHING HABITS

You may now use the information on the functioning of the breathing mechanism as a basis for the analysis of your own breathing habits. Perhaps you will find that your breathing is adequate and controlled for everyday speaking situations. You may not perceive a need for practicing breathing and vocal exercises until finer skills of control are required of you in public speaking, reading, or acting. On the other hand, you may discover that your faults of inaudibility, rapid rate, broken phrasing, or unsteadiness of tone relate distinctly to poor breathing habits, and you will be motivated to practice exercises immediately. Analysis of present habits must, of course, precede improvement.

The Importance of Control of the Breath Stream

The control of breathing, as it relates to effective voice, is vital for the following reasons:

1. It contributes to the steadiness of your vocalization. If the flow of air coming up through the trachea and past the vocal folds is not steady, the vibration it sets up in the vocal folds cannot be steady. If you allow the air to come out rapidly on the first words, little breath will remain to sustain vibration at the end of a phrase. The muscular activity centered in the abdominal and lower rib region can govern the steady flow of breath needed.

2. Control of breath flow is necessary for the increase in strength of tone which enables you to be heard over some distance. If the flow is weak, the vibration is correspondingly feeble. The control also permits the variations in loudness which provide a means of conveying changes in your meaning.

3. Good breathing habits allow you to adjust the amount of air inhaled to the length of phrase and the duration of the words which you emphasize

within the phrase. The manner of breathing will also relate to the general rate of your speech and your ability to vary rate.

4. Control of breathing contributes to a feeling of ease of production. If, as you speak, you experience no gasping for air or feeling of breathlessness, and if you know that because of established control your voice can reach all within the group and can change in loudness and rate to suit your meanings, then you have the confidence which results from the habitually efficient use of the breathing mechanism. The lack of control, conversely, will disturb your confidence. Poor breathing habits often influence detrimentally the pitch changes and quality of tone. They induce muscular tension. Faults of phonation and resonation are frequently traceable to a basic breathing difficulty.

Observation and Self-analysis

1. First duplicate each of the four methods of breathing, exaggerating the movements in order to feel the action of the muscles involved. Raise the collarbone and shoulders as you inhale deeply. Next, place your open palm against the breastbone. Raise the upper chest as you take a breath, allowing the whole rib cage to be pulled up. Now, with the palms pressed against the lower ribs, move the ribs out, first while taking in a breath, and again with no breath being inhaled. Place one open hand over the triangular soft spot where the lower ribs do not join in front, and the other hand against the ribs at the side. As you inhale, observe both the outward and upward movement of the ribs and the outward movement of the abdominal wall. Which of these types of activity seems easiest for you?

2. Repeat several short sentences as you reproduce each type of breathing. Can you analyze your own method?

3. During an animated conversation, for a brief time give attention to your manner of breathing. Are you raising the shoulders or gasping for air?

4. Observe in other speakers any tendency to raise the shoulders on inhalation for speech. Do they have good control over their voices?

BREATH CONTROL FOR STEADINESS OF VOCALIZATION

Self-analysis

1. Read aloud one of the more serious and slow practice selections in the Appendix, such as Number 4 or 23. Is your tone unsteady or weak?

2. As you read, do you tend to exhaust your breath supply quickly at the

initiation of the phrase so that you run out of air and your tone becomes less firm at the end of the phrase?

3. In phrases which contain many of the friction sounds, like H, S, TH, and F, do you waste a great deal of breath? Mark these sounds in any passage and listen critically to yourself. This is in reality an articulatory fault, but it will be related to lack of steady tone on the vowel sounds.

Exercises for Improvement

Before you begin the exercises, make sure that your body is relatively free from tension. Standing on your toes, stretch upward as far as you can reach with your fingers, bringing your hips forward and your abdomen in, so that the entire body falls into line. Repeat several times.

Next, bend forward from the waist, allowing the trunk, arms, and neck to hang down limply. Begin to straighten slowly, inhaling as you come up; feel the pull of the muscles in the hip, thigh, and abdomen. Slowly assume the upright position, making sure that the large muscles of the shoulders and neck are relaxed.

Tighten the muscles at the back of the neck, pull the head back tensely, turn it from side to side, and then let it fall forward gently.

Examine your posture. The body should feel well balanced and at ease, with the weight on the balls of both feet. You should avoid the extremes of either the military or the slouched posture.

1. Place the open palms of your hands tightly against your lower front ribs. Inhale slowly and deeply through both mouth and nose, feeling the push of the lower rib wall against your hands. Hold the breath for about the count of five, noting that your ribs are held up and out. Now exhale slowly, pressing in with your hands but resisting this pressure by the slow lowering of the ribs. Turn your hands so that the fingers point toward the back; the open palms can now feel the rib movement of the side and back of the rib cage. Repeat the slow inhalation, the holding, and the steady exhalation until you are well aware of the desired movement.

2. Repeating this same steady breathing, place your finger tips on your shoulders. Inhale. Your fingers will tell you whether or not your shoulders are relaxed. Place one palm on the sternum. As you inhale, concentrate on the movement of the lower rib cage so that the hand on the upper chest moves only slightly. Repeat, until you can minimize the activity of shoulders and sternum.

3. To correct clavicular breathing, sit upright in an armless chair; grip the legs of the chair low enough so that your chest can remain erect and

your shoulders cannot be raised; in this position, inhale and exhale, concentrating on the movement at the center of your body.

4. Repeat, this time counting aloud on the exhalation.

5. With your open palms again on the ribs, inhale quickly through your mouth, purse your lips, and blow a steady, forceful stream of air, as if you were trying to blow out a candle some distance from you. Continue blowing until most of your breath is exhausted; feel the inward movement of the abdominal wall and the gradual lowering of the ribs. Try this also with an actual candle, this time blowing evenly, with little force, so that the flame is merely made to bend steadily away from you but is not extinguished and does not waver.

6. Inhale to the instructor's count of "one," exhale to the count of "one, two"; inhale; exhale to the count of "one, two, three"; and so forth up to the count of ten, so that the ratio of inhalation-exhalation becomes 1:10. Be aware of steadiness of movement at the ribs.

7. Repeat, this time counting aloud on the exhalation.

8. As you inhale, hands on ribs, yawn gently. Maintain this relaxed openness of throat as you produce a breathy AH. On the second attempt, retain the relaxation in your throat, but consciously increase the clarity of the AH. Keep the ribs elevated without strain as long as possible, bringing the abdominal region in before the descent of the ribs begins. The tone does not have to be loud, but steadiness in flow should be sought. Close your eyes as you vocalize; listen to see if breath is wasted at the initiation of the tone or if the tone becomes faint near the end of the production. If the tone wavers, concentrate on steadiness of movement at the lower ribs, rather than on any muscular adjustment in the throat. This ability to achieve a steady vowel tone without wasted breath or strain is your most important objective at this time.

9. Repeat the above exercise for each of the "long-vowel" sounds: A, E, I, O, OO, AW. Take the breath in quickly, but without exaggerating the amount or permitting audible intake; hold the vowel sound until most of the breath pours out. Do not strain; this is an exercise for steadiness of tone, not for duration.

10. Repeat all of the vowel sounds listed above on one exhalation, keeping the flow of breath steady as you change the position of the mouth.

11. Using long, sustained vowel sounds, chant the following phrases quietly and easily:

> How far away.
> How quiet it became.
> How slowly the waves roll in.

12. Inhale and count aloud from one to ten, from one to twenty, from one to thirty, using a firm, sustained tone. Listen to yourself to see if some of the breath is wasted on F's, TH's, and s's. How far can you count without a feeling of strain?

BREATH CONTROL FOR CHANGES IN LOUDNESS

Loudness, Energy, and Projection

When a situation arises in which you must speak to a roomful of people, or call to someone in the distance, you discover that you must speak louder than you usually do. From a technical standpoint, loudness depends in part on the physical make-up of the speaker, but allowing for individual differences, any speaker may increase or decrease his loudness by increasing or decreasing the breath pressure at the vocal folds. To understand what is meant by this statement, find an opportunity to shout to someone. Notice that inhalation is quick, and if you are going to shout more than one word, somewhat deeper than usual. The muscles of exhalation now contract quickly and firmly, exerting pronounced pressure on the lungs, with a decrease in the size of the thoracic cavity. The breath coming up through the trachea to the vocal folds is thus under more pressure than usual. The sudden tone produced is loud.

A desired degree of loudness can be maintained if the pressure of the muscles of exhalation is firm and sustained during the phrase to be spoken. You should note several facts. First, under such pressure, air escapes from the lungs more rapidly than during quiet speaking. Thus each phrase spoken loudly must be relatively short, so that a new supply of air can be taken in to give support to the next phrase. Second, there must be enough air in the lungs to maintain pressure. For this reason, the inhalation, though quick, is often deeper than average. Third, the control which brings about the firm pressure lies in the diaphragmatic-abdominal region, not in the throat. You can, of course, increase the pressure of the breath stream, and loudness, by increasing tension at the vocal folds. Such tension, however, results in raising of pitch and may induce additional constrictions above the larynx, producing a strident quality.

So far we have been discussing loudness as if it were a factor which existed in isolation. You can, of course, change your loudness by following the suggestions we have given for proper use of the muscles of exhalation. But unless you go beyond this, you are likely to be mechanical and lifeless. If loud tones are to be effective, they must be motivated by a wish to be heard—a desire to communicate your ideas and feelings to your listeners. And your increase in energy must involve not only the muscles of exhalation, but your entire body. Moreover, it is desirable to approach the whole problem of adequate loudness from the point of view of general physical responsiveness and communicative attitudes.

A simple experiment will demonstrate the relationship between general physical energy and loudness. Stand before the class or in your own room at home in an erect, but not stiff, posture. Count rhythmically from one to twenty-five, at the same time striking your fist into the palm of your other hand. Begin gently, then strike with greater energy in the rhythm of you·count. Try to keep your voice at exactly the same level of loudness as you increase the energy of your pounding. Can you do it? Unless you have unusual control over your voice, you probably cannot. If you can, you perhaps do not need this advice.

Of course, you should not pound your palm or the lectern every time you wish to speak more loudly. But if loudness is to be more than mere noise, it must be energetic, involving greater tonicity of the muscles of the whole body. This increased readiness to act affects the muscle tone of the vocal mechanism. Your response to a speaker under these conditions is to note not merely that he spoke loudly enough, but that he meant what he said.

To be most effective, however, energy must be controlled. If one touched a match to the gasoline in a can, the gasoline would burn with an explosive flash. The energy of the explosion, uncontrolled, would be wasted. However, if the same gasoline were used in an automobile, under control in the motor, it would drive the car. In the same way, control and direction of vocal energy are necessary if energy is to serve a purpose in communication.

A speaker who directs his voice with controlled energy is said to be *projecting*. Projection is a difficult concept to define. Psychologically, it depends upon a genuine desire on the part of the speaker to communicate his thoughts and feelings to his hearers. Without this attitude, mechanical adjustments will not make the speaker seem to be projecting. Physically, it depends upon the control of the speaker's bodily activity in response to his desire to communicate. In conversation, discussion, or public speaking, this may take the form of alert posture, responsive facial expression, and eye-to-eye contact with his hearers. On the stage, the orientation may be partly toward the other persons on the stage and partly toward the audience, but the same sense of purposeful activity will be present.

The complex result of these factors emerges in the voice in greater clarity of articulation, more brilliance in resonation, and more efficient use of the breath stream in phonation. For the listener, it seems as if the voice were *aimed* at him. When a mother goes out to call her son to dinner and she does not know just where he is, she will call, "Johnny, Johnny!" loudly, but will broadcast the call diffusely over the whole neighborhood. However, once she has located Johnny, she projects her call with machine-gun accuracy to Johnny so that he hears her and comes home. If the person vocalizing is projecting, you as the listener will feel, "He is speaking to *me!*"

Projection is related to loudness, but it is not loudness alone, nor does it depend upon loudness. You may have a high degree of loudness and no projection, or very quiet speech with projection. Experiment with loudness and projection on this statement: "That's a lie, and you're nothing but a dirty liar!" Shout it as loudly as you can, but do not let the words have any meaning, reality, or aim. Now say it at conversational volume with all of the earnestness and conviction you can muster; try to feel the vehemence of the speaker as you aim the statement at someone. Observe that loudness alone does not project the meaning. Experiment with the phrase to see what different levels of energy and projection you can achieve. Notice the differences in muscle tension in your whole body as you do this.

Notice how mere loudness usually results from increased tension in the muscles which control the exhaled breath stream. For energy and projection, there must be the same increase in muscle tension, but this must be in the mechanisms of phonation and resonation as well. As in all of the other vocal skills, the fine balance of tensions and relaxations must be maintained. Otherwise, faults resulting from overtension will appear in breathing, phonation, and resonation.

In the preceding paragraphs, we have mentioned the skills of phonation, resonation, and articulation, each of which will be discussed in detail in later chapters. Energy and projection are basic to all of them. If you will develop sufficient energy to maintain adequate breath pressure for loudness, and cultivate the mental attitude which is basic to projection, you will discover that many of the problems you have in other areas will also diminish, and less time will have to be devoted to them in later assignments.

Self-analysis

Examine yourself to discover the habits which affect your use of loudness.

1. Can you make yourself heard in a large room? If not, do you really want to be heard? Do you have something to say you think is worth listening to? Are you *aiming* your voice and your ideas at anyone?

2. What is your level of energy when you are speaking? Are you physically alert in posture? Do you feel ready and able to respond to your ideas with physical activity as well as with changes in your voice?

3. When you are trying to make yourself heard, do you take a very deep breath and raise the shoulders and the upper chest?

4. Do you strain to increase loudness, and in so doing tense the muscles of the throat? Does your pitch rise? Does your quality of tone become harsh, strident, or squeaking?

5. Does a quantity of air pour out as you produce the first loud tone? Are you breathless, so that you immediately have to gasp for air?

6. Does the tone waver as it becomes louder? Does it diminish in volume, so that you start with a loud tone and then fade into an inaudible one?

7. Do you tire after the first four or five sentences? Does your voice break?

Exercises for Improvement

As you practice each of the following exercises, work for general physical responsiveness. Assume an alert posture and get the feeling that any muscle in your body could respond quickly if you needed it. At the same time, do not become tense or strained. Alertness, not tension, is the goal.

1. With the palms of your hands on the lower ribs, and your tongue tip behind the lower front teeth, yawn gently as you inhale; exhale slowly and steadily as you produce the long I sound. Inhale quickly and somewhat more deeply; exhale with more vigorous pressure at the central region of the body. Repeat a third time, being conscious of even greater muscular contraction. The last I will be energetic and short, and should easily reach across a large room without straining your throat muscles. Your mouth, of course, should be sufficiently open to permit the sound to escape without being muffled.

2. Repeat the above exercise, using the word "one" for vocalization. Hold the tongue in the position of the final sound until the breath stream has finished its objective of carrying the tone. Imagine on the first vocalization that you are speaking firmly to someone next to you and that this listener moves farther away for each of the succeeding four vocalizations. Be careful not to raise the pitch for each louder tone.

3. Run five "ones" together on one breath, steadily increasing the pressure of the muscles of exhalation so that the tone gradually and smoothly builds up in loudness.

4. Repeat Exercise 9 on page 34. Gently commence a yawn and produce a steadily controlled AH sound. Next, with the mouth wide open, yawn gently and produce a faint AH; gradually, through pressure at the central region,

swell this tone in a crescendo without raising the pitch. As you gain skill in doing this smoothly and without straining the throat muscles, learn to start the faint tone, swell it gradually, and then allow it to diminish slowly. This may be practiced with all long-vowel sounds.

5. Contrast the fault of breath wastage with clarity of tone during loud production. Repeat the following sentences, pouring out excessive breath at the initiation of each phrase. Then, with the hands on the lower ribs, repeat the sentences in a clear, loud, sustained tone, getting full phonation from all exhaled breath on the voiced sounds.

> How do you expect me to go?
> He had to see the man today.
> We can't believe in this plan.
> I have told you again and again.
> Each of you must understand.

6. Repeat short phrases, such as "I know," "I will," using three degrees of loudness for each. Imagine you are talking to listeners at different distances. Keep the throat relaxed.

7. Read aloud a selection in the Appendix, such as Number 15 or Number 19: first, as if you were talking sincerely to one person; second, as if to a small group of people; third, as if to a large auditorium of listeners. In addition to the general increase in energy of production, you will notice that the larger and more extensive the speaking situation, the shorter the phrases become. Loudness uses up breath supply. The articulation must also be more exact so that the sounds of speech can be recognized easily at a distance.

After practice at home, read other similar short selections to the class, first speaking to those in the first row, then increasing the distance your voice can be made to cover until the audience finally indicates that you are speaking too loudly.

CHANGES IN LOUDNESS FOR MEANING

Increase in general loudness is necessary to meet the requirements of audibility as the size of the audience or the room increases. To communicate specific meanings to the listeners, however, you need the additional skill of being able to change the loudness within the spoken passage to suit the meanings you wish to convey. For this purpose, a desire to project the ideas and a constant feeling of physical alertness and energy are even more important than for audibility.

The use of loudness to express strong feeling is an elementary skill learned early in life. If it remains on the primitive level of childhood, however, it is likely to suggest emotional instability rather than force of ideas. On the other hand, controlled loudness, blended with changes in timing, pitch, and quality of tone, may be useful in conveying changes in meaning to listeners. Skillful control of loudness is dependent upon change, rather than upon the number of decibels produced. If a speaker has been explaining facts at a level of loudness suited to the situation, and then drops his volume so that his listeners have to lean forward and attend carefully, he produces the effect of presenting valuable, exciting, and somewhat private data. The attention of the listener is caught immediately, if the device is not used too frequently. Again, an experienced speaker may, as he presents a series of ideas, build from a quiet level of loudness, increasing the intensity with each idea, until at the climax the audience is carried toward emotional conviction by his vocal energy. Any change in loudness will attract the listener's ear momentarily; whether or not his attention is held will depend upon the speaker's ideas and his other skills of delivery.

Changes in loudness for emphasis contribute to the intelligent interpretation of an idea. The words which carry the greatest importance within the phrase are usually produced with the greatest energy. For example, read the following sentence, giving a different pattern of emphasis by means of increasing loudness on different words for each reading: "I saw you with him last night." Note how the meanings vary. The changes need not be pronounced or extreme.

If you overuse loudness for emphasis, you may fall easily into a pattern of loudness changes. Any repeated way of emphasizing, such as making the first words the most prominent in the sentence, or hitting too many words in the phrase with a sudden increase in loudness, will become monotonous for the listener and thus will interfere with your communication. The use of mono-loudness is just as ineffective. If no word is louder than any other, meaning is obscured. In any case, do not depend on loudness changes alone for meaning. Learn to temper loudness with the more subtle changes in timing, pitch, and quality developed later in the book.

Self-analysis

The faults of extreme vocal energy and of lack of energy both call attention to themselves and away from meaning. Examine your speech critically to ascertain whether any of the following are true:

1. When you are earnest and emotional in proving a point, do you shout

the whole idea, or do you confine the greatest display of energy to the most important part of the idea?

2. Do you hit words you want to emphasize with sudden changes in loudness? Have you heard another speaker do this?

3. Do you have a pattern of emphasis?

4. Do you speak all the words in a phrase with equal loudness so that, although the words may be said at different pitch levels, none is made with more energy than another?

5. Have you ever used gradually increased or decreased loudness for effect in building to a climax in a speech or argument? Have you ever been aware of this skill in the speech of others?

Exercises for Improvement

Continue the exercises for breathing and for control of increase in loudness.

1. Count from one to five, increasing the loudness steadily, as if the *five* were the climax of an idea. Keep the tone firm by steady pressure at the central region. Count steadily from one to ten, increasing loudness to a peak at five, diminishing volume on the succeeding numbers, but keeping the tone unwavering.

2. Repeat the letters of the alphabet through F. State the letters as if they were: first, a casual idea; second, an increasingly vital concept; and third, in a loud, clear tone, as if they represented a main convincing argument.

3. Repeat the following groups of three sentences; increase the energy of production and loudness from the first to the third in each group.

  a. I believe in this man.
      What he says is true.
      I will follow his plan of action.
  b. I have come here today.
      I will come back tomorrow.
      I will stay until this is settled.
  c. There are five points to this plan.
      Not one can be discarded.
      Discount one, and you weaken the whole structure.

4. Try to reverse the process in Exercise 3, and produce a convincing effect by starting with average loudness and decreasing it on each of the three sentences in the group.

5. Read the following passage, increasing your energy and sense of pro-

jection on the important words. Be aware of the changes in breath control as the sounds become louder. Repeat the reading, this time being conscious of the value of phrases rather than of individual words. Make the changes in energy and loudness smooth and firm, rather than sudden and sharp.

JOHN BROWN'S SPEECH

I have, may it please the Court, a few words to say.

In the first place I deny everything but what I have all along admitted: of a design on my part to free slaves . . . .

Had I interfered in the matter which I admit, and which I admit has been fairly proved . . . had I so interfered in behalf of the rich, the powerful, the intelligent, or the so-called great . . . and suffered and sacrificed, what I have in this interference, it would have been all right. Every man in this Court would have deemed it an act worthy of reward rather than punishment.

I see a book kissed which I suppose to be the Bible, or at least the New Testament, which teaches me that all things whatsoever I would that men should do unto me, I should do even so to them. It teaches me further to remember them that are in bonds as bound with them. I endeavored to act up to that instruction. I say I am yet too young to understand that God is any respecter of persons. I believe that to have interfered as I have done, as I have always freely admitted I have done in behalf of His despised poor, I did no wrong, but right. Now, if it is deemed necessary that I should forfeit my life for the furtherance of the ends of justice and mingle my blood further with the blood of my children and with the blood of millions in this slave country whose rights are disregarded by wicked, cruel and unjust enactments, I say, let it be done.

Let me say one word further. I feel entirely satisfied with the treatment I have received on my trial. Considering all the circumstances, it has been more generous than I expected. But I feel no consciousness of guilt. I have stated from the first what was my intention and what was not. I never had any design against the liberty of any person, nor any disposition to commit treason or incite slaves to rebel or make any general insurrection. I never encouraged any man to do so, but always discouraged any idea of that kind.

Let me say also, in regard to the statements made by some of those connected with me, I hear it has been stated by some of them that I have induced them to join with me. But the contrary is true. I do not say this to injure them, but as regretting their weakness. Not one but joined me

of his own accord, and the greater part at their own expense. A number
of them I never saw, and never had a word of conversation with, till the
day they came to me, and that was for the purpose I have stated.

Now I have done.

The voice ceased. There was a deep, brief pause.

The judge pronounced the formal words of death.

One man, a stranger, tried to clap his hands.

The foolish sound was stopped.

There was nothing but silence then.—BENÉT *

6. Write out a statement of belief, working up to a climax, with the aim
of convincing your listeners. The following may serve as suggestions:

a. I believe that racial discrimination exists in this community . . . .

b. I believe that the present system of marking is unfair . . . .

c. I believe that this university should . . . .

Ask for criticism from your listeners. Did your level of energy and loudness reflect the strength of your feeling? Was the tone steady? Were you
clearly audible? Did you use changes in loudness effectively to bring out
differences in meaning? If you have had poor breathing habits, have you now
been able to improve them in this real-life situation?

7. The following selections in the Appendix are recommended for practice
on variation in loudness: Numbers 2, 12, and 22*b*.

TIMING AND BREATH CONTROL

Several factors contribute to the timing of your oral communication: the
speed with which the phrase is presented, the interval of silence between
vocalizations, and the duration of the individual sounds which make up the
words. These three factors operating together determine the general rate or
number of words spoken within a given time period.

All of these elements are affected by the control of the breath stream. If
you run out of breath quickly or cannot sustain enough air in the lungs to
support the tone adequately, you cannot achieve skill in the manipulation of
timing and thus may not become effective in the expression of your meanings.

Counting the number of words which you speak within a minute gives
you only a general notion of the effect which your time pattern produces

* Stephen Vincent Benét, *John Brown's Body,* Farrar and Rinehart, Inc., New
York, 1936. (By permission.)

upon your hearers. One speaker may utter 120 words a minute, hurry the phrases, give staccato production to all vowels, and yet allow long pauses between phrases. His timing may be interpreted by the ear as being too fast for intelligibility. Another man may repeat the same passage with slow phrases and long vowels but no appreciable pauses. Although the number of words produced per minute by both men is exactly the same, the interpretation of the meaning and the effect on the listener will be very different.

General Rate

The general rate for unemotional, spontaneous material presented in a situation with only a few listeners is between 120 and 140 words per minute. Reading rate is usually considerably faster, the average being about 160 words a minute. Rate, of course, is influenced by the nature of the idea and the emotions inherent in the situation.

Thus, as you describe an action scene, your fast rate indicates that you want your listeners to share your feeling of excitement and animation. If the topic is solemn or sad, the slow rate used can suggest the quietness or lethargy of the body in experiencing such a situation. Your feeling states are conveyed by this skill of changing general rate to suit your emotion. The listener responds quickly to such indications.

If you use a gradual increase in loudness to build to a climax, you will find that you often couple this with an increase in the rate of speaking. This means of displaying energy can arouse emotions and carry the listener forward to the climax of the idea.

Rate is influenced by the complexity of the thought you present. A simple report, well known to the listeners, can often be speeded up. A new problem, with aspects hitherto unanalyzed by the audience, will require time for comprehension.

It has already been mentioned that the size of the audience and of the room will affect timing. A dramatic scene upon the stage, while seeming to move swiftly, must still allow time for the lines to reach the audience. An angry question, such as "What do you mean by that?" is said at great speed to the single listener. To a large audience, the intensity of the utterance must often supplant the natural inclination to hurl the words out quickly.

You may now argue that another factor influences general rate profoundly: the characteristics of your own personality. "I am excitable," you may say. "My rate is always fast." Or, "I am naturally slow moving." The type of person that you are will modify your general rate, but the assumption that your personality characteristics are static and cannot be varied when the need arises will interfere with the growth of your skill. Your purposes for using your speech fluctuate from hour to hour. The adaptation of your speaking habits to those purposes is your goal.

In practicing speech, you need to analyze your immediate purpose or intent in reading, speaking, or acting, and to think how changes in timing may be suited to the emotional content, the complexity of the idea, and the audience situation, so that the listeners can receive the full implication of your communication.

Analyze yourself to see if poor breathing habits are affecting your rate. If you have the habit of taking a breath and then speaking as long as seems physically possible before you gasp for air, you will tend to speak rapidly, particularly if you do not have control over the breath stream. The result is an uncertain and breathless production. Often, practice in improving breathing habits will overcome the excessive rate. The breathy, unsteady tone associated with clavicular breathing may cause the speaker to feel unsure of his voice, and self-consciousness will induce him to use a fast rate to get through the speaking situation as soon as possible.

Phrasing and Pauses

The phrase is the thought unit of speech. Phrasing refers to the process of grouping words together so that the relationship between the words will convey your immediate meaning. No criticism of "correct" or "incorrect" can be placed upon oral phrasing, provided that the grouping of the words fulfills your purpose and is meaningful to the listener.

Pauses, which serve to separate phrases from one another, are oral punctuation marks. Originally, written punctuation was a set of symbols designed to represent the oral grouping of the words. In recent writing, however, punctuation has become formalized, and the marks are not always accurate representations of the oral thought groupings. In reading aloud, therefore, you should not rely on punctuation alone to determine where to pause, although punctuation marks are usually helpful.

The oral phrasing of the first sentence below quite logically follows the written form:

1. John,/ unaware that they had gone,/ continued to talk.

The second sentence, with a more personal or emotional connotation, will need your own way of phrasing:

2. We are now far into the fifth year since a policy was initiated with the avowed object and confident promise of putting an end to slavery agitation.—LINCOLN

The way in which a passage is phrased, then, depends upon the meaning intended by the reader, actor, or speaker. Good phrasing contributes both to intelligibility and to emotional expression. Poor phrasing tears down the meaning and produces a feeling of confusion in the listener. As a matter of fact, poor phrasing is used deliberately in a dramatic production to indicate the uncertainty or emotional tension of the character.

While you must remember that length of phrase and use of pause are governed by meaning, you must also recognize that there are physical limitations to the use of these devices. You cannot prolong a phrase without adequate breath. Pauses must occur frequently enough for you to renew your breath supply. For skill in speaking, you must learn to combine the interpretations of meaning with efficient use of the breathing mechanism.

Phrases can be fast, slow, or average in speed. The timing of a particular phrase will depend on the specific emotion to be conveyed, the complexity of the idea, or the relative importance of the phrase in relation to those surrounding it. Vary the rate of the following phrases until the most meaningful combination is achieved. Make sure that breathing is controlled.

1. He was shouting wildly, and even though I could not hear the words, I knew what I had to do.
2. Language grows out of the social context.
3. Because of this, I understood his plan.

Notice that if you wish to subordinate a phrase, you hurry over it.

4. As I mentioned before, there are five points to remember.
5. You should repeat, whenever possible, the main points of your argument.

This ability to vary the timing of phrases makes your meaning clear, through the use of contrast, and also continually attracts the listener's ear by the variety of expression.

Pauses may be used for emphasis and dramatic effect. If, with the intent to be forceful, you declare, "These—are mine," you make the first word stand out with great significance. You may build toward an effect, directing your listeners, by your manner of presentation, to take particular notice of the final words in a sentence. "What you may be experiencing is a will—to fail." Pauses before, after, or around single words or short phrases will attract attention to the specific idea.

The length of the pause is dictated by the effect you seek. If your idea has been profound or new, for example, you may wish to pause for some time so that your listeners can consider the thought and continue to "think with you" as you go on. The size of the room will also affect the pause. If the sound does not carry well, it will be necessary for you to have frequent and long pauses so that the sounds of speech may be understood.

The average speaker is unwilling to pause for even a short time. He feels that, in this competitive society, the conversation will be taken away from him if he permits a break to occur. In the speaking or reading situation, he believes that attention will lag. An actor often places a more accurate interpretation on the pause; he knows from experience that its use will contribute to suspense—provided, of course, that he has the attention of the listeners in the first place. Probably the use of AH or ER to fill what would otherwise be a natural pause comes from the unfortunate feeling that some noise must be made continually to indicate that the speaker has not yet finished.

A pattern of pauses is often just as detrimental to meaning as the use of too infrequent or too short pauses. The speaker who says a phrase, pauses, says another, and so forth, and the speaker who gives the same-length pause and the same-length phrase over and over are both monotonous.

Two common breathing faults are frequently associated with poor timing. If your supply of breath is inadequate, you may break the phrase by gasping for air in the middle of a logical grouping of words. On the other hand, too deep an inhalation may induce you to use an interminable phrase while your listener waits anxiously for you to run out of breath.

In practicing phrasing and use of pauses, you need to be highly aware of the effect you wish to produce on the listener. A responsiveness to the implications of your idea and your purposes in speaking will frequently give you skilled variations in timing without any analysis of techniques. The techniques stand you in good stead when the responsiveness is temporarily disturbed by some factor in the immediate speaking situation.

Probably a recording of your reading and of your spontaneous speech is the best way for you to study your habits of phrasing and pausing and their relationship to breathing.

Duration of Sounds

The sounds of the language vary normally in length or duration of production. An isolated AH, as in *father*, is longer than the I in *sit*. An L has greater duration than a T. The length of sounds, particularly of vowels, will change with the accenting of the syllable. The material on articulation of sounds will present some of these factors later in the text.

The duration of the sounds of speech often relates to the speaker's general rate. If a person speaks rapidly, he may have the habit of clipping, or short-ening, all of his sounds, thus producing a staccato effect. If he is a slow speaker, he may drag out, or drawl, all of his vowels regardless of the mean-ing of his communication.

The basic meaning of the sentence will suggest the general duration of all the sounds in a passage. For instance, you would get a very strange effect if you produced the sounds of the following line in a staccato manner:

Roll on, thou deep and dark blue Ocean—roll!

Nor can you suggest excitement and action if you lengthen all the sounds in the sentence: "As he raised his arm to strike, the other man suddenly darted away."

The vowel sounds of speech can be classified, in rather a loose way, as *long* and *short*. Poets are well aware of this fact and use it to achieve certain emotional effects in their poems. Notice the use of long vowels in the poem by Tennyson:

And slowly answered Arthur from the barge,
"The old order changeth, yielding place to new . . . ."

An opposite staccato effect is sought by Browning:

Kentish Sir Byng, stood for his king,
Bidding the crop-headed Parliament swing . . . .

The variation of the duration of sounds is one of the main ways of em-phasizing ideas. Read the following sentence with conviction and then de-cide which of the vowels are the longest: "I know that this story is true."

In everyday conversation, we continually give longer duration to the words or the accented syllables of the words within the phrase which carry the most meaning. The natural rhythm of spoken language evolves from this variety of emphasis. Sometimes a speaker can make his communication more effective by reviewing his habits of the use of duration to see if he lengthens sounds in too rhythmic a pattern or if he gives most of his sounds equal duration.

For your own practice, mark a reading selection to indicate phrasing, pauses for emphasis, and increased duration of key words within phrases. Devise your own system. A well-written advertisement, conversational and interesting in context, will serve your purpose. Reread it after marking. Do these visual indications remind you to make the vocal changes?

Self-analysis of Timing

Examine your speech objectively as you consider the following questions:

1. Is your speech to the single listener, before the small group, or in front of the large audience too fast for comprehension? Is it too slow to maintain interest? Do you always hurry or drag out your words no matter what the topic?

2. Do you take a deep breath and continue to speak until the breath is exhausted, then break the phrases in the middle to gasp for air? Do you consistently break phrases to search for a word? Are all your phrases long or all short?

3. Does your rate vary from phrase to phrase so that a listener can tell that some are more meaningful than others?

4. Are you willing to pause long enough between phrases to look at the listeners and to judge their reactions to your ideas, or do you hurry on? Do you fill the natural times for pauses with a vocalized AH or ER? Do you permit time for comprehension of complex or new ideas?

5. Is your speech staccato in effect? Do you have a pattern of timing? Does your speaking sound so even and rhythmical in timing that the effect is monotonous?

6. Listen to recordings of your speech made when you were reading and when you were talking spontaneously. How many words did you speak a minute? Does the general rate permit intelligibility and is it suited to the idea expressed? Are your phrasing and use of pauses effective?

Exercises for Improvement

1. By timing yourself as you read the following passage aloud, ascertain your general rate on simple material. The average reader will not complete the 185 words within the minute, but will reach the dash in the last sentence (160 words per minute). If you finish some time before the minute limit, you are probably going too fast for the audience's comprehension. If you do not finish the first sentence of the third paragraph, you are going too slowly for interest.

Your rate, when you read factual material, is faster than your rate for factual, spontaneous speech. The words are provided for you on the page, and even though you take time to react to the ideas and to make sure that the listeners respond, the words will still flow out faster than they would if you were creating your own phrases.

If the reading material is simple, your speed may even approach 180 or 190 words per minute. At these faster rates, articulation must be particularly clear to permit understanding.

The moment the spoken material suggests an emotion, changes in rate occur. If you describe a quiet scene, you allow time for your listeners to react to your appreciation of the details. Introduce a horseman galloping across this scene, and your rate must change. Philosophize about the desolation of the picture, add a humorous detail, follow the horseman on to a climax in action—for each aspect of the idea you present, you will use a rate suitable to the feeling states you wish to evoke in your listeners.

If you are told that your rate is rapid, practice the selection until the time limit catches you in the middle of the last paragraph. The insertion of longer pauses alone will not change the listener's criticism. The phrases themselves must be slower and the words within the phrases longer in duration, to decrease the effect of hurrying.

2. Go back over the same selection and mark the phrases. Indicate where you would take a breath. Reread the selection, observing the breath marks.

3. Several selections will now be presented, each quite different in complexity of idea and in emotional connotation. Analyze each selection according to the following plan:

a. Should the general rate be fast, slow, or intermediate? Should there be progressive changes in rate within the passage? Why?

b. Mark the phrasing given in several of the selections, rereading the material as marked, until the grouping of the words seems logical and the length of the phrase is adjusted to your breathing habits.

c. Where might pauses longer than usual enhance the effectiveness of the reading?

d. In Selection 5, underline the phrases which, because of their importance, should be spoken more slowly than surrounding phrases. Reread the selection until you can hear your use of contrast between fast and slow rate on phrases.

SELECTION I

The changes wrought by death are in themselves so sharp and final, and so terrible and melancholy in their consequences, that the thing stands alone in man's experience, and has no parallel on earth. It outdoes all other accidents because it is the last of them. Sometimes it leaps suddenly upon its victims like a Thug; sometimes it lays a regular siege and creeps upon their citadel during a score of years.—STEVENSON

SELECTION 2

Then there is the beefsteak. They have it in Europe, but they don't know how to cook it. Neither will they cut it right. It comes on the table in a small, round, pewter platter. It lies in the center of this platter, in a bordering bed of grease-soaked potatoes; it is the size, shape, and thickness of a man's hand with the thumb and fingers cut off. It is a little overdone, is rather dry, it tastes pretty insipidly, it rouses no enthusiasm.

Imagine a poor exile contemplating that inert thing; and imagine an angel suddenly sweeping down out of a better land and setting before him a mighty porter-house steak an inch and a half thick, hot and sputtering from the griddle; dusted with fragrant pepper; enriched with little melting bits of butter of the most unimpeachable freshness and genuineness; the precious juices of the meat trickling out and joining the gravy . . . and imagine that the angel also adds a great cup of American home-made coffee, with the cream afroth on top, some real butter, firm and yellow and fresh, some smoking hot biscuits . . . —could words describe the gratitude of this exile?—MARK TWAIN

SELECTION 3

The ring was empty now, terribly and completely empty, a circle of sparkling golden sand waiting to blot up his blood. The drum rolled and the crowd hushed. The bugle bleated out, cracking on the last note, the rope that went to the latch was jerked, and the toril door swung open.

Nothing happened.

Cascabel, safely behind the fence, swung his cape several times in front of the dark tunnel. Suddenly a greenish-black shape exploded from the darkness and skidded out into the sun. Babilonio, number 55 branded big on his side, was low in the haunches, swelling up to great shoulders and the angry hump of tossing muscle. The dust from the corral blew off the muscled back as it ran fast around the ring, feinting with its horns and looking for something to kill. It had not been goaded or irritated or injured in any way—not even by the sting of the identifying "divisa" ribbons which most other plazas jabbed into the bull's shoulders—yet it knew what it was in this arena for. It was a Toro Bravo, a separate breed from the domestic bovine, and its natural instinct, plus centuries of careful breeding behind it, told it that it was here to fight and kill. It hadn't eaten this day, any more than the men who were to fight it had, but its fat barrel and sleek hide showed that all its life it had had plenty of the best food. Though it was fairly small, the audience applauded the bull's conformation, the small hoofs, the uniform horns, the silky tail that almost touched the ground. It could turn faster than a polo pony and beat any race horse in the world for a hundred feet. Here was a good example of the most perfect living instrument for killing that man could devise.—CONRAD*

SELECTION 4

The President stood before us as a man of the people. He was thoroughly American, had never crossed the sea, had never been spoiled by English insularity or French dissipation; a quite native aboriginal man, as an acorn from an oak; no aping of foreigners, no frivolous accomplishments, Kentuckian born, working on a farm, a flatboatman, a captain in the Black Hawk war, a country lawyer, a representative in the rural legislature in Illinois;—on such modest foundations the broad structure of his fame was laid. How slowly, and yet by happily prepared steps, he came to his place.—EMERSON

SELECTION 5

I am credibly informed that there is still a considerable hitch or hobble in your enunciation, and that when you speak fast you sometimes speak unintelligibly. . . . Your trade is to speak well, both in public and in private. The manner of your speaking is full as important as the matter, as more people have ears to be tickled than understandings to judge. Be your productions ever so good, they will be of no use, if you stifle and strangle them in birth. . . . Remember of what importance Demosthenes, and one of the Gracchi, thought ENUNCIATION; and read what stress Cicero and Quintilian lay upon it; even the herb-women at Athens were correct judges of it. Oratory, with all its graces, that of enunciation in particular, is full as necessary in our government as it ever was in Greece or Rome. No man can make a fortune or a figure in this country, without speaking, and speaking well in public. If you will persuade, you must please; and if you will please, you must tune your voice to harmony, you must articulate every syllable distinctly, your emphasis and cadences must be strongly and properly marked, and the whole together must be graceful and engaging. If you do not speak in that manner, you had much better not speak at all. . . . Let me conjure you, therefore, to make this your only object, till you have absolutely conquered it, for that it is in your power;

* Barnaby Conrad, *Matador*, Houghton Mifflin Company, Boston, 1952. (By permission.)

think of nothing else, read and speak for nothing else. Read aloud, though alone, and read articulately and distinctly, as if you were reading in public, and on the most important occasion. Recite pieces of eloquence, declaim scenes of tragedies to Mr. Harte, as if he were a numerous audience. If there is any particular consonant which you have difficulty in articulating, as I think you had with the R, utter it millions and millions of times, till you have uttered it right. Never speak quick, till you have first learned to speak well. In short, lay aside every book, and every thought, that does not directly tend to this great object, absolutely decisive to your future fortune and figure.—LORD CHESTERFIELD

4. To gain a better appreciation of the duration of sounds, read the following selection. Lengthen all of the vowels, with the exception of those in unimportant words. Do not drawl, but sustain the tone steadily for each long-vowel sound. Be aware also of control over your breathing.

Life is a narrow vale between the cold and barren peaks of two eternities. We strive in vain to look beyond the heights. We cry aloud, and the only answer is the echo of our wailing cry. From the voiceless lips of the unreplying dead, there comes no word; but in the night of death, hope sees a star, and listening love can hear the rustle of a wing.

He who sleeps here, when dying, mistaking the approach of death for the return of health, whispered with his latest breath: "I am better now." Let us believe, in spite of doubts and dogmas, of fears and tears, these dear words are true of all the countless dead.—INGERSOLL

5. Read an excerpt from a modern story to the class. Choose a selection which will show your skills in suiting rate to type of material and in varying timing for effect.

6. Describe an action scene for the class, building to a climax through increase of rate and loudness.

These selections in the Appendix are suggested for practice on timing: Numbers 2, 8, 11*b*, 20, 23, and 25.

SUMMARY

In the production of your voice, the exhaled breath passes between your vocal folds. Control over steadiness, loudness, and timing of the vocalization will then depend, in great part, on control of the breath stream which sets the folds into vibration.

The structure of the breathing mechanism includes the rib cage, which is comprised of backbone, sternum, and twelve pairs of ribs; the diaphragm and tendons which provide a dome-shaped floor for the thoracic cavity; the two large conical-shaped lungs; the bronchial tubes; and the trachea, which leads up to the larynx.

When you inhale, the large diaphragmatic muscle contracts and descends; by means of muscle contraction, the ribs are raised and lifted slightly, and the sternum rises a little. This process increases the size of the thoracic cavity in three directions: up and down, side to side, and back to front. Air rushes in to fill the lungs. On exhalation in life breathing, the diaphragm and muscles between the ribs relax, the raised structures descend, and with this increased pressure upon the lungs, the breath pours out. In breathing for speech, however, the breath stream must be expelled more slowly. The abdominal muscles assist in control. As they contract, they exert steady pressure on the viscera within, which are thus forced back up against the diaphragm. The diaphragm and rib muscles relax slowly, so that there is a nice balance achieved between the relaxation of the inhalation muscles and the firm pressure of the abdominal muscles. The breath now moves steadily upward under this controlled pressure.

There are four general types of breathing for voice production: clavicular, upper thoracic, medial, and diaphragmatic-abdominal. Clavicular breathing, which involves elevation of the shoulders and collarbones, is to be avoided because it usually results in tension, fatigue, and poor control over the exhalation. The medial and diaphragmatic-abdominal are the most similar to the natural breathing-for-life process.

The control of breathing is important because (1) it contributes to steadiness of vocalization; (2) it permits the use of increased loudness when the speaking situation and the meaning necessitate this; (3) it allows you to vary the timing of your material, permitting changes in the length of phrases and pauses and in duration of words which you emphasize; and (4) it brings with it a feeling of ease and a growing assurance that you can develop skill of varying loudness and rate to suit your particular meanings.

In practice, drills for improvement of phonation and of breathing complement each other. Consequently, as you read in this book the material on phonation and resonation, you will find it helpful to go back over the exercises on breathing. Respiration, phonation, and resonation are not three independent processes. Much of your skill in the other phases of vocalization will depend upon control of breathing.

4

Tone Production

The tones of human voices are mightier than strings or brass to move the soul.—KLOPSTOCK

When the noisy welcome of a recent national political convention had died away, the governor of a prominent state stepped up to the rostrum to make the most important nominating speech of the convention. He began with energy and enthusiasm, but in a high-pitched voice. As he proceeded, his voice became higher and higher until it went above its normal pitch level to at least three tones above middle C. Finally he was able to speak only in a shrill and hoarse whisper, stopping at the end of every sentence in an attempt to relieve the evident distress of his strained vocal folds. He was barely able to finish his ten-minute speech because of the unnatural strain which he had placed upon his vocal folds and the muscles of his larynx.

A good sportscaster, on the other hand, can speak with enthusiasm, vigor, and excitement for two and a half or three hours, reporting a football game, at a pitch level which is easy for him and pleasant to the ears of his listeners. He will still have plenty of voice left when the game is over and will feel little strain on his vocal folds or the muscles of his larynx. He has achieved the fine balance of tensions and relaxations necessary for the production of excellent tone. The governor, however, upset that balance with extreme tension.

Faulty muscular control of the vocal folds as they vibrate to produce sound, through too much tension, too little tension, or improper adjustment, makes for poor tone production. This chapter is designed to help you achieve tones which may be "mightier than strings or brass to move the soul."

PHYSICAL BASES OF TONE PRODUCTION

To understand how tone is produced, we need to know something of the nature of sound itself. On any given day, most of us hear an infinite variety of sounds. The hum of automobile engines, the chirping of birds, the clatter of dishes in a restaurant, the blare of music from a juke box, the drone of a professor's voice in a dull lecture, the yelling of the crowd at a football game—these are only a few of the sounds that form a part of our everyday experience.

The sounds to which we give most frequent and careful attention are those of articulate speech. But all sounds have certain common characteristics: they are formed by the action of some force upon an object capable of vibration; they pass through some transmitting medium (usually, but not always, the air) in the form of waves; these waves set up similar vibrations in the receiving object, ordinarily the ear. When sounds have a clearly identifiable pitch, or a harmoniously blended series of tones, they are called musical sounds; when the pitch is confused or dissonant, sounds are termed noise.

Sound Waves

In ordinary transmission of sound the vibrations of the sound sources are communicated to the surrounding air and carried as *sound waves* to the ear of the listener. Sound waves are characterized by differences in *frequency*—the number of vibration cycles per second emanating from the sound source—and by differences in *wave length*—the distance between the vibration impulses as the wave moves away from the sound source. The frequency and the wave length are inversely proportional to one another, their product always equaling the speed of sound.

The speed of sound varies with the temperature of the air, the altitude, and other factors, but it is roughly 1,100 feet per second. Obviously sound could not be carried at such a speed by a continuous forward motion of the air, for that would imply winds many times faster than the most furious typhoon every time a sound was made. Sound waves are simply alternate periods of condensation and rarefaction (thinning out) of the air molecules. The initial energy derived from the sound source is transmitted from one particle to another, with only slight forward motion, and with each particle rebounding to its first position before the next condensation strikes it.

The movement of a single period of condensation in a sound wave may be illustrated by standing a number of dominoes on end at a distance from each other slightly less than the length of one domino. By touching the first piece, you may push over the whole row, as the initial energy is transmitted from one to another until all are down. If the dominoes could be made to return immediately to an upright position, another touch would start a second wave after the first. If this were done at regular intervals, the number of

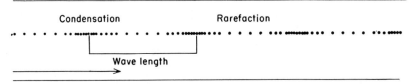

Fig. 4. *Diagram showing condensation and rarefaction of air in sound waves*

times it was repeated in a given period of time would be the *frequency*, and the distance between the impulses on the row of dominoes would be called the *wave length*. To put the figure back into terms of the sound wave, the distance between two condensations is the wave length, and the number of condensation-rarefaction cycles per second is the frequency.

Frequency and Pitch

The frequency of a sound wave is determined by the frequency of vibration of the object from which the sound comes. It is interpreted by the ear as the *pitch* of the sound, the same number of vibrations per second being heard as the same pitch, regardless of the source or loudness of the sound. A good point of reference in interpreting pitch is to locate middle C, a pitch made readily by both male and female voices. This pitch is approximately 256 to 260 vibration cycles per second, depending upon the musical standard adopted. The vibration rate doubles with each octave of the musical scale. Thus one octave below middle C is approximately 130 cycles, and one octave above is approximately 520 cycles. A few individuals are able to detect frequencies as low as 12 or as high as 50,000, but there are wide variations in perception, particularly in the high frequencies. It is the exceptional ear which can hear frequencies higher than 20,000.

In vibrating objects like the human vocal folds, frequency is determined by four factors: (1) length—the pitch is lowered as the length increases; (2) thickness—the pitch is lowered as the thickness increases; (3) tension—the pitch is *raised* as the tension increases; (4) density—the pitch is lowered as the density increases. The force which sets the vibrating object into motion does not directly affect the frequency, although in the human voice an increase in force is almost always accompanied by increased tension and a consequent rise in pitch. It is possible that there may be a causal relationship between these two conditions, but because the vocal folds are difficult to observe in a natural state, it is hard to determine how closely they are related.

All four factors are involved in the differences between any two voices. Thus the lower pitch of men's voices, as compared with those of women and children, is the result of longer and thicker vocal folds. In an individual voice, changes in length and thickness tend to cancel each other, and variations in pitch are largely the product of differences in the tension of the folds.

STRUCTURE AND FUNCTION OF THE LARYNX

In Chapter 3, we showed how the controlled exhalation of the breath provides motive power for vocalization. When the breath leaves the lungs, it goes through the many small bronchial tubes to the two large bronchi, through the open tube of the trachea, and into the larynx. As this stream passes through the larynx and activates the vocal folds within this structure, the sound begins. To locate your larynx, place your fingers in the region of the Adam's apple and hum vigorously. You will feel the vibration of the folds attached to the inner side of the Adam's apple.

STRUCTURE

The framework of the larynx is composed of cartilages connected by ligaments, membranes, and muscles. You will find the whole structure far from rigid if you place your hand on your throat as you swallow or as you move your head.

The main cartilages of the larynx are the thyroid, the cricoid, and the arytenoids. The *thyroid cartilage* is the largest; the Adam's apple is its front projection (see Figures 5 and 6). This structure, which serves as a shield for the delicate mechanism inside, is made up of two plates of cartilage fused in front and diverging at the back. Examine your own mechanism. Put your thumb and forefinger on your Adam's apple and move them back and apart; you will feel the sides of this shield in your neck. Move one finger upward from your Adam's apple; here is the notch of the thyroid (see Figure 5).

The sides of the thyroid cartilage extend backward at an angle from the point of fusion at the Adam's apple. At the back of each side, horns project upward and downward. Above the larynx, at the intersection of neck and chin, the horseshoe-shaped hyoid bone lies embedded at the root of the tongue with the open end at the back. The upper horns of the thyroid cartilage connect with the posterior ends of the curving hyoid bone by means of ligaments and small additional cartilages. A curtain of muscles extends from the hyoid bone to the thyroid cartilage, so that the entire larynx is suspended from the hyoid bone.

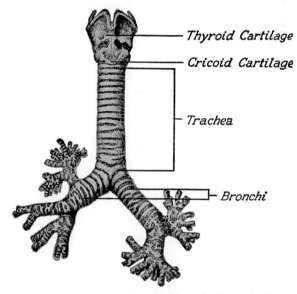

Fig. 5. Larynx, trachea, and bronchi (front view)

Below the thyroid cartilage is the *cricoid*. This cartilage is a complete circle resembling a signet ring with the narrow part in front just below the thyroid cartilage and the large signet at the back. The cricoid forms the top ring of the trachea.

The lower horns of the thyroid articulate with the sides of the cricoid cartilage. The joint is not fixed; the thyroid can tilt back and forth on this small joint and can also slide a short distance.

The upper edge of the signet part of the cricoid forms a small platform in the space between the spreading sides of the thyroid. Resting on this platform are two small, paired cartilages called the *arytenoids*. These are shaped like irregular three-sided pyramids and articulate with the cricoid on their fourth or base side. The arytenoids, by means of their muscular attachments, can be pivoted toward and away from each other and drawn back a short distance over the edge of the cricoid cartilage. These small cartilages are important to speech because they form the posterior attachments of the vocal folds, and by means of their movements manipulate the folds.

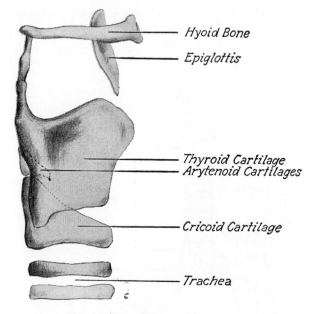

Fig. 6. The cartilages of the larynx

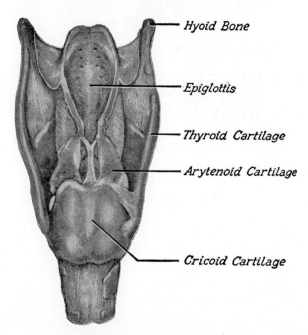

Fig. 7. The larynx (back view)

Inside the larynx, the two *vocal folds* extend from the inner front prominence of the thyroid cartilage back to the two arytenoid cartilages. These
are not "cords," as an older terminology would imply, but folds of muscle
and membrane which close like lips. When they are brought together, the
entire opening in the larynx is obstructed. When the arytenoid cartilages
are moved apart, the folds open to form a triangular slit called the *glottis*.

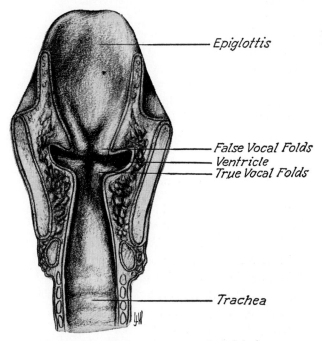

Fig. 8. The anterior transverse section of the larynx

The folds have thin inner edges at the glottis but become thicker toward
the sides, where they are attached to the inside of the cricoid cartilage (see
Figure 8). The folds are covered with mucous membrane which forms a continuous lining for the larynx, pharynx, and oral cavity. The thin inner edges
of the folds are of fibrous tissue, pearly white in color.

The arytenoids which move the folds are operated by a complex system
of muscles. Muscles between the arytenoids, or extending from their sides
down to the cricoid, or underlying the folds between the arytenoids and the
thyroid, can pivot the arytenoids on their bases and move them apart and
together. By these actions the vocal folds can be made to assume varying
degrees of openness and closure. The shifting position of the arytenoids in

relation to the thyroid, the movement of the thyroid in relation to the cricoid, and the contraction of muscles underlying the vocal folds can all combine to set up different states of tension in the folds themselves.

Figure 8 shows the larynx from the rear as if a vertical cut had been made perpendicular to the folds at their center. This is called a transverse section. The false vocal folds which lie directly above the true folds are not subject to a high degree of control. They assist in protecting the vocal folds during swallowing.

Also attached to the thyroid cartilage is the *epiglottis*, a leaf-shaped cartilage. It is connected by its stemlike lower part to the inside of the thyroid directly above the front attachment of the vocal folds, and extends at an upward angle beneath the base of the tongue. It does not contribute to voice production. The horseshoe-shaped hyoid bone partially encircles the epiglottis. Directly behind the larynx is the *esophagus*, or food passage, a tube of muscle and connective tissue which leads from the level of the top of the larynx to the stomach.

BIOLOGICAL FUNCTION

The basic function of the larynx is to act as a valve at the entrance to the trachea. When you swallow, the tongue rides back, the larynx is raised, muscle action diverts the food away from the entrance of the larynx, and both false and true vocal folds are brought together to close off the larynx at its top. If, in spite of this protective action, food or other foreign matter enters the larynx, an instantaneous reflex is set up to expel it. The vocal folds are closed tightly, air pressure is built up by the contraction of the abdominal muscles, the vocal folds are forced apart, and a blast of air is released under pressure, forcing out the foreign matter. This is what you label a *cough*. Similarly, by closing the glottis and contracting the abdominal muscles, pressure can be maintained in the chest to give a firm base for lifting or for other heavy strain.

These biological functions of the larynx take precedence over the functioning of the larynx for speech, making phonation an overlaid process. When it is necessary to use the larynx for any of them, speech functions of the larynx are disrupted.

FUNCTION IN PHONATION

The whole adjustment and movement of muscles and cartilages in phonation will be oversimplified in the following discussion so that you can understand the most important activities and those over which you have some conscious control.

During breathing, the glottis is open and is triangular in shape, with the apex of the triangle at the front. The arytenoids are separated and rotated slightly outward to maintain this opening. To produce tone, the *intrinsic muscles* of the larynx (those connecting cartilages of the larynx with each other) act upon the arytenoids to slide them together and rotate them inward, thus closing the glottis. When the edges of the folds are brought together, air pressure is built up beneath the glottis by the action of the muscles controlling exhalation. Because they are taut, the folds resist this pressure and are forced apart by it and set into vibration. This vibration is

Breathing   Whispering   Phonation

Fig. 9. The glottis during breathing, whispering, and phonation

the action which produces tone. It occurs simultaneously in both folds and moves outward from the glottis in a wavelike motion of the entire fold. The vibrations are transmitted to the air column as a sound wave. In the rapid vibrations of phonation, the edges of the folds may touch hundreds of times a second as the glottis is opened and closed. An antagonistic set of muscles returns the arytenoids to the open position when phonation is finished.

The tone produced by the folds in vibration is determined principally by the action of the various intrinsic muscles of the larynx altering the position of the thyroid and arytenoid cartilages. Muscles which stretch and elongate the vocal folds are called *tensors;* those which relax and shorten the folds are called *relaxors;* those which bring the folds together are known as *adductors;* those which swing the folds apart are termed *abductors.* These muscles produce the fundamental movements necessary for the production of tone. As we cannot consciously control the action of these individual muscle groups, it is not necessary to name them or to discuss their individual functioning. However, their activity determines the condition of the folds at any given instant, and, therefore, the pitch level of the tone produced.

The *extrinsic muscles* of the larynx are those which connect the larynx to other parts of the mechanism, such as the sternum or the hyoid bone. They serve chiefly to raise and lower the larynx from its normal position in relaxed breathing. Their main activity is related to such life processes as swallowing. Place your fingers on the thyroid cartilage and swallow; you will notice that the whole larynx rides up with the pull of the extrinsic muscles. Any marked raising or lowering of the larynx in phonation will, undoubtedly, affect the tensions in the larynx and, hence, the pitch. Some upward and downward movement of the larynx is necessary to good phonation, as you can feel if you place your fingers on the thyroid cartilage and speak a sentence or two. However, extreme movements, especially if the larynx is held at the top or bottom of its range of action, are to be avoided.

As a number of different forces are at work at the same time influencing the conditions of the folds, it is difficult to decide which influence determines a specific pitch level. The relationship of the various factors determining pitch has never been fully determined by research. While the length and thickness of the vocal folds help to determine the pitch, they tend to cancel each other in influence; the final pitch is probably determined largely by tension. In whispering, the glottis is only partially closed, and friction noises, instead of tone, make up the vocalization (see Figure 9).

For phonation, the glottis must be closed; air pressure must be built up beneath the folds, forcing them apart and setting them into vibration. The action of the intrinsic and extrinsic muscles of the larynx sets up conditions of length, tension, thickness, and density in the folds which determine the pitch produced.

Selective Activity of Muscles

In order to produce the best vocal tone, you must be free from unnecessary tensions. Obviously, however, since every aspect of voice production involves muscular activity, speech itself would be impossible if all the muscles were relaxed. Relaxation for speech simply means that you should activate *only* those muscles which are necessary to the production of the effect you desire.

This selective activity is the same process of learning used in acquiring any motor skill. A newborn baby, for instance, responds to every stimulus with his entire body. When he is uncomfortable, he cries, but his crying involves every muscle of his face, contortions of his body, and even the wriggling of his toes. An older child will repeat this identical over-all activity when he is in a temper tantrum; an unstable adult in hysteria will also react with every muscle of his body. A skilled athlete, on the other hand, improves in proportion as he eliminates unnecessary motions and muscle tensions. He learns to bring into play only those muscles which contribute to the goal for which he is striving. The same holds true for the skilled speaker or actor. A common term for any one of these performers who is off form is that he is "tied up." He is using too many muscles.

Your aim in voice production, therefore, should be to relax all the muscles of the throat which are not actually used in the formation and resonation of tone. This particularly refers to the heavy throat muscles used in chewing and swallowing, as well as to the muscles which raise the shoulders or tighten and draw down the chin. Relaxation of the general throat region is necessary so that the tone passage may be free from any interference by the biological functions; it is also necessary so that the highly delicate adjustments of the larynx and the resonating cavities may occur. In emotional states, temporary or chronic, these adjustments break down, and the more fundamental biological reactions tend to reassert themselves. Thus, people with poor physical coordination and people who are emotionally unstable tend to have unpleasant voices.

If you are successful in effecting this type of selective relaxation, you will produce the best tone of which your individual vocal mechanism is capable. And if your vocal mechanism is not impaired by the presence of some organic abnormality, this will usually be a pleasing tone.

ANALYSIS OF PHONATION HABITS

Since you have limited conscious control over specific muscle movements in phonation, you must learn to feel the presence or absence of muscle tensions in the mechanism of phonation as you speak. You must learn to associate particular kinds of muscular activity with the characteristic sounds which these activities produce. In this way you will develop a feeling sense for the muscular contractions necessary for good tone production, for the unnatural tensions which distort tone, and for the variations in tension responsible for pitch changes.

The Importance of the Control of Phonation

Learning to control phonation is important to the speaker for the following reasons:

1. Improper phonation may influence your breath control. If too much air escapes between the vocal folds as you phonate, no matter how good your breathing habits, you will run short of breath, lack control for changes of loudness, and interrupt your control for proper timing.

2. If there is muscle strain in either the intrinsic or the extrinsic muscles of the larynx, you cannot have easy vocalization. This tension may upset

you and make you lose confidence in your own abilities. It will make phonation an effort instead of an easy, pleasant process.

3. Faulty phonation resulting in hoarseness, harshness, or raspiness will have an unpleasant effect on the ear of the listener and may be a distinct barrier to social acceptance and even to efficient communication.

4. Inefficient phonation often results in the inability to control and vary pitch for connected speech. When this occurs, the melody changes which suggest the variations in meaning are absent; communication is thus interfered with.

Self-analysis and Listening

Intelligent analysis of tone production through ear training is of major importance. Until you can hear critically the skills and faults of phonation in the voices of your classmates and in your own voice, you can do little toward self-improvement.

1. You should begin with an analysis of the muscle tensions present in your own phonation.

a. With your finger tips on the thyroid cartilage, produce an easy, pleasant, sustained AH sound loud enough to be heard easily by a person six feet from you. Notice the position of the larynx; are the extrinsic muscles above and below it tense or relaxed?

b. Without moving your fingers, sustain AH on as high a pitch level as you comfortably can. Notice how the larynx moves up. Is there tension in any of the extrinsic muscles?

c. Keep the fingers in position and sustain AH on your lowest comfortable pitch level. Notice how the larynx moves; note the tensions in the extrinsic muscles below it.

d. On one breath go from the low to the high AH sound without interrupting the tone. Do you feel muscle movements and changes in tension within the larynx as the pitch changes? On which pitch level do you feel the greatest tension? On which the least?

2. Listen to your phonation while sustaining AH at a conversational level of loudness, while reading aloud at conversational level, while reciting or performing in class, and while you are conversing with your friends. Does the phonation sound easy and pleasant? Do you sound hoarse or harsh to yourself by comparison with a voice which you judge as excellent? Do you feel any marked tensions in the extrinsic muscles? Within the larynx?

3. Do you hear in your own voice the same factors in tone production which your instructor and classmates report?

4. Listen to the recording of your voice which you made at the beginning of the semester. Do you hear any faults in your phonation? What are they?

5. Listen carefully to the normal phonation of your friends and that which takes place in the exercise assignments in class. Can you recognize clear, pure, unstrained production? Does your ear distinguish better phonation in the speech of one person than in that of another? When you hear phonation which is not pleasant and which sounds strained, try to imitate in your own mechanism the muscle tensions which the other person has in his; duplicate the tensions and phonate. Does your tone ordinarily sound like his?

PROBLEMS OF PHONATION

You should be acquainted with several specific and common voice problems which arise from improper phonation. We are not concerned with problems caused by organic defects of the larynx and the associated mechanism, such as paralysis of the folds, vocal nodes (corns on the inner edges of the folds which prevent their approximation), or malformation of the laryngeal structure. These are problems for the physician or the speech pathologist. We are interested here in the malfunctioning of the "normal" structure which can be corrected through training. While there is a wide variety of such difficulties, we shall classify them into a few general categories for analysis and retraining.

BREATHINESS

Breathiness is a condition caused by an incomplete closure of the glottis in phonation. The vocal folds are not brought together completely before air pressure is built up beneath them. As a result, there is air escaping which is not being used. This may happen on all phonation or, as is common, only on the initiation of a vowel. The person with a breathy tone seems to be whispering everything he says; there is a fuzzy or feathery edge to all of his vocalization. The tone is not necessarily unpleasing, but it lacks carrying power, gives the impression that the speaker is airing his secrets in public, and frequently leads to monotony. The speaker who uses it puts forth a tremendous amount of effort in attempting to project with sufficient volume to an audience of any size.

GLOTTAL SHOCK

Glottal shock is a condition which is almost the direct opposite of breathiness. It is a staccato click, or tight, coughlike explosion of the vocal folds, frequently observed on the initiation of vowel sounds. Its presence is an indication that tone is begun with the throat in a strained condition.

This phonatory fault is caused by a tense, complete closure of the glottis under breath pressure. The vocal folds are then blasted apart, as in a light cough, when tone is initiated. In normal vocalization, the vocal folds touch each other lightly without the need of any pressure from the external throat muscles. Any voluntary cramping of the throat muscles interferes with this normal functioning, and a harsh, unpleasant initiation of tone results. The same tensions which produce glottal shock frequently lead to high pitch and to a flat tone which is deficient in resonance and tone color.

HARSHNESS

Harshness is related both to tone production and to resonation. It is the result of excessive muscle constriction throughout the vocal mechanism from top to bottom, and not in the larynx alone. The tension is particularly notice-able in the extrinsic muscles of the larynx; ordinarily, the larynx is held at the top or bottom of its range of movement. These tensions do not allow free and easy vibration of the vocal folds, and extraneous friction noises may be introduced in the passages immediately above the folds. The woman who talks at the top of her range with a shrill, high quality, or the man who forces his voice to the bottom of his range, so that it sounds gravelly and harsh, are both examples of this type of phonation.

HOARSENESS

Hoarseness is generally associated with some abnormal physiological con-dition of the vocal folds, which may be either temporary or chronic. A temporary condition in the folds may cause them to swell, and the muscles may become less responsive to stimulation than normally. When you have a severe cold which "goes down your throat," the folds swell; they will not approximate easily or vibrate freely. When you yell continuously at a football game, you strain the muscles of the larynx and irritate the vocal folds by rubbing their edges together, so that hoarseness or complete loss of voice results. In the same way, if you give a speech with unnecessary tension in the larynx and strain the folds, you will become hoarse before you are through and may find it difficult to speak at all. A common cause of prolonged hoarseness is postnasal drip from hay fever, sinusitis, or other infection which causes constant inflammation of the folds.

These more or less temporary conditions, which have brought on the irritation in the larynx, may disappear and the irritation go away; yet you may continue to be hoarse. In this instance, either you have set up a pattern of muscle response which maintains the temporary tensions or you are still trying to adjust to an irritation which no longer exists. When a prolonged irritation of the folds leaves, you may still be trying to protect the folds as you did when they were sore, and so the hoarseness continues even though there is no longer a physical cause for it. The voice sounds raspy and strained.

Self-analysis and Listening

1. Read aloud a selection of vigorous, direct, communicative speech. "A House Divided," Number 18 in the Appendix, is that type of material. Record the selection and play the recording for analysis.

a. Are you breathy? Do you sound as if you were whispering?

b. Notice the vowel sounds at the beginning of words, particularly when a vowel begins a sentence. Is it initiated easily and smoothly? Do you hear a "click" or "shock" as you start it? Do you feel any unusual tension in the larynx as you start the vowel sounds?

c. Do you hear strain in your voice? Does the tone sound clear and pleasant? How does your tone sound by comparison with the best voices in the class?

d. Try to remember how the tone of your voice sounded when you had a bad cold, hay fever, or after you had done a lot of cheering at a ball game. Was it unpleasant? Was there a feeling of strain or tension in the muscles of the larynx?

2. Do you hear any of the four problems of phonation in the voices of your friends or classmates? How do you react to the faults when you hear them? Do the faults seem to interfere with efficient communication?

3. Do you hear in your own voice any of the problems of phonation which your classmates and instructor report?

Exercises for Improvement

Exercises for both general improvement and correction of specific defects are presented here. They should prove helpful to all of you, regardless of your individual problems. The exercises should be regarded not only as remedial measures, but as tests of your ability in phonation. Plan and carry out a regular program of practice.

Breathing exercises should be continued as part of the work on phonation. It will be difficult for you to produce a pure and relaxed tone unless there is proper breath support. The most helpful exercises are those listed under *Breath Control for Steadiness of Vocalization* in the preceding chapter.

FOR RELAXATION

Relaxation is basic to good phonation. It is necessary that the mechanism use only those muscles which are needed in each act and use them with the minimum of strain. Hence, the first exercises in this section are designed to relax the mechanism of phonation. Use these exercises each time before you do those for specific phonation faults.

1. Hold the head upright. Relax the muscles holding it and let it fall forward with the chin touching the chest. Be sure that it is falling forward of its own weight and that you are not pulling it forward. Repeat this several times.

2. Let the head fall forward as in Exercise 1, and then rotate it slowly and with as little muscular effort as possible up to the right shoulder. Now let the head fall backward and then rotate it forward over the left shoulder, letting it fall forward again. See that the jaw drops open of its own weight as the head falls back. As you rotate the head backward, inhale. Exhale as the head moves forward. Repeat this slowly; reverse the direction and do it several times more.

3. Relax the jaw by letting it fall open of its own weight as the head is held upright. Be certain that you are not pulling the jaw down, but letting it fall. Close the mouth and repeat the exercise several times, getting the feeling of relaxation in the jaw muscles as the mouth falls open.

4. Repeat the syllable SUH, keeping the tongue relaxed and letting the relaxed jaw fall open after the consonant sound. Repeat this several times.

5. Take a deep breath; by relaxing as completely as possible, let out a deep sigh. Try to let the muscles of the throat and mouth go as you release the air. Feel that those muscles are relaxed. Repeat several times and then vocalize an easy, soft AH sound as you sigh. Try for pure tone without increased tension. Repeat, using the vowel tones OH, AW, OO, and EE.

FOR BREATHINESS

Breathiness may be corrected through the systematic use of the following exercises.

1. Start a whispered AH; gradually add phonation on the sustained whisper until you have a clear and nonbreathy tone. Repeat this several times, being sure each time that the final tone has no breathiness in it.

2. Practice the sounds AH, OH, OO, and EE, starting each one with a firm

glottal closure; sustain each for at least a count of three. Be sure that there is neither leakage of breath on the initiation of the sound nor breathiness as you hold the tone. Repeat several times with each of the sounds.

3. Starting with the lowest tone which you can produce with ease as *do* and sounding each note as a sustained AH, sing up the scale. Make each tone as long and loud as possible without strain, and be sure that it is not breathy. When you reach the top of the octave, reverse the scale and go back down to your original note. Breathe between tones. Repeat the exercise several times.

4. In reading the following paired words, pay no attention to breathiness on the vowel in the first word, but be sure that there is none on the vowel in the second word of the pair. Read through the list again and reverse the words in each pair. This time, eliminate the breathiness on all vowels. Do this a number of times.

hair	air	hat	at	hate	ate
hold	old	helm	elm	harm	arm
hit	it	high	eye	heel	eel
had	add	heat	eat	hall	all

5. Read the following words, guarding against all breathiness: *who, home, hunt, him, hem, whole, hand, wreck, wave, this, them, thick, several, finish,* and *stool.* Repeat a number of times, lengthening the vowels on some of the trials.

6. Read the following paragraph as loudly as possible and without breathiness; then reread it, gradually reducing the loudness until you reach a conversational tone. Reread it as many times as is necessary to reduce the volume to the desired level. Be sure that there is no breathiness at any time. Making a record of this will assist you.

If you have breathy tone quality, you must make every effort to correct the fault. Hearing the defect is the first step toward this rehabilitation. A thorough course of exercises, practiced every day, will help to establish the new habit. Have your classmates check on the progress which you think you are making.

FOR GLOTTAL SHOCK

If glottal shock is one of your problems, then you should work with the following exercises to help eliminate it.

1. Whisper the AH sound and gradually begin to phonate the tone at your habitual pitch level and with conversational volume. Be sure that

the sound is easily initiated and that there is no click as the folds approximate on the initiation of the tone. Hold the sound steadily for a count of three. Repeat on the sounds OH, AW, OO, and EE.

2. Practice starting the vowel AH a number of times. Be sure that you get a smooth, easy initiation of tone without noise. Hold the sound, as in Exercise 1. Repeat on OH, AW, OO, and EE.

3. Use the paired words in Exercise 4 under *Breathiness* as the basis for this exercise. Read the first word of the pair, breathing the H sound and sliding easily without shock into the vowel; now read the second word of the pair without the breathed H, but with the same easy initiation of the vowel sound.

4. In the following sentences, the sounds on which you are apt to have glottal shock have been italicized. Read the sentences aloud, paying particular attention to the marked sounds, trying to get an easy initiation of sound on them. In each phrase, be sure that you blend the words so that the sounds flow smoothly without any break between them.

a. *I*mmediately *a*fter the *e*nthusiastic *e*ncore, the *a*rtist *a*nswered his *a*pplause.
b. *O*ur *a*unt *e*mphasized the *i*dea that *a*n *a*ttitude *o*f *a*ttentiveness *i*s *o*bligatory.
c. *E*ach *o*rator *o*ught to *o*utline *a*n *a*lternate *a*rgument.
d. His *i*naccurate *e*stimate *o*f expenses was not *o*nly *e*xaggerated but *a*nnoying.
e. *I* *i*nvited *I*rene *a*nd *E*mma to *a*ccompany *u*s *a*ll *a*long the *a*venue.
f. *H*onest *e*ffort *i*s *i*ts *o*wn reward, *a*sserted the *o*ld *O*riental.
g. *I*s *A*lex *a*n *e*xpert *a*t *a*crobatics?
h. *I*nsist *u*pon *i*nclusive *i*nformation *i*n *a*ppraising *a*ny *i*nsurance.
i. *E*lla *a*greed to *a*ssist *a*ll *e*ligible *a*mateurs.
j. *E*very *a*lley *e*ntering the *a*venue *i*s *o*pen to *e*veryone.

FOR HARSHNESS

Harshness can be materially helped through the use of the following exercises. You will find that the exercises for relaxation and for glottal shock are also helpful.

1. Place the tip of the tongue behind the lower front teeth; open the mouth and throat as if to yawn. Maintaining this relaxed position, phonate an easy AH sound and sustain it for the count of three. If you feel any tenseness or rigidity in the muscles at the back of the throat, as you do in a completed

yawn, relax and begin again. Practice the same exercise with OH, AW, OO, and EE.

2. Following the same directions as for Exercise 1, start with the OH and gradually blend it into the AH sound. Start with OO and EE and blend in the same way. Keep the tone free and relaxed.

3. Keep a relaxed throat and repeat the following sentences slowly, sustaining all of the vowel sounds, being sure that they are not harsh.

a. Where are you?
b. Green grow the lilacs.
c. The moon is mellow tonight.
d. Few were ready to go.
e. Aim high if you are in earnest.
f. Roll on, thou deep and dark blue Ocean—roll!
g. Thou art merciful unto him.
h. Blow a low, low tone.
i. Hear how the sea moans today.
j. Hold high the hero.

4. The following selections provide good practice for eliminating harshness. Practice them, sustaining the vowels and listening for any sign of harshness.

a. Sweet and low, sweet and low,
    Wind of the western sea,
  Low, low, breathe and blow,
    Wind of the western sea!
  Over the rolling waters go,
    Come from the dying moon, and blow,
  Blow him again to me;
    While my little one, while my pretty one, sleeps.
                  —TENNYSON

b. Blessed is the man that walketh not in the counsel of the ungodly, nor standeth in the way of sinners, nor sitteth in the seat of the scornful.

But his delight is in the law of the Lord; and in his law doth he meditate day and night.

And he shall be like a tree planted by the rivers of water, that bringeth forth his fruit in his season; his leaf also shall not wither; and whatsoever he doeth shall prosper.

The ungodly are not so: but are like the chaff which the wind driveth
    away.
Therefore the ungodly shall not stand in the judgment, nor sinners in
    the congregation of the righteous.
For the Lord knoweth the way of the righteous: but the way of the
    ungodly shall perish.

—PSALMS I

c. Teach me your mood, O patient stars!
    Who climb each night the ancient sky,
Leaving on space no shade, no scars,
    No trace of age, nor fear to die.

—EMERSON

d. Selection 12 in the Appendix.
e. Selection 21 in the Appendix.

FOR HOARSENESS

If your hoarseness is pathological, caused by chronic infection or irritation, you have more need for medical care than you do for voice exercises. If it is not pathological, then you should use the relaxation exercises and those for glottal shock and harshness. It is not necessary to set up new exercises for this condition. The following exercises are particularly useful.

1. *Glottal Shock:* Exercise 1.
2. *Glottal Shock:* Exercise 3.
3. *Harshness:* Exercise 1.
4. *Harshness:* Exercise 2.
5. *Harshness:* Exercise 3.

PITCH

Harshness and hoarseness are often found in voices which are pitched too high or too low for the most efficient use of the muscular structure which produces tone. It is therefore important to discover at what pitch level your vocal mechanism functions best. This level is called your *optimum pitch*. At this level, tone may be produced with a minimum of muscular activity, and with the selective process of relaxation and tension operating efficiently. Because of this, the purest, richest, and fullest tones can be produced at the optimum pitch of your voice.

Unfortunately, however, the optimum pitch is not necessarily your *habitual pitch*. Physical or emotional tensions may have created a habitual pitch well above your optimum. Or a desire to emulate someone you admire may have forced your pitch lower than is suitable for your physical structure. Many conditions of habit and training influence your habitual pitch. General health, specific conditions associated with the larynx, general emotional states, and the immediate emotional condition all go toward determining this level. Your habitual pitch may change from day to day, or even from hour to hour, as you become tired, ill, emotionally upset, or depressed, or, conversely, elated or excited.

In the foregoing discussion, habitual pitch and optimum pitch do not, of course, mean unvaried pitch. Rather these are the levels to which the voice returns after each variation to express a change in meaning. We will discuss these changes later under the heading of *melody*. What we are concerned with here is to discover the best basic pitch level for your voice. For maximum efficiency of operation and the most pleasant phonation, the optimum pitch and habitual pitch should be the same.

Finding the Habitual Pitch Level

It is difficult to discover your habitual pitch level without aid from the instructor or a member of the class. A piano or a pitch pipe is almost a necessity for accuracy. Three methods are suggested below for you to try.

1. Read a selection of prose in an easy, conversational voice. As you go along, try to hear the level of pitch which you use most often and to which you return after any variation up or down the scale. Pick a word or syllable which seems to be on that note, and prolong the sound. Locate the pitch on the musical scale. Try the experiment several times, and average the results to get an approximation of your habitual pitch level.

2. Read a selection as suggested above while sitting at a piano. As you read, try various tones on the piano around middle C (or C below middle C for a man's voice) until you find the one which comes closest to your habitual level. Repeat the experiment several times to be sure you have the right tone.

3. If you do not have a piano available, but do have a pitch pipe, try Exercise 2, using the pitch pipe instead of the piano. It is possible to do this by yourself, but much easier if someone else uses the pitch pipe to help you locate the pitch level.

4. Read a selection and have someone else at the piano lightly sound the notes around middle C. The person at the piano should be able to locate your habitual pitch level. Repeat several times. Naturally, this experiment will be the most successful if the person helping you is trained in voice, particularly in listening.

Finding the Optimum Pitch Level

Generally the optimum pitch level is about one-third of the way up from the lowest note to the highest note you can produce comfortably. If you will experiment, you will find that your tone is more easily sounded, fuller, and richer at one pitch level than at any other; that is your optimum pitch. At best, any method available to you for finding it is crude and only approximate. Three possible methods are suggested.

1. Sing down to the lowest note you can comfortably produce. Let this be *do*. Sing up the musical scale to *sol*. Your optimum pitch should be at or near this tone. Using this pitch, say, "I am going home," on a monopitch. Try the same exercise one tone higher, and then one tone lower. Listen to your voice and have some other person listen, to determine which pitch produces the purest and fullest tone with the least effort. The tone which meets these requirements should be your optimum pitch.

2. Stop up your ears with your fingers and hum M up and down the scale until you find the pitch level at which the sound seems to ring the loudest in your head. This will be approximately your optimum pitch. Test your ability to use this pitch by repeating the procedure suggested in Exercise 1.

3. Using a piano, go down to the lowest note which you can comfortably produce; follow along on the piano note by note. Now sing back up the scale, as suggested in the first exercise, sounding each tone on the piano as you do so. When you reach the *sol* in this experiment, try sounding it with the piano, and then sounding tones just above and below that level. Listen to hear which one sounds the richest and fullest; that is your optimum pitch. It is best to have someone with a good ear to assist you in this exercise.

If your habitual pitch level and your optimum pitch level are the same, then you need not be concerned about your voice in this regard. However, if there is any wide discrepancy between the two, then you must work to reconcile the difference and bring your habitual pitch closer to the optimum pitch for the most efficient, effective, and pleasant phonation.

MELODY: VARYING PITCH FOR MEANING AND FEELING

Pitch variations in speech are called *melody*. The term is borrowed from music, and like the original, it refers to the flow of sounds from one pitch to another. Speech melody is less regular than song melody, and its pattern is determined by the speaker at the moment of utterance rather than being preordained by a composer. It is thus a spontaneous reflection of the thoughts and feelings of the speaker. Perhaps more than any other type of variety in speech, melody tells something of the personality and temperament of the speaker and his attitude toward his listeners. But even more, it indicates his evaluation of the importance and emotional significance of ideas, words, and phrases. If your melody pattern causes your listeners to make wrong judgments about you or your ideas, you are as much at fault as if you had misled them by inaccurate choice of words, for meanings and feelings are carried by the melody as well as by the words which are spoken.

Melody changes may appear alone, or in combination with modifications in loudness, timing, or quality. Like other forms of emphasis, the effectiveness of pitch variation depends upon an alert and active body responding to the thought and feeling you wish to express. Changes in the total energy pattern of the body make it easier to adjust the muscles of the larynx for best use of the elements of melody: key, inflection, step, and range.

THE ELEMENTS OF MELODY

Key

The term *key* means the average pitch at which you speak a phrase, a sentence, or a longer passage. In ordinary communicative speaking or reading, the most effective key will center on the optimum pitch, with suitable variations from that level to give emphasis to important words and ideas. On the other hand, when the emotional, rather than the intellectual, content of what you speak or read is dominant, the mood may often be better communicated in a higher or lower key. Consider, for example, the effect you create if you read this sentence from Poe's *Fall of the House of Usher* in a high key and at a fast rate:

> There was an iciness, a sinking, a sickening of the heart, an unredeemed dreariness of thought which no goading of the imagination could torture into aught of the sublime.

Now slow the rate, and speak in a low key. Note how much better you can portray the mood.

Reverse the procedure for the following lines from Shelley's "To a Skylark." Read them first in a low key, and then in a high one. Which is better?

> Hail to thee, blithe spirit!
> Bird thou never wert,
> That from heaven, or near it,
> Pourest thy full heart
> In profuse strain of unpremeditated art.

> Higher still and higher
>   From the earth thou springest
> Like a cloud of fire;
>   The blue deep thou wingest,
> And singing still dost soar, and soaring ever singest.

Often imaginative literature offers sharp contrasts between adjacent passages. This is particularly true of sonnets, and key changes may frequently be invoked to develop the shift in mood. Experiment with key changes in reading Shakespeare's "Sonnet XXIX" (Appendix, Number 7) and Shelley's "Ozymandias" (Appendix, Number 5).

The Inflection

Inflection is one of the methods through which you achieve variety of melody. An inflection is an upward or downward glide—a change in pitch within a single phonation. It is a change accomplished by sliding through the intervening pitch levels in moving from one pitch to another, without any cessation of tone. The rising inflection is an upward glide. Such an inflection usually denotes doubt, uncertainty, indecision, questioning, suspense, or unfinished thought. The falling inflection, ending on a lower pitch level, denotes certainty, positiveness, finality, or finished thought. The rising inflection is frequently used to end a question, while the falling inflection generally ends a positive statement of fact. You will impair the effectiveness with which you can use inflections, however, if you fail to note that there are many exceptions to these generalizations.

The circumflex inflection is a subtle inflection used to express fine shades of meaning. It may be a rising inflection followed by a falling one; it may be a falling inflection followed by a rising one; or it may be any one of a number of combinations of the two. A circumflex inflection may give an idea a double meaning, or one which is not inherent in the words but which the speaker wishes to imply. A classic example is the line from Shakespeare's *Julius Caesar* when Antony is addressing the crowd, saying, "For Brutus is an honorable man." The use of rising and falling inflections, particularly on the word "honorable," gives the listener the subtle meaning exactly opposed to what the words say, but which Antony wishes to convey.

Inflections help to convey the logical meaning and mood of the speaker to his listeners. They suggest the attitude of the speaker toward his ideas. By means of inflections, the speaker can give different meanings to the same words. Try saying "no" or "yeah," first with a falling, then a rising, and finally a rising and falling circumflex inflection. Note the differences in meaning achieved by the inflectional changes alone. It is important for you to be able to produce these various types of inflections so that your vocal instrument will be responsive to the changes in thought and feeling as they occur in your materials.

The general changes in pitch within a group of phonations are called an *intonation*. You must be careful not to repeat the same intonation pattern in each phrase or sentence you speak. If you are responsive to the fine shades of meaning and allow individual inflections to express them, you will avoid this pitfall.

The Step

In the inflection, the change in pitch is gradual, but in the *step* there is an abrupt change without a noticeable glide. In the transitions between words or syllables, and even more frequently between phrases, a skilled speaker will change his pitch because of a shift in thought or feeling. Between the major tonal elements of adjacent syllables there is a clear and discrete pitch change. In the following examples, the position of the words indicates the places where steps might be used in speaking.

```
                        red,
                             white,
        The colors are               and
                                          blue.
        This is the
                      place!
                  far,
                       far
        It was           away.
```

The speaker may use the step to give emphasis to a word or group of words by placing them on a higher or lower pitch level than the remainder of the phrase. Also, it may help the speaker to convey emotional mood and atmosphere, and at the same time, to fix spatial relationships for the listener. The step is more direct, positive, and assertive than the inflection. As it is one of the methods for achieving variety, you should test your ability to use and hear the step. Further examples of the use of the step will be found in

Exercise 9, page 84. In many of these sentences you will be able to note the significance of the step when it is used between phrases.

Pitch Range

You will be most effective in using melody if you are able to use a fairly wide pitch range. This range is determined by the limits from the lowest to the highest pitch which you use in speaking. Persons whom you would judge as having good voices have a pitch range of an octave or more, while a highly trained voice will often have a range of at least two octaves. President Roosevelt's normal speaking range was from 96 to 256 cycles, a range of about one and a half octaves, with the top tone at about middle C. On the other hand, many persons with poor voices have a pitch range which is limited to not more than two full tones each way from the habitual pitch level. The mechanism of the larynx is capable, if it is in good physical condition, of operation which will give a range of at least an octave. Research has shown that there is little if any difference in the muscular development of the larynx in the person with a wide pitch range and one with a narrow range. It is up to you to discover whether your pitch range is adequate for good vocalization, and if it is not, to make every effort to increase it.

Determining the Speaking Range

At best, the two exercises below are not entirely satisfactory methods ot determining your range. However, without the aid of instruments such as those in a voice laboratory, they are the best methods available to you.

1. Read a prose selection which, by its very nature, seems to call for variation in pitch level. Try to locate the highest tone which your voice reaches while reading, and sustain that tone; that is the top of your reading range. Do the same for the lowest note which you reach in reading. Repeat the experiment several times and with different materials. If possible, record the reading in order to hear your range more objectively.

2. Using a piano, repeat the reading, or listen to the recording you made for the first exercise. When you hear the tone which you think is the highest, sustain it and locate it on the piano. Do the same with the lowest tone. This will give you your range. Try the experiment with several different selections and with conversational speech; note the differences in range and try to strike an average.

There is a distinct relationship between habitual pitch, optimum pitch, and range. If the habitual pitch is either so low or so high that it is near the bottom or the top of the range, then no matter how wide the range may be, it will be difficult for you to achieve real variety; all of the change of pitch will be either up from the bottom or down from the top. However, if you are using your optimum pitch level as your habitual one, then, even though the range is limited, there will be an opportunity for variety both up and down the scale within the range of your voice. Naturally, the wider your range, the greater chance there will be for effective variety. Hence, it is important for you to explore your habitual and optimum levels and your range and, if necessary, work to change or broaden them.

MELODY AND PERSONALITY

Your own emotional responsiveness will in large part act as a determining influence for variations in speech melody. If you are emotionally unresponsive, you will not have much melody change, and what you have will be in a narrow range. If you are excessively responsive, you are likely to have changes which are too abrupt and too wide and sweeping. Your habitual tensions will be reflected in your basic pitch and the pattern and variety of your melody. This is something which you must listen for in your own speech and ask others to criticize. If such patterns are present as the result of your personality, you must analyze yourself to find the root cause, and then make conscious efforts to break the old habits.

Subtle cues to the personality of the speaker are given by his use of melody. Consider the speaker who has many positive, falling inflections; generally, other things being equal, he will give the impression that he is a positive, even a didactic, person. Mr. Milquetoast will use many rising inflections, indicating his doubt and uncertainty about everything. When a man overuses a subtle pattern of combinations of circumflex and rising inflections, a certain femininity in character will be suggested. A constant series of rising inflections and a song pattern on the high pitch level associated with the gushy hostess denote the insincerity inherent in such an individual. These patterns limit the effectiveness of the speaker, because they all tend to impose themselves upon speech regardless of the meaning required by the words spoken. The effective speaker, therefore, must work not only to modify the pattern itself, but to change the personality traits from which it is derived.

Your emotional state in the speaking, reading, or acting situation may influence the melody, too. If you feel no unnatural tensions in the situation and have a responsive mechanism, you will probably make the changes necessary for meaning. However, if you feel unnatural inhibitions, engendered by the immediate situation, your mechanism may not respond freely; the variation in melody will be restricted to a narrow range, be almost entirely absent, or fall into a distorted pattern.

Self-analysis and Listening

1. Listen to yourself in three typical speaking situations: reading aloud, performing in class, and conversing with friends. Does your habitual pitch sound right to you? Is it too high or too low? You will be able to analyze yourself more effectively by recording your voice.

2. Can you find a level where the tone is easier, richer, fuller, and more pleasant than any other? What happens when you try to use that level as your habitual level? How does your fullness of tone then compare with that of your friends and classmates?

3. Is the pitch monotonous as you read aloud? Is there change from the highest to the lowest tone you produce? Do you have as great a range as others in the class with good voices?

4. Read aloud a selection such as "Hamlet's Advice to the Players," which is given on page 200. Listen to the melody as you read. Is there variety of melody, or does all of the vocalization center around one or two tones? Do you start most of your phrases on a relatively high pitch and then work your way down in pitch to the end of the phrase? Or do you have other melody patterns?

5. Listen to the recording you made at the beginning of the semester. Try to plot a curve on paper representing your changes in melody as it moves up and down the pitch scale within your range. Is there easily recognizable variation? Does the variation follow any set pattern from phrase to phrase? Do you use both steps and inflections?

6. In your conversational speech, can you recognize inflections? Steps? Do they occur frequently or rarely? Do these pitch changes help you to express your meaning?

7. Listen to your friends and classmates. Do you hear Mr. Milquetoast, the didactic informer, or the gushy hostess? What melody factors contribute to making the impression? Are any of those factors present in your own voice?

8. Can you hear in your own voice the things about habitual pitch, pitch range, and melody which the instructor and your classmates report to you?

Exercises for Improvement

1. Beginning at your lowest comfortable pitch, intone the sound OH. Glide up to your highest comfortable pitch, take a breath, and glide down again. Listen to yourself to see if there are any breaks in pitch level. Repeat several times, trying to extend the range in both directions, but do not strain.

2. Starting at a comfortably high pitch, count down the scale, using speaking rather than singing tones. Repeat, extending the scale at both ends, as far as you can without strain.

3. The following drills are useful in testing your ability to achieve variety in pitch. Be sure that each tone is easily initiated, full, and clear. Do not strain or go beyond the easy limits of your speaking range.

a. Chant the vowel sound AH in steps through the middle octave of your speaking range, from the lowest to the highest tone, taking a fresh breath on each pitch. Hold each tone for a duration of three seconds. Repeat with OH, OO, EE, and AW.

b. Inflect each of these vowel sounds through the same octave to the top note and continue down to the lowest one. Repeat from top to bottom and back to the top.

c. Try Exercises *a* and *b*, exploring the full limits of your speaking range.

4. Using a low pitch level, read the following passage (*a*) in a monotone; (*b*) with a limited pitch range; (*c*) with the widest possible range.

The speaker who has a very narrow pitch range will have difficulty giving full expression to his ideas. If your mechanism is in good physical condition, you can extend your range through careful exercise. While it may be difficult to do this without the aid of the piano, still you can train your ear to help you. A few minutes each day is all that you need to use on this type of exercise.

5. Repeat the three different types of reading of the above passage, using a high level of pitch. Repeat again on an intermediate level.

6. Repeat the passage in Exercise 6, starting on a monotone near your optimum pitch and gradually widening the range to your broadest one before you reach the end.

7. Read each of the following words and phrases with a final falling inflection, a final rising inflection, a circumflex inflection, and on a monopitch without inflection. Try each of the phrases with a rising step and then with a descending step to the final word. Notice the various shades of meaning which you give to the material with the melody changes.

a. Please	*i.* Friend	*q.* You would
b. Yes	*j.* Go	*r.* Keep quiet
c. Where	*k.* Now	*s.* Not at all
d. See	*l.* Thief	*t.* Oh, look
e. Why	*m.* Look out	*u.* Children play
f. Fire	*n.* Don't go	*v.* We stand
g. No	*o.* See here	*w.* Follow me
h. Help	*p.* Who's there	*x.* Page thirty

8. Read each of the following sentences in the upper, middle, and lower keys of your speaking voice. Introduce all of the melody changes which are essential to meaning. Strive for variety and freedom from pattern. Decide in which key you are most expressive.

a. It was a foggy, gray day, and I felt especially low as I realized that I had flunked two of my midsemesters.

b. First you could hear the low roll of the muffled drums, and then the funeral procession came slowly around the corner with the flags draped in crepe and the hero's body on the flag-covered caisson.

c. He jumped into his convertible and raced to the beach where he knew he would find his gang waiting for him.

d. In this class tomorrow we will have a discussion and demonstration of the uses of melody in connected speech.

e. What a party! Everything seemed to go wrong! No one had the right address, half of the food was missing, and everyone was fighting with everyone else.

f. Another verse of the hymn arose, a slow and mournful strain, such as the pious love, but joined to the words which expressed all that our nature can conceive of sin, and darkly hinted at far more.—HAWTHORNE

g. A ship captain is a good man to marry if it is a marriage of love, for absences are a good influence in love and keep it bright and delicate.—STEVENSON

h. If one is to improve his speaking voice, he must constantly strive to establish new vocal habits in place of old ones.

9. In the following sentences, be sure that you are getting variety through the full use of the inflection and the step. Analyze each sentence, marking the places where you might use an inflection or a step for meaning; indicate the type of inflection or step which you would use. Practice the sentences, following your markings and revising them as necessary.

a. Before him lay the river; beyond it the yellowing fields of the farm; and in the distance the blue hills which he had never explored.

b. She posed before the mirror, admiring the fluffy yellow folds of her first real evening dress, showing off the gold slippers, adjusting her brown hair just so, and trying on the little white fur jacket.

c. When the brilliant orange, red, and yellow of the sun had faded from the sky, the clouds were tinged with purple and gray which added to the somberness of the fog sweeping in from the ocean.

d. The garden was laid out in a formal pattern with the low flowers in prim beds in the foreground, backed by rows of tidy, clipped shrubs, and the whole topped by regularly spaced oaks and elms.

e. Far, far in the distance she could hear the low moan of the train whistle, reminding her that she could never go home again.

f. In a riot of red, yellow, and blue the gypsies whirled in the dance, going faster and faster to the ever-increasing tempo of the music.

g. He was only three, so he had never gone alone beyond the garden fence to the distant henhouse, nor the even more distant barn, which lay before him like a foreign land.

10. Strive in the following selections to achieve variety of melody for meaning; avoid mono-melody or pattern.

a. Sometimes when winds are variable and breakers run at long angles to the foam-line, strange sights are to be seen. Unknown perils of the abyss, mysterious panics, drive whole nations of fish to flee from the profundities, and infinite multitudes rush to the shallows,—even to the shore itself—followed by enemies in legion. Then begins the gigantic massacre of an entire population,—the destruction of an innumerable race. Pursuers and pursued spring high into the daylight;—millions of iridescent creatures, mad with fear, leap far out onto the sand,—while behind them the armies of porpoises and of sharks slaughter savagely and silently. And above where the sea is most thickly seamed with those sharp fins that sailors fear,—above the churning and foaming and the prodigious quivering of terror, triumphantly ride the murderous bands of air,—squadrons of shrieking gulls, the wheeling eagles, and fish-hawks, and frigate birds, hideous of foot and huge of wing. Keen-eyed gulls drop swift as lightning from the storm-cloud of beating wings, and dive, and seize, and tear, and soar again to devour some palpitating silver life between sun and sea,—while pirate birds, seeking to snatch the hard-earned meal, pursue them through the great blaze of blue light. Soon along the great beach is spread so mighty a feast that the birds may sicken themselves with luxuries;—they feed upon the eyes only, and only devour one eye of most victims, not seeking even to overturn the flat body in order to tear out the other. Enormous slaughter!—appalling cruelty!—destruction symbolizing grimly the great contests of human life in which the fiercest and strongest and swiftest survive. . . .—HEARN*

b. First a shiver, and then a thrill,
Then something decidedly like a spill,—
And the parson was sitting upon a rock,
At half-past nine by the meet'n house clock,—
Just the hour of the Earthquake shock!

—What do you think the parson found,
When he got up and stared around?
The poor old chaise in a heap or mound,
As if it had been to the mill and ground!
You see, of course, if you're not a dunce,
How it went to pieces all at once,—
All at once and nothing first,—
Just as bubbles do when they burst.

End of the wonderful one-hoss shay,
Logic is logic. That's all I say.

                                                —HOLMES

c. With malice toward none; with charity for all; with firmness in the right, as God gives us to see the right, let us strive on to finish the work we are in; to bind up the nation's wounds; to care for him who shall have borne the battle, and for his widow, and his orphan—to do all which may achieve and cherish a just and lasting peace among ourselves, and with all nations.—LINCOLN

d. The Lord is my shepherd; I shall not want.
  He maketh me to lie down in green pastures: he leadeth me beside the still waters.
  He restoreth my soul: he leadeth me in the paths of righteousness for his name's sake.

* "Torn Letters," in Lafcadio Hearn (ed.), *An American Miscellany*, vol. II, Dodd, Mead, and Company, Inc., New York, 1909. (By permission.)

Yea, though I walk through the valley of the shadow of death, I will fear no evil: for thou art with me; thy rod and thy staff they comfort me.

Thou preparest a table before me in the presence of mine enemies: thou anointest my head with oil; my cup runneth over.

Surely goodness and mercy shall follow me all the days of my life: and I will dwell in the house of the Lord for ever.

—PSALM 23

e. Old Euclid drew a circle
On a sand-beach long ago.
He bounded and enclosed it
With angles thus and so.
His set of solemn greybeards
Nodded and argued much
Of arc and of circumference,
Diameter and such.
A silent child stood by them
From morning until noon
Because they drew such charming
Round pictures of the moon.

—LINDSAY *

f. I have, myself, full confidence that if all do their duty, if nothing is neglected, and if the best arrangements are made, as they are being made, we shall prove ourselves once again able to defend our Island home, to ride out the storm of war, and to outlive the menace of tyranny, if necessary for years, if necessary alone. At any rate, that is what we are going to try to do. That is the resolve of His Majesty's Government—every man of them. That is the will of Parliament and the nation. The British Empire and the French Republic, linked together in their cause and in their need, will defend to the death their native soil, aiding each other like good comrades to the utmost of their strength. Even though large tracts of Europe and many old and famous States have fallen or may fall into the grip of the Gestapo and all the odious apparatus of Nazi rule, we shall not flag or fail. We shall go on to the end, we shall fight in France, we shall fight on the seas and oceans, we shall fight with growing confidence and growing strength

* Vachel Lindsay, *Collected Poems*, The Macmillan Company, New York, 1925. (By permission.)

in the air, we shall defend our Island, whatever the cost may be, we shall fight on the beaches, we shall fight on the landing grounds, we shall fight in the fields and in the streets, we shall fight in the hills; we shall never surrender, and even if, which I do not for a moment believe, this Island or a large part of it were subjugated and starving, then our Empire beyond the seas, armed and guarded by the British fleet, would carry on the struggle, until, in God's good time, the New World, with all its power and might, steps forth to the rescue and liberation of the old.—CHURCHILL

11. The following selections in the Appendix are particularly good for work on melody: Numbers 5, 9, 10, 17, and 22.

12. Analyze the speech melody of the recording which you made at the beginning of the term. Answer the following questions about it:

a. Does the analysis you made in Exercise 5 of the self-analysis section (page 82) suggest that you are responding mentally, emotionally, and physically to the ideas to be communicated? Are the pitch changes pleasant and interesting?

b. What changes might occur in the melody to make your voice more pleasing, interesting, and communicative?

c. Read the selection again, trying to change the melody as your analysis suggests, responding more fully to the ideas. Record the new reading on a tape recorder and compare it with the first reading. Experiment until you are satisfied that you have made substantial improvement.

13. There is a strong correlation between colorful language and interesting melody. Materials which are phrased in a dull fashion seldom inspire a speaker to lively delivery. The following narrative has been purposely written in a colorless fashion. Potentially it is a lively and entertaining story, ending with a "shaggy dog" punch line. If it is to be interesting to listeners, it needs much more detail and vivid, descriptive language building up the picture leading to the final line.

A man got on the subway and took his seat. After a few minutes he heard an unusual noise behind him. He turned around and was surprised to see a man reading a newspaper. The man had a pigeon seated on each shoulder. They were also looking at the paper. This continued for a long time until the crowd thinned out near the end of the line. At that point, the first man decided to inquire the reason for such odd events. The second man looked up from his paper and said he didn't know; the pigeons had boarded the train at 14th Street.

a. Now that you know the story, tell it to the class, but dress it up. Supply additional details about the characters and the subway ride. Insert direct conversation between the men. Use vivid, descriptive language. Enjoy yourself as you speak. Use variations in melody, timing, and loudness to reflect that enjoyment to your listeners.

b. Using the same approach, tell a narrative of your own choosing.

14. Prepare to give a two-minute speech based on a personal experience. If possible, try to work in a description of some action. When you give it in class, keep the delivery alive and animated. What do your instructor and classmates say about the melody variety in your voice? Record the speech and do your own analysis of your use of melody.

PHONATION AND LOUDNESS, TIME, AND QUALITY

Changes in loudness are the result of changes in amplitude of vibration of the vocal folds. Increased amplitude is brought about by greater breath pressure at the glottis. For the best phonation, as we have already noted, control of this pressure should be achieved by control of breathing. It is perfectly possible to increase the pressure, however, by narrowing the opening of the glottis through increased tension of the vocal muscles. This tension, of course, inevitably produces higher pitch, and if it is the only method of increasing pressure, the tones will be harsh and unpleasant. We do not mean to suggest that a controlled rise in pitch should not be used simultaneously with an increase in loudness, as a means of interpreting meaning. These changes will be both effective and pleasant, however, only when they are attained without excessive tension in the laryngeal muscles.

The problem of duration involves both time and phonation. You must be able to maintain a steady, pure tone for a sound of any length. If the sound is short, you must be able to initiate it easily and smoothly. The sound of long duration requires not only easy initiation, but also the ability on your part to maintain the tone steadily and evenly. Exercises under both phonation and melody deal with this problem.

Phonation and quality are closely connected. In the discussion of optimum pitch, it was suggested that optimum pitch was the product of both phonation and resonation. What the ear hears as tone is the result of both the action of the vocal folds and the influence of the resonation cavities on that sound. It is necessary that the proper relationship be maintained between the tensions in the folds determining the basic pitch and the adjustments of the resonating cavities. If you were able to find your optimum pitch, you noted that one tone was fuller and richer than all of the others when you reached the ideal relationship between the vibration of the folds and the action of the resonating cavities. The discussion of quality in the next chapter will make this problem clearer to you.

SUMMARY

The larynx is the housing for the vocal folds; it is composed of four major cartilages: the thyroid, the cricoid, and the paired arytenoids. The vocal folds are flaps of muscle attached in front to the inner edge of the thyroid, in the rear to the arytenoids, and at the sides to the inner edges of the cricoid. The entire larynx and associated structures are interlaced with muscles and connective tissue, and the interior surfaces are covered with mucous membrane. The basic biological function of the larynx is to act as a valve at the entrance to the trachea.

For phonation, the glottis must be closed; air pressure must be built up beneath the folds, forcing them apart and setting them in vibration. Conditions of length, tension, thickness, and density in the folds will determine the pitch produced. When the vocal folds do not function properly, such problems of phonation as breathiness, glottal shock, harshness, or hoarseness may arise.

In your vocalization, you have a habitual pitch level and an optimum one; as nearly as possible these should be identical. Yet pitch must not be unvaried, even at the optimum level. Meaning in speech depends strongly upon the many variations in melody which can reflect your estimate of the importance and emotional value of the words you speak. Melody may also give some indication of your personality and your attitude toward yourself, your listeners, and your ideas.

As you do not hear the tone directly as it comes from the vocal folds, but only after it has been resonated, an understanding of resonation is necessary for the complete analysis of tone production. If you find that you have a phonation problem, read ahead in Chapter 5 to see how poor resonation may be contributing to it.

5

The Resonating Process

The art of delivery deals with the voice: how we ought to manage it to express each several emotion.—ARISTOTLE

Voices sing, whine, snarl, murmur, chortle, chuckle, roar, rant, and gurgle. They are melodious and raucous, gentle and fierce. The qualities of voices soothe, stimulate, rouse, and anger us. They are pleasing and displeasing, interesting and dull, strange and familiar. We recognize at once the voice of a friend on the telephone by its distinctive quality. At the same moment, we can and often do make an accurate evaluation of his mood, regardless of the words he speaks.

In part, these distinctive characteristics of voice depend upon the factors of timing and melody which we discussed in Chapters 3 and 4. But in large part they also depend upon a less tangible element—the process known as *resonation*. This is the means whereby the weak, colorless, laryngeal note is amplified and modified as it passes through the cavities of the throat, mouth, and nose.

THE NATURE OF RESONATION

To understand how resonation operates in voice production, we need to know something of the principles which govern it. We noted in Chapter 4 that sounds are produced when some force acts upon an object and sets it into vibration. During the vibration cycle, the extent of displacement of the vibrating object from its normal position is the *amplitude*. The greater the amount of force exerted upon the object, the greater the amplitude. These pulsations set the surrounding air into vibration in regular waves, and the ear interprets varying amplitudes of the sound waves as different degrees of loudness. Thus, in voice production, initial loudness is determined by the amount of force exerted upon the vocal folds by the breath stream. However, since sound waves (unless prevented by reflection or absorption) move in all directions from the source of the vibration, the initial energy is dissipated rapidly. The amplitude of the wave decreases as the square of the distance from the sound source. If sound waves are to be used for communication, therefore, they must be controlled and directed to prevent the amplitude of the wave, and hence the loudness, from decreasing so rapidly that sounds cannot be heard by the listener.

Fundamental and Overtones

Few vibrating objects produce pure tones. They have one frequency which is dominant and determines the pitch you hear—the *fundamental* tone. But they also produce other frequencies, known as *overtones*, or partials, which are not heard as separate pitches, but which determine the distinctive quality of the tone you hear. Thus the conductor can pick out of the orchestra the particular instrument which is off key, since he can recognize the overtones of that instrument. Similarly, no two voices, even in the same pitch range, have identical quality; you can easily recognize a familiar voice without seeing the speaker.

Usually the strongest overtones are those produced by segmental vibrations of the vibrating object. A violin string, for example, may vibrate not only over its full length, but also over one-half, one-third, or one-fifth its length, simultaneously with the stronger fundamental vibration. Segmental vibrations of this kind blend harmoniously with the fundamental and change its quality without the hearer's being particularly conscious of the existence of additional pitch levels. A complex vibrator like the human vocal folds, however, produces many more overtones than the simple string. When these are amplified in different combinations, great varieties of voice quality become possible.

Neither the fundamentals nor the overtones produced by musical instruments or the human voice are strong enough to carry any distance without some form of amplification. The overtones are so weak that without some way of increasing their intensity they may be lost altogether. Such a method of amplification is provided by the phenomenon called *resonance*.

The Types of Resonance

Resonance is the result of three forces, usually acting together, although they may act independently. The first is the principle of *reflection of sound waves*. You enjoy singing in the bathtub because the hard walls of the tub and the room itself reflect the sound waves back to your ear and give the illusion of a much more resonant tone than you actually possess. If you try singing in a closet filled with clothes, the tone will seem stifled and dull, although the initial sound in the two cases may be exactly the same. The difference lies in the reflection of the waves, a phenomenon which does not occur in the closet because the waves are absorbed by the soft surfaces instead of being returned to you. In a band shell or a megaphone, sound waves are reflected and concentrated in one direction. The tone is loudest in front of the opening, and its carrying power is greater, because the initial energy has been increased by preventing its dissipation in other directions. It should be noted that hard surfaces, smooth contours, and open passages reflect a wider range of sounds more efficiently than their opposites.

In the human voice, reflective resonance is the primary means by which the fundamental tone is amplified. It follows that the best amplification and projection of tone will occur when smooth contours and open passages are maintained between the larynx and the mouth opening. Later in the chapter you may put this concept to work in the exercises dealing with *open throat*.

The second principle is that of *forced vibration* (sometimes called *sounding-board vibration*). When a tuning fork is struck and held in the air, its tone is barely audible at close range. When its base is held against a table top, however, the table is also set into vibration at the same frequency, and the tone may be heard at much greater distances. The vibrations of a piano string are communicated to the sounding board of the instrument, and those of the violin string to the wood of the violin. The differences in quality between clarinets made of wood, metal, and plastics are largely traceable to the different vibration traits of the respective substances, although they may be due in part to different reflective traits of the surfaces. Different overtones are given prominence, and the quality varies. In addition to such vibrations induced in solid objects, a body of air in a partially enclosed cavity may also be set into forced vibration if it is in close proximity to the sound source. There is much controversy about the role of forced resonance in the production of voice. There can be little doubt that the bones of the head and chest are set into forced vibration by the action of the vocal folds, but it seems quite dubious that much of this vibration is transformed into audible sound through layers of soft flesh, membrane, and skin, to say nothing of clothing. Certainly this is the least important to voice production of the three types of resonance.

The third principle is *sympathetic vibration*. If two sound sources are tuned to the same frequency, and one of them is set into vibration, the other object, if it is nearby, will also begin to vibrate. You may note this principle by singing one or more notes while seated at the piano with the damper pedal depressed. The strings corresponding to the tones you sing will vibrate in response to your voice.

More important to the production of voice, however, is the fact that not only solid objects, but bodies of air in a cavity may be set into sympathetic vibration by vibrating objects near them. The natural frequency of the air in a cavity is determined by the volume of the cavity and the shape and size of its openings. A cavity may be of a fixed size and shape or it may be capable of great variations, as in the vocal mechanism; but in any given form, it will respond sympathetically only to a narrow range of pitch.

If you take a number of large jars of the same size and shape and fill them with water to different levels, you can observe this fact for yourself. Strike a tuning fork and hold it over the mouth of each jar in turn. The vibrations of the fork will be amplified only by those jars whose water level is such that the natural frequency of the cavity is approximately equal to that of the fork. In the same way, in the marimba, each tone is produced by the vibration of a bar which is struck, reinforced by the sympathetic vibration of a column of air, directly beneath it, tuned to the same frequency.

The fact that a cavity responds most efficiently to a narrow range of pitch is important both to the quality of the voice and to the complex series of resonances that distinguish the vowels and some consonants from one another. The general shape and size of the resonance cavities of the nose, throat, and mouth determine the basic quality of the voice. The nasal cavity may be shut off from the other resonators and the size and shape of the mouth and throat cavities may be changed greatly by various muscle movements. As the cavities vary in size, shape, and interrelationship, different overtones are resonated sympathetically, and the quality of the voice is modified. Similarly, movements of the tongue and jaw change the oral cavity to produce the characteristic resonances of the various vowels and consonant sounds. Thus sympathetic resonance gives variety, color, and articulate quality to the vocal sounds produced at the larynx.

STRUCTURE AND FUNCTION OF THE RESONATORS

STRUCTURE

We shall now examine the structure of each of the resonance cavities and indicate what modifications in their size and shape are possible. We shall also discover what effects such modifications produce in the fullness and quality of the tones heard by the listener.

The Oral Cavity

If you take a mirror and hold it before your open mouth, you will observe that the outer boundary consists of the mobile lips, behind which are the fixed gums and teeth. Move the tip of your tongue back from the inner side of your front teeth. Here you will notice a definite gum ridge, called the *alveolar ridge*. In back of this is the bony, rigid, concave roof of the mouth

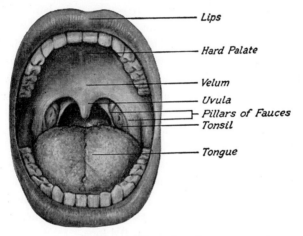

Lips

Hard Palate

Velum
Uvula
Pillars of Fauces
Tonsil

Tongue

Fig. 10. The oral cavity

known as the *hard palate*. Behind the hard palate and continuing in what appears to be part of it is the sheet of muscle fibers covered, like the hard palate, with mucous membrane; this is known as the soft palate or *velum*. This can be further identified by its terminal pendent tip, called the *uvula*. Unlike the hard palate, the velum is flexible and may be raised or lowered. This action, together with the movement of the upper pharyngeal wall, can open and close the entrance into the nasal passageway directly behind and above the velum.

In examining your own structure, notice that double arches border the back edges of the velum and extend downward from the uvula. These are called the *pillars of fauces* (see Figure 10). You will see the opening into your throat between these pillars and above the back of your tongue; this is known as the *isthmus of fauces*. As you yawn, vocalize with an oral or a nasal tone, or raise or lower the tongue, you will perceive that this opening into the pharynx can vary greatly in size. The activity in this area has considerable influence on the resonation of the tone.

The *tongue* consists of a large mass of muscular fibers tapered at the front tip and widening and thickening at the back. It goes much farther down into your throat than you realize, and its root connects with the lower jaw and the hyoid bone. It possesses extreme agility, being able to stretch forward, draw back, thin or thicken, broaden or groove, and raise and lower itself in part or as a whole. Because of its extensive ability to alter its shape and position, the tongue serves greatly to change the size and shape of your oral cavity. The activity of the *lower jaw*, of course, does much to determine the vertical dimensions of the cavity. If you have the habit of tensing the muscles of the jaw as you speak, the cavity space needed to amplify the tone efficiently will be restricted. The tongue will also be limited in action and the lips may become tight. The quick movements of tongue, lips, and jaw which contribute to clear articulation as well as to the shaping of the oral resonator will not take place effectively. On the other hand, smooth but energetic downward movements of the jaw will provide space for full oral resonation and will assist in maintaining the open passageways necessary for good resonation.

The interaction of all these structures of the mouth enables the oral cavity to undergo considerable variation in size, shape, surfaces, and openings. It may also be linked directly with the pharyngeal cavity and indirectly with the nasal. Because of these numerous and complex adjustments, it may improve or distort the quality of the resonated tone.

The Pharyngeal Cavity

The pharynx, or throat, is a passageway approximately five inches long. It extends from the area just above the false vocal folds and the esophagus up to the posterior opening of the nasal passage. The pharynx communicates with the larynx, the esophagus, the mouth, the nose, and the Eustachian tubes leading to the ears. Three sheets of paired, overlapping muscle fibers, called the *constrictor* muscles, contract the walls of the pharynx in swallowing.

The three main divisions of the pharyngeal cavity are known as (1) the *laryngopharynx*, which is immediately above the false vocal folds; (2) the *oropharynx*, which is behind the mouth in back of the pillars of fauces, reaching from above the epiglottis to just below the velum; and (3) the *nasopharynx*, which is just above the velum, continuing on into the nasal passage.

The size, shape, and adjustability of the pharynx enables it to function admirably as a resonator. The pharynx may be shortened by raising the larynx on high-pitched sounds, thus contributing to the brilliance of the resonated tone. It may be lengthened by lowering the larynx on low-pitched sounds, thus influencing the mellowness of the resonated tones. A reduction in the length of the pharynx may also be effected by raising the velum against the back wall of the pharynx, thus blocking off the nasopharynx and eliminating the top section of the pharyngeal tube. Because of the adjustability of the velum, the pharynx can employ the mouth and the nose, either separately or together, as its opening. This action will obviously affect the quality

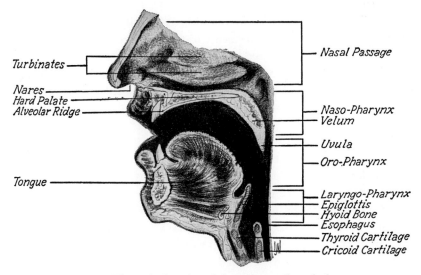

Fig. 11. The sagittal section of the nose, mouth, and pharynx

of the resonated tone. In addition to these changes in size, shape, and openings, the pharynx has the muscular ability to vary its diameter, surface tension, and texture, further affecting resonation. Relaxed pharyngeal musculature promotes a rich, mellow tone by damping out the high frequencies and strengthening the fundamental and lower overtones. Tense, constricted pharyngeal musculature, on the other hand, has a tendency to produce a hard, harsh quality by reflecting the higher overtones as well.

It may be seen, then, that the great adjustability of the pharyngeal cavity enables it to function as our most efficient and important resonator.

The Nasal Cavity

The nasal cavity continues the tube of the nasopharynx on out through the anterior *nares*, or nostrils. The nasal cavity might more accurately be referred to as two cavities, since it is divided into two sections by a thin bone, called the *medial septum*. Each of these sections contains three shell-like bones, called *turbinates*, which project horizontally into the cavity. Although, on most drawings showing the various cavities of the head, the nasal cavity appears to be much larger than either the oral or the pharyngeal cavity, actually it is considerably smaller because of the presence of the septum and turbinate bones. Its size is further decreased by the fact that, like the other cavities, its entire surface is covered with thick mucous membrane.

In addition to its limitation in size, the nasal cavity is further restricted as a resonator. Except for movements of the velum which change its posterior opening, and muscular constrictions at the region of the nostrils which slightly change its anterior opening, it is unable to vary its shape. The nasal cavity, therefore, is our least adjustable and least versatile resonator. Of all English speech sounds, only three, the nasal continuants M, N, and NG, are primarily, if not completely, the product of nasal resonation.

Considerable difference of opinion exists as to the extent to which the nasal cavity contributes to the resonation of the oral vowel sounds. Many of the older textbooks stipulate that a complete closure must take place between the velum and the nasopharyngeal wall to prevent escape of air into the nose and consequent nasality. Research has shown, however, that most speakers do not make a tight closure. Because a small opening into the nose is maintained during speech, the nasal passageway serves as a sympathetic, supplemental resonator to the mouth. Test this out in your own voice production: if you talk as if you had a cold in the head, the vowels sound different than they will when you speak in a normal relaxed manner. Without that slight amount of nasal resonance, even on oral sounds, the tone will seem dull.

The sinus cavities which are connected with the nasal chamber are sometimes said to act as resonators. Although the sphenoidal, ethmoidal, maxillary, and frontal sinuses are of appreciable size, the last two being an inch or more in height, depth, or breadth, the ducts connecting them with the nasal cavity are probably too small and too long to accommodate the sound waves. Their main function appears to be that of lightening the bone weight of the head; in this respect they may influence the degree of forced vibration of sounds. But it is extremely doubtful whether the sinus cavities themselves function as resonators.

Biological Function of the Cavities and Structures

Resonation, like all other aspects of voice, is an overlaid function of the vocal mechanism. The cavities, structures, and muscles involved in resonation are biologically intended to serve the primary purposes of breathing and eating. Furthermore, these biological activities frequently are in conflict with the muscle movements necessary to produce good, resonant tone.

The muscles we use for tone production and resonation are the same muscles which are used for gagging, coughing, sucking, chewing, and swallowing. Some individuals who otherwise are well adjusted have never mastered the small muscular coordinations needed for a good voice. Some of the muscular activities of coughing, chewing, and swallowing have not been eliminated; they intrude upon the speech process. The coughing and gagging muscles constrict the opening from the larynx to the laryngopharynx and also unduly tense the vocal folds, the chewing muscles tighten the jaw and constrict the mouth opening, and the swallowing muscles raise the larynx and crowd it against the base of the tongue. Each of these actions tends to narrow the space available for resonation, interfering with the normal resonance channels and constricting the passageway for the breath stream so that friction sounds may occur.

Function in Resonation

In order to secure normal resonation of the human voice, your throat, mouth, and nose must not be constricted or distorted by any interference from the biological functioning just described. The structure of these cavities is such that the tones of speech are reflected and are concentrated as they are released through your mouth and nose, thus providing the primary resonance of the fundamental tone. If these passageways are constricted, the desired reflection and amplification of tone will not take place.

You must realize that your pharyngeal and oral cavities are capable of wide variation in size and shape, and thus can respond sympathetically to many different overtones. Moreover, the breadth of range to which they respond is further increased by the fact that, as your velum is raised or lowered, your pharynx may be coupled either to your oral or your nasal cavity. The openings at the isthmus of fauces and at the lips can also vary greatly. This flexibility of adjustment, when not interfered with by excessive muscular tensions, enables your cavities to function admirably as sympathetic resonators.

We have noted earlier that the extent to which forced resonance contributes to the quality of the voice is a matter of considerable dispute. Certainly the bones of the head and chest, the teeth, and the walls of the pharyngeal and laryngeal cavities are set into forced vibration by the action of the vocal folds. There is much doubt, however, that these vibrations are transmitted to the outer air and actually contribute to the sound we hear.

In the absence of conclusive evidence as to the function of forced resonation in contributing to the production of voice, we must assume that probably the principal factor in *resonating the fundamental tone* in most voices is the reflection and concentration of sound in the open-tube structure of the pharyngeal and oral cavities. On the other hand, research has shown that the distinctive quality of a voice is primarily the product of sympathetic vibrations set up in the cavities in response to overtones ranging between 400 and 2,400 vibrations per second. Different qualities of the same voice and the special characteristics which distinguish one speech sound from another are the result of modifications in size and shape of the resonance cavities, which cause them to respond sympathetically to a different set of overtones.

We have said that in order to secure a full and pleasant tone, your throat, mouth, and nose must be free from constrictions; yet the admonition that complete relaxation is needed is not true. As in tone production (see page 64), desirable functioning involves selective relaxation of muscles. The tensing of the jaw, the stiffening of the lips, the riding back of the tongue, and the contracting of the throat will all distort size, shape, and surface texture of the resonance cavities. Activate only those muscles necessary for the production of the vocal effect you want. If you speak in a relaxed and easy way, the jaw and lips will tend to remain more open than when you speak with tension. The passageway between the oral and the pharyngeal cavities will also be larger.

Principle of Open Throat

Because so many people have faults of resonance due to excessive tension, the concept of *open throat* should be examined. Open throat is a condition of wideness and openness in the oral and pharyngeal passageways. Inhale through your mouth as though commencing to yawn gently. Feel the air passing through the isthmus of fauces and back into your pharynx. As you watch in the mirror, you will notice how the back of your tongue lowers, your velum rises, and the opening into the throat widens. Maintain this openness as you say AH. Notice that there will be a greater fullness than usual to the tone.

What has actually happened is this: by lowering the jaw and the tongue you have provided an extensive cavity in the mouth for resonance; the opening into the throat has widened and the back throat wall, although you will have difficulty in discovering this, has moved back slightly. As you produce tone, the larger resonance cavities in mouth and throat will amplify the lower overtones as well as the fundamental. You have prevented the constrictions that occur when swallowing and chewing muscles come into play.

Provided you do not overdo this widening and thus produce a hollow, unnatural tone, practicing open throat in an easy, relaxed way will demonstrate for you the resonance it may be possible for you to acquire. You cannot maintain this wideness on all sounds as you speak, but an endeavor to speak with greater openness will prevent tensions in tongue, jaw, lips, and throat.

Tone placement is a term commonly encountered in singing instruction, the direction being that the tone must be "placed" in the front of the mouth instead of in the back of the throat. The term "frontal placement" has no basis in physiology, but it may prove useful in providing a distractive technique. In the effort to place the tone forward, "behind the front teeth," the speaker or singer will open the mouth more widely than usual, lower the tongue, and probably make a multitude of small muscular adjustments which will result in open throat and a clearer, more fully resonated tone.

Adjustments of the resonators alone, however, will not produce good voice. As you analyze your resonation habits and try to improve them, remember that good resonation is dependent upon controlled flow of the breath stream, steady and energetic vibration of the vocal folds, and a pitch level produced without excessive tension. Effective resonation, then, must supplement the efficient functioning of the breathing and phonation mechanisms.

ANALYSIS OF HABITS OF RESONATION

As you examine your speaking habits, consider again what contributes to pleasing voice quality. Your resonating cavities should be free from any constricting muscular tension. The mouth and throat, when the tone is oral, should be open. The nasal passageways, particularly for the nasal sounds, should be unobstructed.

In order to maintain open passageways and to vary their size, shape, and relationships quickly, you must have a responsive and healthy organism. Sluggish muscular activity will impair both vocal quality and articulation.

The many changes in the relative positions of these organs must be made quickly and exactly if sounds are to be meaningful, pleasant, and full. Weak and indefinite movement will produce only muffled and dull sounds because oral and pharyngeal cavities will not be properly adjusted.

Control of your resonation then means that you speak without excessive tension or extreme lassitude, and that you move the needed structures freely and strongly to maintain openness of the resonators and to modify their size and shape quickly and smoothly.

You should check, too, on the control of your breathing. A review of exercises on page 32 can be coupled with practice to improve resonation. You may also need to continue practice to establish optimum pitch. If you are using a pitch level higher or lower than your optimum, the resulting tension in the larynx will often be transmitted to the pharyngeal and oral areas and affect resonation. The use of your optimum pitch, with its assured ease in production, will enable you to amplify your tones with the least expenditure of effort.

In Chapter 2, we noted that a frequent cause of poor voices is to be found in temporary or chronic emotional tension. Nowhere is this more important than in its effect on vocal quality. If you discover that your quality is impaired because facing an audience is a trying emotional experience, remember that you are not unique. In greater or lesser degree, all your classmates feel just as you do. Indeed, even experienced speakers approach an audience with some trepidation. But a skilled public speaker, reader, or actor learns to divert his emotional excitement into constructive channels. He uses it to heighten his response to his materials and to sharpen his interest in his listeners. In doing so, he forgets himself, his unwanted tensions are relieved, and the quality of his voice is benefited. As you develop your skill in speaking, you can do likewise.

Of far greater concern is the habitual nervous tension with which some individuals respond to all social situations. This problem is less widespread than the nearly universal response to the stimulus of an audience, but it is more difficult to deal with. If you are one of those whose unresolved social tensions impair their vocal quality, review the analysis of influences on your speech habits suggested in Chapter 2. Understanding the causes is the first step in eradicating disturbing feeling states which result in qualities often described by such terms as whining, strident, or raucous.

Self-analysis

Examine your own speech habits critically and try to determine if they are in accord with the principles of good resonation presented in this chapter.

1. Take a small mirror and observe the changing shape of your lips and the movements of your jaw as you repeat various familiar phrases, such as: "What are you going to do?"; "My name is . . . "; etc.

2. Tighten the jaw muscles; swallow and maintain the muscular contractions in throat and jaw as you repeat these same phrases. Place your hand at the junction of your chin and neck and feel the constriction of your throat muscles. Listen to the tone: this is what happens when you fail to relax your swallowing muscles. Now say the phrases in as relaxed a way as possible. Become aware of the contrasting sensations of tension and relaxation in throat and jaw.

3. Assume the position for the open AH sound, with the tip of your tongue resting against the lower front teeth. Observe the size and shape of the megaphonelike opening of your mouth. Phonate and sustain the AH. See whether the jaw and throat muscles remain relatively relaxed as vocalization takes place.

4. Facing a good light, hold the mirror before your open mouth; locate the velum, uvula, and pillars of fauces. Discover how these structures and the back of the tongue can move into various positions in relation to each other. Now crowd the tongue back toward the pharynx and talk with it in this position. Have you ever heard anyone using this squawking, strained quality?

5. Assume the position for the AH. Yawn gently. Notice the movements of the velum and the back of the tongue; see the widening of the isthmus of fauces. Observe the pharyngeal wall directly behind the opening. As you watch, vocalize; do you maintain an open throat when tone is produced?

Listening and Observation

1. Listen to class members and friends when they speak. Watch mouth, throat, and jaw areas. Do their face and neck muscles seem unduly tense? Are their voices muffled and dull, strident and harsh, or fully resonated and pleasant in quality?

2. Listen critically to various speakers and actors and try to evaluate the resonance characteristics in their voices. Compare their voices with your own. What resonance traits are present that you would like to emulate? What faults would you like to avoid?

Exercises for Improvement

1. Place the tip of your tongue against your lower front teeth. Gently inhale through your mouth; then easily roll your head toward the right, allowing it to fall toward your chest; exhale through your mouth as your head falls. Repeat, moving toward the left. Continue in this fashion until you experience a feeling of ease and relaxation in the region of your throat.

2. Assume the basic AH position with the tip of your tongue against your lower front teeth. Inhale through your mouth as though commencing to yawn. Feel the current of air passing through the isthmus of fauces and into your pharynx; this sensation indicates one of the desired conditions for openness of throat. Repeat this action until you establish the feeling of a rising soft palate and an open throat.

3. Repeat the conditions described in Exercise 2. Keeping your throat passage as open as possible, chant an easy, sustained AH sound. Prolong it for the approximate count of five. Repeat, changing to an AW sound. Next, practice gliding from AH to AW and retain the feeling of an open, relaxed throat.

4. With the tip of your tongue against your lower front teeth and your jaw as relaxed as possible, practice the following sounds, employing a fresh oral inhalation for each sound: HAH, PAH, BAH, FAH, VAH, YAH. Repeat several times.

5. Keep your jaw as open, relaxed, and motionless as possible. In this position, repeat the following sounds with gross movements of your tongue but keep the tongue tip against your lower front teeth: HAH-HAH-HAH-HAH, YAH-YAH-YAH-YAH, YAW-YAW-YAW-YAW, YOH-YOH-YOH-YOH, YAH-YEA-YEE-YEA-YAH-YAW-YOO-YAW.

6. Test the operation of what is called "tone placement" by phonating the vowel AH in such a manner that it appears to be produced far back in your throat. To facilitate this, pronounce AH and try to imagine that you are making the sound AW. You will notice that the sound acquires a throaty, muffled quality. Follow this by phonating the same AH sound as though you were producing it at the upper front gum, and imagine that you were making the vowel sound EE. In this instance, you will notice that the same AH sound now acquires a firm, brilliant quality.

7. With the tip of your tongue against your lower front teeth, pronounce the word *we* several times. Carefully produce the vowel sound of this word

so that it seems to achieve great fullness of tone toward the front of your mouth.

8. With the tip of your tongue against your lower front teeth and the sounds as though aimed at your upper front gum, repeat the following: WAH, WAY, WE, WAY, WAH, WAW, WOO, WAW. Chant these singly and as a continuous phrase.

9. Chant the vowel sounds AH and OO alternately on different pitch levels. Try to concentrate the tones in the front of your mouth by aiming at your upper front gum. Carefully keep these tones full and open and keep your throat muscles relaxed.

10. Repeat Exercise 4, using the vowels EE and AH. Also practice these sounds as a single chant, carefully gliding from EE to AH.

11. Keeping your throat open and relaxed, practice the following sentences.

a. Hello.
b. How are you?
c. May I go too?
d. How will I know what to do?
e. The ball rolled away.
f. High on a hill.
g. Over the valleys and over the plains.
h. I like to ride in this car.
i. Find the house for me.
j. Cool, blue, evening shadows slowly moved across the green lawn.
k. The university team easily won the contest.
l. A little learning is a dangerous thing.

12. Read the following selections, responding fully to the ideas. Concentrate on open throat and ease of production.

a. A corn-field in July is a sultry place. The soil is hot and dry; the wind comes across the lazily murmuring leaves laden with a warm, sickening smell drawn from the rapidly growing, broadflung banners of the corn. The sun, nearly vertical, drops a flood of dazzling light upon the field over which the cool shadows run, only to make the heat seem more intense.

Julia Peterson, faint with hunger, was toiling back and forth between the corn-rows, holding the handles of the double-shovel corn-plough, while her little brother Otto rode the steaming horse. Her heart was full of bitterness, her face flushed with heat, and her muscles aching with fatigue. The heat grew terrible. The corn came to her shoulders, and not a breath seemed to reach her, while the sun, nearing the noon mark, lay pitilessly upon her shoulders, protected only by a calico dress. The dust rose under her feet, and as she was wet with perspiration, it soiled her till with a woman's instinctive cleanliness, she shuddered. Her head throbbed dangerously. What matter to her that the kingbird pitched jovially from the maples to catch a wandering blue-bottle fly, that the robin was feeding its young, that the bobolink was singing? All these things, if she saw them, only threw her bondage to labor into greater relief.

Across the field, in another patch of corn, she could see her father—a big, gruff-voiced, wide-bearded Norwegian—at work also with a plough. The corn must be ploughed, and so she toiled on, the tears dropping from the shadow of the ugly sunbonnet she wore. Her shoes, coarse and square-toed, chafed her feet; her hands, large and strong, were browned, or more properly, *burnt*, on the backs by the sun. The horse's harness *"creak-cracked"* as he swung steadily and patiently forward, the moisture pouring from his sides, his nostrils distended.—
GARLAND *

b. The splendour falls on castle walls
    And snowy summits old in story;
The long light shakes across the lakes,
    And the wild cataract leaps in glory.
Blow, bugle, blow, set the wild echoes flying,
Blow, bugle; answer, echoes, dying, dying, dying.

                    —TENNYSON

c. She walks in beauty, like the night
    Of cloudless climes and starry skies,
    And all that's best of dark and bright
    Meet in her aspect and her eyes;
    Thus mellowed to that tender light
    Which heaven to gaudy day denies.

                    —BYRON

* Hamlin Garland, "A Corn-field in July," *Main-travelled Roads,* Harper & Brothers, New York, 1909. (By permission.)

d. Willows whiten, aspens quiver,
    Little breezes dusk and shiver
    Thro' the wave that runs forever
    By the island in the river
        Flowing down to Camelot.
    Four gray walls, and four gray towers,
    Overlook a space of flowers,
    And the silent isle embowers
        The Lady of Shalott.

                —TENNYSON

13. Selections 3, 9, 12*b*, and 23 in the Appendix are also recommended for practice.

PROBLEMS OF FAULTY RESONANCE

STRIDENCY AND THROATINESS

Stridency is a fault of resonance. The prominence of the higher overtones produces a harsh, sharp quality. It is usually caused by excessive tension in the pharynx and in the muscles of the soft palate. The firm surfaces of these areas contribute to mechanically "efficient" resonation so that, instead of many of the higher overtones being damped out by the relaxed soft surfaces of the oral and pharyngeal cavities, most of the overtones are reflected. The throat may be held open, but the whole area is tense. The tension may be observable in the restriction of jaw and lip movement and even in excessive action of the external throat muscles. You may have heard strident voices in political speeches, particularly among speakers accustomed to speaking to large audiences who have not yet tempered their method of voice production to the requirements of public-address systems.

In some individuals the strident tone is high; if it is accompanied by a drawing out of the vowel sounds, it can be called whining. In others, the tensing of the pharyngeal muscles may so constrict the opening that a friction sound accompanies phonation. The tone then becomes grating as well as sharp, made more unpleasant by the additional noise components.

Stridency frequently occurs with rapid rate, since both may be due to habits of nervousness and excitability.

The *throaty tone* may be produced when the lower part of the pharynx is constricted and when the back of the tongue crowds into the throat. A speaker may have the habit of holding his chin down and back as he speaks, assuming, for reasons best known to himself, a dignified and pompous manner. Another person may allow his head to drop down and may raise only his eyes when he speaks. These positions of the head will change the size and shape of the pharyngeal resonator. The tone is often low in pitch, probably well below the optimum, with a guttural quality produced by constrictions in the pharynx and with the same grating and friction sounds which may accompany stridency. The riding back of the tongue will also muffle the tone.

Throatiness is sometimes the response to the effort to lower the general pitch. The external muscles of the larynx may contract and pull down on the entire larynx, holding it in this lowered position while voice is produced. This, coupled with the inner pharyngeal constriction, will interfere with good resonance.

Either stridency or throatiness may result when the speaker tries to project the tone but lacks the necessary control over the breath stream. He attempts to create subvocal pressure, not by diaphragmatic control over breathing, but by constricting the passageway directly above the larynx. Breathing examination and exercises should precede attempts to correct these faults of resonance. If the breath cannot be controlled either for steadiness of tone or for increased loudness, the speaker almost always responds with tenseness of the throat area.

The presence of physical differences may cause the initial use of the generally harsh tone. If the throat is inflamed and sore, the speaker may try to protect it by preventing movement in the area. If there is a great deal of mucus on the vocal folds or the pharyngeal wall, the person may clear his throat frequently, an activity which tends to keep the muscles of the velum and pharynx in a state of tension.

Listening and Self-analysis

1. In the Columbia album *I Can Hear It Now*, Volume I, listen to the voices of Adolf Hitler, Wendell Willkie, and Fiorello La Guardia, watching for elements of stridency and throatiness.

2. Listen to the voices of your classmates and see if you can hear faults of stridency or throatiness. Observe any unusual muscular actions accompanying these qualities.

3. Listen to the record you made at the beginning of the semester. Do you have either of these faults?

Exercises for Improvement

1. Review all the exercises in Chapter 3 dealing with steadiness and loudness of tone.

2. Review the exercises in Chapter 4 dealing with glottal shock, harshness, and optimum pitch.

3. Practice the exercises for open throat on page 104. Both stridency and throatiness are the antithesis of open throat.

4. Practice speaking or reading with the chin up, the shoulders relaxed, and the body in an erect but easy posture.

5. Examine your own case history to discover possible causes for excessive tension.

Nasality and Denasality

The quality known as *nasality* results from the entrapment of the vibrating breath stream in a cavity in which the entrance is substantially larger than the exit, or in which there is a narrow common entrance and exit. This blind-alley, or cul-de-sac, type of resonance is produced most frequently in the nasal resonator, from which the term nasality is derived. When the velum is relaxed, leaving a wide opening from the oropharynx to the nasopharynx, the narrow exit through the nares completes the factors characterizing nasality. The three normal nasal sounds in English speech, M, N, and NG, are all resonated in the nasal cavity, with a supplemental cul-de-sac provided by the oral cavity. The differences in quality among these three nasal sounds are created by the changes in size and shape of the oral cul-de-sac. The whole cavity is used for M, a smaller part for N, and a narrow pocket at the back for NG.

The basic characteristic of nasality is a foghorn quality. If this quality appears on sounds other than the three nasal continuants, it is generally regarded as a fault in English-speaking voices. Normally, nasality is the result of excessive relaxation of the velum, but speech clinicians have also recognized nasality in cases where the subject clearly made an adequate closure of the soft palate. In such instances, the cul-de-sac must be sought elsewhere. One obvious answer in many cases is an inadequate mouth opening. A small mouth opening clearly duplicates the conditions for nasality produced in the nasal resonator by providing a wide entrance into and a narrow exit from the oral cavity.

A special problem in nasality is the so-called "nasal twang", which is usually accompanied by high pitch and stridency. Although this problem is not fully understood, it is probable that the same tensions which produce the other faults also operate to create pockets along the sides of the resonance passages in which cul-de-sac resonance occurs. At any rate, it is certain that in such cases relaxation of the throat muscles will usually remedy the condition.

It is important to distinguish between the fault of nasality and the use of the nasal resonators as a normal supplement in the resonation of primarily oral sounds. So long as the posterior opening of the nasal cavity is smaller than the opening of the nares, nasal resonance is a positive contributing factor to fullness of tone, and the foghorn quality of nasality is not heard. Careful listening to the tones you produce will help you to distinguish between supplemental nasal resonance and the fault of nasality.

Denasality is the lack of nasal resonance—cold-in-the-head speech. Any blockage of the nasal passage, caused by a cold, hay fever, deviated septum, broken nose, or enlarged adenoids blocking the nasopharynx, may produce this quality. If any of these factors persist for some time, inactivity of the velum may become so habituated that removal of the obstruction may be followed by marked nasality until new habits can be formed.

It should be noted that both nasality and denasality, under certain conditions, may be present in the same voice. If the temporary or permanent blocking of the nasal passageway is in the anterior portion of the nares and the soft palate is inactive, the vocalized breath for vowel tones may be entrapped in the posterior portion of the passageway. Such a condition causes vowel sounds to become nasal and at the same time blocks and distorts the normal nasal-resonance character of the M, N, and NG sounds.

Listening and Self-analysis

1. Listen to a recording of your voice. Do the M, N, and NG sounds have a clear nasal quality? Are your vowel sounds free from nasality?

2. Observe the movement of your lips and lower jaw as you speak in front of a mirror. How wide is your mouth opening? Does it seem to be as wide as the posterior opening into your oral cavity?

3. Looking into a mirror, open your mouth wide. Hold your tongue down and forward. If you have trouble doing this, use a tongue depressor or spoon handle to keep your tongue down. Now inhale sharply through your mouth, and exhale through your nose, keeping your mouth wide open. Notice the movement of your velum as it rises on inhalation and moves down in contact with your tongue on exhalation. Observe the same phenomenon as you phonate NG-AH-NG-AH. If you can get vigorous action of your velum, you should have no difficulty controlling nasal resonance.

Exercises for Improvement

1. Practice the exercises for open throat given earlier in this chapter.

2. Sound AH at your optimum pitch. Without stopping the tone, close

your mouth to get M. Move back and forth from one sound to the other several times, without allowing nasality to creep into the vowel sound.

3. Repeat the procedure of Exercise 2, using the vowels AW, OH, EE, E (as in *bet*), and A (as in *bat*). Repeat the same procedure for each vowel, using N and NG.

4. Pronounce each of the following words slowly, and then repeat more quickly, giving full value to the M, N, and NG sounds, but eliminating nasality from the vowels: *am, time, gone, sang, fine, dance, seem, soon, song, moon, mat, gnat, neat, singing, finger, can, ram, ran, rang, ten, met, fame, rain, length, land, friend, spend, lame, mean.*

5. The following sentences contain no nasal sounds. Speak them without nasality.

a. He was awake at five o'clock.
b. He walked to the store and asked for cigarettes.
c. They hurriedly left for the gold fields.
d. Be sure to go to bed early.
e. This is the house that Jack built.
f. Today is the last day to go to the Catskills.

OTHER PROBLEMS

Some teachers of voice use additional terms to refer to vocal faults, such as *flatness* of voice, *thinness*, and so forth. The faults covered by these terms usually involve the functioning of the entire vocal mechanism. If you can learn to develop an adequate breath stream, to initiate tones without shock, and to sustain full tones through open resonance passages, you should have little difficulty in overcoming these problems.

We cannot emphasize too strongly that defects in vocal quality, except those caused by physical differences, are often deeply rooted in early habits based on environmental influences, in fundamental personality problems, or in emotional disturbances. If you have serious problems in vocal quality, therefore, you should reread Chapter 2, examine your whole background of habit and emotional response, and try to make adjustments which may remove tensions contributing to poor vocal quality.

VOCAL QUALITY

Up to this point we have presented resonation as a mechanical process If the mechanism is operating effectively, with the resonators free from con striction and capable of smooth, quick changes, the tone is well resonated.

The quality that you hear is likely to be pleasant. If faults of resonation are present, you will hear defective voice quality. In this sense, quality of tone is the listener's interpretation of how the tone is resonated. Physically, it is the complex result of the selective combination of the fundamental and the overtones.

However, the word "quality" has more extensive connotations. As the speaker responds to the ideas he wishes to convey, his emotions affect his body and make changes in the size, shape, and tension of his resonators. The resulting variations in quality will be expressive of his feeling states. As you listen to another person, therefore, you may comment that he has good or poor quality evident in pleasant or unpleasant resonance aspects in the voice. You may also call his voice quality responsive to and expressive of his emotions or unresponsive and lacking in communication of his feelings.

The terms used to represent what quality is heard have, over a long period, become exceedingly subjective. They may report the emotional effect produced in the listener, or suggest the psychological or physical condition of the speaker. For instance, you may have used many of the following terms to describe quality: friendly, soothing, exciting, smooth, complaining, antagonistic, shrill, mellow, metallic, muffled. The list could be continued at length. Of course, every time you make a judgment on quality, you must recall that the speaker's voice is also characterized by his habits of manipulating loudness, timing, and pitch to communicate meaning. For instance, if you say that a tone is whining, you refer probably to unpleasant nasal quality and to habits of maintaining a high pitch and of dragging out the vowel sounds. The emphasis in this chapter, however, will be on the quality aspects of voice.

Your quality of voice is influenced not only by your emotional state at the moment of speaking, but also by the structure of your particular resonators, your general health, your long-standing habits of tension and relaxation in the entire body, and your habitual emotional responses. These can all serve to make your quality different from that of anyone else, and different from situation to situation.

As you listen to others, notice the variety of interpretations you place upon quality. Without opening a door to peer into a room, you can say, "That's my friend in there. I'd know his voice anywhere."

If a student standing out of sight around the corner in the hall suddenly exclaims, "Ah," without looking further, you decide that he is disappointed over a poor grade. You do not know either the student or the circumstances, yet you have defined the nature of his emotion on the basis of his voice.

You may turn on the radio or hear the sound on television before the picture becomes clear. An actor announces that he wants action immediately. If you are interested, before you hear the next character's response, you will think, "He's a decisive, arrogant man who easily loses control of his temper." You are not surprised that your conjecture is correct, even though you knew neither actor nor story.

First of all, you have long been aware of the fact that quality of tone can identify the individual. When you were a small child, you responded to the tone of the voice before you could understand words. You could soon identify family members and friends by their voices alone.

Secondly, early in life you discovered that it was important to your comfort to identify the nature of emotion by the tone quality. As a child, you depended for so long a time upon the assistance and good will of other people that their emotional reactions became exceedingly vital to you. You used both your eyes and ears to determine whether your father was in good humor, whether your mother felt loving toward you, or whether your teacher would let you get away with throwing a spitball. You also listened to yourself in a variety of emotional states. Now, in adulthood, when you hear a tone of anger, without even seeing the speaker, you call upon your experience; you have heard and produced that emotional tone before. You may also respond empathically to what you hear; you unconsciously imitate the muscular contractions of the speaker. You recognize the physical sensation of anger and combine this with what you have heard. You then come to the conclusion that you know how the other person feels.

Lastly, through years of association with other people, you have noted that physical characteristics and personality factors are often associated with certain kinds of voice quality. Since you have frequently been successful in gauging one from the other, you may conclude that voice quality can identify the type of person. You will find that this is often, but not always, true. In any case, such judgments are constantly made—about you as well as about others.

By your own experience, then, you know that quality of voice enables you to recognize a person, perceive an emotion, and even surmise something about the personality of the individual speaking. A judgment of tone quality will therefore be more than a judgment of the efficiency of the resonation process. It will include your interpretation of the individual's responsiveness to the immediate situation and of his personality traits in all social situations.

CHANGES IN VOCAL QUALITY TO EXPRESS MEANING

When you read or speak, the ideas you wish to communicate carry a multitude of subtle connotations. No idea spoken can appeal only to logic and reason. You hold personal attitudes toward everything you say, whether it be an argument over the honor system, an account of a strange experience, or the presentation of a logarithm. If you are reading, you should realize that the author of the selection also had his own feelings about his material. You cannot fully communicate what you are saying or reading unless you respond to the emotions inherent in the content.

If the ideas spoken are your own, you usually recognize your feelings without stopping to analyze them. If the material is written by someone else, however, you must try first to gain a thorough understanding of the meanings to be conveyed before you can present them effectively. Such an analysis is not enough, however. As you speak, an emotional response must take place physically. Your attitudes must show not only in the changes that occur in facial expression, body movement, timing, loudness, and pitch, but also in responsive variations in vocal quality. The listener needs to see and hear your emotional reactions if full communication is to take place. Without this physical expressiveness, you cannot make clear all the implications of what you say, and you will often fail to interest and stimulate your listener.

Consider vocal quality in relation to muscular tension and emotions. In speaking, reading, or acting, you must engage in body tensions and relaxations corresponding to the tension and relaxation of the emotional states to be expressed. These physical responses are not tensions of the resonators alone, or even of the whole vocal mechanism, but must be of the entire body. In the discussion of the other elements of voice, you have seen how the functioning of the whole body operates in determining the vocal result. The effect of the gross muscles—those of the arms, legs, and torso—on the fine muscles of the vocal mechanism, especially on the resonators, is of tremendous importance for vocal quality.

If you are angry, you are angry with your whole body, not with only a part of it. The muscles of your extremities are set to fight, and the effect of these tensions makes itself felt on the vocal mechanism. You cannot say, "I am so angry I could knock his head off!" and give full significance to the words unless you respond with body tensions of anger. If you try to say this sentence with your body as relaxed as possible, you will fail to express the full meaning of the phrase. However, if you actually engage in the muscle tensions of the emotion, attempting to "suit the action to the word, the word to the action," your words will increase in meaning. The states of anger, anxiety, and fear are generally expressed as the result of strong, positive, muscular tensions affecting your vocal mechanism, while depressing states of grief, sorrow, or boredom generally receive their appropriate tone color as the result of the relaxation of muscular tensions.

You will find that the emotion must be genuine; you cannot assume or imitate a feeling or achieve an emotional expression mechanically. If you should say to yourself, "Since this passage calls for an expression of fear, I will use such and such a tone quality," you will succeed only in being patently artificial. Because you have had a great deal of experience in responding to emotional expression, you quickly hear falseness in the tone and are likely to reject both the speaker and his ideas.

You often hear similarity in emotional quality changes from one speaker to another in like situations. Because of this, you may assume that there is "a tone of grief," "a tone of surprise," and so on. Out of this mistaken concept stereotypes in quality develop: the petulant woman always whines; the gangster gives his orders in a throaty, gruff voice; and the heroine, like the cowboy on the white horse, speaks in happy, ringing tones. Definite and strong emotional qualities too often are classified as "the frightened cry," "the angry roar," and "the joyous greeting." Actors and readers, when they lack true artistic skill, often make use of these stereotypes, but as you listen your ears will tell you that the emotion is mechanically contrived. Instead of imitating expressions of emotion which you have observed, examine and respond to your own sincere feelings about your ideas.

The concept of empathy will help you to understand the relationship between your expressiveness and the reactions of your audience. When you become engrossed in watching or listening to an individual, you tend to follow his muscular activity with contractions or relaxations in your own muscles. Your physical responses may be minimal, and you may not even be aware of your reactions. If you watch a man struggle to close a window, and you are interested in the outcome, you will find yourself contracting the muscles of arms and hands as if you were pulling with him. On the platform, once the speaker has gotten your attention, he can make use of empathy. For instance, you may be listening to a speaker appealing for funds for the March of Dimes and describing a child taking his first step in braces. If his emotion is genuine and fully expressed, you may find yourself frowning with anxiety, leaning forward, and even moving your hands slightly as you observe his body movements and listen to the tone of his voice. If this is true of you as a listener, when your turn comes to speak, you can appreciate how valuable it will be to you to be able to start this empathic response in your listeners.

In addition to the expression of the general emotion involved in an entire idea, you should be able to respond to the meanings of single words. The quality change on the word becomes an aspect of emphasis and is called *word color*. For example, in a descriptive passage certain words will have a strong appeal to the senses. In phrases like "the *warmth* of the sun," "the *dark* clouds," "the *screaming* siren," "the *acid* taste," and "the *bright blue* of the summer sea," you must add quality responses to the sensations involved, besides your meaningful variations in duration of vowels, in loudness, and in pitch. You must show a physical response to words which convey action, like "the *swift flight* of the bird," "the *sudden rush* of air," and "the *stunning blow* of his fist." You may make quality changes on colorful words which attempt to show the emotional impact of events on the individual, like "the *soothing* tone of the old mandolin," "the *frightening* blast of sound," and "an *exciting* message." Whatever the meaning, the responsive change in quality on the single word or phrase points up the attitudes of the speaker and of the writer and catches the ear of the listener.

Read aloud the following selection from "The Eve of St. Agnes" by Keats. Think through the meanings carried by single words and phrases and listen to yourself respond to the variety of images.

> And still she slept an azure-lidded sleep,
> In blanchéd linen, smooth, and lavendered,
> While he from forth the closet brought a heap
> Of candied apple, quince, and plum, and gourd;
> With jellies smoother than the creamy curd,
> And lucent syrups, tint with cinnamon;
> Manna and dates, in argosy transferred
> From Fez; and spicéd dainties, every one
> From silken Samarcand to cedared Lebanon.
>
> —KEATS

For a more familiar pattern of speech, turn to the selection by Mark Twain on page 51. At the end of this passage, note how quality changes can make the concluding statement stand out from the rest. The device of using a final climactic sentence is often useful in public speaking situations, particularly if you have skill in making communicative quality changes.

Changes in quality, as they occur in response to the entire passage or to single words, must make plain your genuine and personal feelings. Your listener will hear and see these expressed attitudes and react, sometimes empathically, and always with increased understanding of your meanings.

Self-analysis and Listening

1. In analyzing your own vocal quality as you express meaning, remember that the tone is the result of the interaction of a number of factors. Examine your own quality in relation to these:

a. *The way your vocal mechanism is constructed.* There may be just as many physical differences between any two vocal mechanisms as you might find between two pianos or two cellos.

b. *Your general health.* Muscular or surface irritation or inflammation in the throat area will seriously affect voice quality. Most of you are familiar with the change in quality that accompanies a cold. You may also find it difficult to respond to emotional meanings in material if you are weak or ill.

c. *Your habitual manner of vocalization.* Your posture may be poor, your chest slumped, your breathing shallow. You may have acquired poor habits of phonation which can influence resonation. You may have habits of habitual tension in all social situations.

d. *Your habitual attitudes toward other people and toward yourself.* You have all heard complaining, aggressive, fearful, friendly, and excitable voices. Instead of responding to their immediate ideas, some people sound the same on all occasions. Their personal problems make them rigid in behavior; they lack the vocal flexibility needed to express the variety of meanings inherent in all communications.

e. *Your immediate responsiveness.* If you read mechanically or pour out memorized lines, the quality will be poor. If you inhibit your emotional expression, the tone will sound dull and incommunicative. You must respond quickly and sensitively to the implications of what you say.

2. Listen to the first recording you made for this class. As you read or spoke, what attitudes did you convey? If you were an unbiased listener, would you be stimulated by what you now hear? Could you have communicated your meanings more surely by responding further to your ideas?

3. In listening to several television programs, such as westerns or stories

of intrigue, list the actors who use stereotypes in emotional expression. Be prepared to discuss these in class.

4. Listen to commercials on television and radio. If an announcer or actor is particularly convincing or unconvincing, listen carefully to the quality of his voice. Is the emotion contrived; does he seem to believe what he says? Discuss commercials in class.

Exercises for Improvement

1. Read each of the following sentences as if it were spoken under a variety of emotional circumstances. For instance, create in your own mind a situation in which you would say the first sentence with feelings of (*a*) anger, then (*b*) anxiety, (*c*) pleasant excitement or amusement, (*d*) hopelessness. You will, of course, vary pitch, timing, and loudness to convey your meanings, but listen particularly to the tone quality and feel the muscular changes which will indicate the nature of your emotion. Proceed through all the sentences in the same way.

  a. You should have known better.
  b. This is a strange situation.
  c. They went to the show with him.
  d. How much money did he finally raise?
  e. Didn't you ever do something that you immediately regretted?
  f. I've never met a person like that before.
  g. We had a wonderful time last night.
  h. If you don't enjoy the work, I don't think you should go on.
  i. What are you up to now?
  j. All that I wanted was at the end of that road.

2. Read again the exercises for melody on pages 83 to 85 (7, 8, and 9). Maintain the effective pitch changes, but add your emotional response to the ideas through subtle quality changes.

3. As you study the following selections, analyze and understand the emotions involved. Select key words which depict or induce specific feeling states. Read the selections aloud several times as you judge your ability to convey the mood and the attitudes behind the words.

  a. The curfew tolls the knell of parting day,
    The lowing herd winds slowly o'er the lea,
    The ploughman homeward plods his weary way,
    And leaves the world to darkness and to me.

Now fades the glimmering landscape on the sight,
And all the air a solemn stillness holds,
Save where the beetle wheels his droning flight,
And drowsy tinklings lull the distant folds:

Save that from yonder ivy-mantled tower
The moping owl does to the moon complain
Of such as, wandering near her secret bower,
Molest her ancient solitary reign.

—GRAY

b. Our revels now are ended. These our actors,
As I foretold you, were all spirits and
Are melted into air, into thin air:
And, like the baseless fabric of this vision,
The cloud-capped towers, the gorgeous palaces,
The solemn temples, the great globe itself,
Yea, all which it inherit, shall dissolve
And, like this insubstantial pageant faded,
Leave not a rack behind. We are such stuff
As dreams are made on, and our little life
Is rounded with a sleep.

—SHAKESPEARE

c. Boot, saddle, to horse, and away!
Rescue my castle before the hot day
Brightens to blue from its silvery gray.

CHORUS—

Boot, saddle, to horse, and away!

Ride past the suburbs, asleep as you'd say;
Many's the friend there, will listen and pray,
"God's luck to the gallants that strike up the lay—

CHORUS—

Boot, saddle, to horse, and away!"

Forty miles off, like a roebuck at bay,
Flouts Castle Brancepeth the Roundheads' array;
Who laughs, "Good fellows ere this, by my fay,

CHORUS—

Boot, saddle, to horse, and away!"

Who? My wife Gertrude; that, honest and gay,
Laughs when you talk of surrendering, "Nay!
I've better counselors; what counsel they?

CHORUS—

Boot, saddle, to horse, and away!"

—BROWNING

d. I should like to rise and go
Where the golden apples grow;—
Where below another sky
Parrot islands anchored lie,
And, watched by cockatoos and goats,
Lonely Crusoes building boats;—
Where in sunshine reaching out
Eastern cities, miles about,
Are with mosques and minaret
Among sandy gardens set,
And the rich goods from near and far
Hang for sale in the bazaar;—
Where the Great Wall round China goes,
And on one side the desert blows,
And with bell and voice and drum,
Cities on the other hum;—
Where are forests, hot as fire,
Wide as England, tall as a spire,
Full of apes and coconuts
And the negro hunters' huts;—
Where the knotty crocodile
Lies and blinks in the Nile,
And the red flamingo flies
Hunting fish before his eyes. . . .

—STEVENSON

e.   Hear the mellow wedding bells,
    Golden bells!
What a world of happiness their harmony foretells!
  Through the balmy air of night
  How they ring out their delight!
    From the molten-golden notes,
      And all in tune,
    What a liquid ditty floats
To the turtle-dove that listens, while she gloats
    On the moon!
  Oh, from out the sounding cells
What a gush of euphony voluminously wells!
    How it swells!
    How it dwells
  On the Future! how it tells
  Of the rapture that impels
  To the swinging and the ringing
    Of the bells, bells, bells,
Of the bells, bells, bells, bells,
    Bells, bells, bells,—
To the riming and the chiming of the bells!

                —POE

f. The day is cold, and dark, and dreary;
  It rains, and the wind is never weary;
  The vine still clings to the mouldering wall,
  But at every gust the dead leaves fall,
    And the day is dark and dreary.

My life is cold, and dark, and dreary;
  It rains, and the wind is never weary;
  My thoughts still cling to the mouldering Past,
  But the hopes of youth fall thick in the blast,
    And the days are dark and dreary.

Be still, sad heart! and cease repining;
  Behind the clouds is the sun still shining;
  Thy fate is the common fate of all,
  Into each life some rain must fall,
    Some days must be dark and dreary.

            —LONGFELLOW

g. You've seen the snow
Fall softly, lightly
In the dreamy rhythm
Of a spirit dance;

But have you seen it
Show its fangs,
A serpent, wriggling,
Belly to the road,
Gliding eastward,
Driven by the wind?

I did today!
                    —COLLINS *

h. . . . Beyond the pale and pitted undulations of the dunes,—forming
a billowy cemetery for countless dead and drifted things,—ponderous
tides compress the sand to the solidity of pavement, and lick the brown
slope till it shimmers. When the southeast wind piles back the waters
of the Gulf, the great waves flock to shore with magnificent tumultu-
ousness, in infinite green herds, to be shorn of their fleece of foam. But
in those summer days when soft warm breezes blow off the shore, the
sea dozes in oily silence,—there is scarcely a whispering of ripples, huge
crabs crawl out from beneath the creamy ribbon of spume,—opaline
fins wrinkle the surface within a few feet of the shore. And when night
opens all her violet immensities, the foam takes flame,—the ripples
have luminous bursts,—a shell flung out of the warm flood, shine like
infernal spiders. . . .—HEARN †

i. I do much wonder that one man, seeing how much another man is a
fool when he dedicates his behaviours to love, will, after he hath laughed
at such shallow follies in others, become the argument of his own scorn
by falling in love: and such a man is Claudio. I have known when
there was no music with him but the drum and the fife; and now had
he rather hear the tabor and the pipe: I have known when he would
have walked ten mile a-foot to see a good armour; and now will he lie
ten nights awake, carving the fashion of a new doublet. He was wont

---

* Virginia Grant Collins, *The Cricket and the Star*, The Author, East Orange,
N.J., 1946, p. 60. (By permission.)

† "Torn Letters," in Lafcadio Hearn (ed.), *An American Miscellany*, vol. II,
Dodd, Mead & Company, Inc., New York, 1909. (By permission.)

to speak plain and to the purpose, like an honest man and a soldier; and now he is turned orthography; his words are a very fantastical banquet, just so many strange dishes. May I be so converted and see with these eyes? I cannot tell; I think not: I will not be sworn but love may transform me to an oyster; but I'll take my oath upon it, till he have made an oyster of me, he shall never make me such a fool. One woman is fair, yet I am well; another virtuous, yet I am well; but till all graces be in one woman, one woman shall not come in my grace. Rich she shall be, that's certain; wise, or I'll none; virtuous, or I'll never cheapen her; mild, or come not near me; noble, or not I for an angel; of good discourse, an excellent musician, and her hair shall be of what colour it please God.—SHAKESPEARE

4. Attempt to arouse in your listeners an appreciation of the emotions you experienced in a particular incident. Recall a situation in which you felt annoyed, indignant, relieved, or triumphant. Tell of this situation, implying your reactions but avoiding such artless statements as: "I was so mad." "This made me happy." Instead of these, describe your emotion in terms of your physical reactions to the situation and allow the tone of the voice to convey your feelings. Watch your listeners closely. Do you notice empathic responses? Are they sharing your emotions?

5. Prepare a short, argumentative speech in which you support some cause or demand an action. Are your feelings clear to your audience? Do your listeners respond to what you are saying?

6. All of the selections in the Appendix demand an emotional response from the reader. Examine these again and practice those which seem the most stimulating to you. Particularly notice the value of quality changes in Numbers 1, 2, 12, 15, 19, and 23.

SUMMARY

Resonance is the product of three physical phenomena: the reflection and concentration of sound in a single direction through open passages; the forced vibration of solid objects in contact with the vibrating body; and the sympathetic vibration of solid bodies, or partially enclosed cavities filled with air, in response to a vibrating object tuned to the same frequency. In the human voice, the sound waves which start at the vocal folds pass through the pharyngeal, oral, and nasal cavities. Through reflective resonance in these cavities, adequate loudness of the fundamental tone is assured; through sympathetic resonance, the quality of the voice may be modified as the size and shape of the cavities change.

The muscles we use for tone production and resonation are the same as those used for gagging, coughing, sucking, chewing, and swallowing. Some individuals speak with such tension that the contractions of these muscles interfere with good resonance. If the cavities are constricted, either because of emotional disturbance or long-standing habits of response, the tone quality is likely to be unpleasant.

Your aim in voice production should be to achieve "open throat" through the relaxation of all muscles which are not actually used in the formation and resonation of tone. The energy needed to produce good voice can then be concentrated on those muscles which bring about the many quick changes necessary for effective resonation. If you are successful in achieving selective relaxation, and if no organic abnormalities are present, you will produce the best tone of which you are capable and it will be pleasant to hear.

There are several definite faults of resonance. Stridency is caused by excessive tension in the walls of the pharynx and in the muscles of the velum. A harsh, sharp quality results from the prominence given to the higher overtones. Throatiness is a tonal characteristic produced when the back of the tongue narrows the pharyngeal passage. The tone is often low and muffled and possesses a guttural quality.

Nasality is a foghorn quality resulting from the entrapment of the vibrating breath in a resonance cavity. It is most frequently produced when the velum is not raised high enough to make a partial closure with the pharyngeal wall. Denasality is the lack of nasal resonance resulting from any blockage of the nasal passageway, caused by a cold, hay fever, deviated septum, or enlarged adenoids.

Vocal quality is the listener's interpretation of resonation. It is the identifying characteristic of an individual's voice in its habitual pattern or in response to an emotional stimulus. Vocal quality should be considered in relation to muscular tensions and emotion if it is to be successfully employed in speaking, reading, or acting. Your physical response to the emotions involved in your ideas must be genuine rather than assumed. You should react not only to the emotional content of the entire passage, but to the "color" of individual words as well. Such quality responses will enable you to communicate your meanings fully.

6

Articulation

Speak the speech, I pray you, as I pronounced it to you,—trip-pingly on the tongue.—SHAKESPEARE

In campaign speeches, occasionally a candidate must speak to a crowd out in the open, in a park, or at a railroad station. As you stand on the outer fringes of the group, you hear his voice in the distance, going up and down as he gestures violently, increasing in energy as he gives a fine show of enthusiasm. You may be impressed with his delivery and wonder what he is saying. You have heard only the sound of his voice. You do not receive complete meaning from what you hear until you become aware of the symbols of language created by the patterning of articulated sounds.

WHAT IS GOOD ARTICULATION?

Articulation is the process of forming meaningful oral symbols by the manipulation of the tongue, lips, lower jaw, and soft palate. Because these involve elaborate adjustments, they can best be illustrated by two examples. A high-school student was heard to remark one day, "If I ever get elected to the school board, I'm going to fire the math teacher." This sounded like personal prejudice, but actually it was not. "I think any teacher ought to be able to speak the English language so that I can understand him, and he mumbles and runs his words together so that half the time the students don't know what he is saying."

This instructor was not an English or speech teacher, of whom high standards of articulation should be expected. Yet he was failing in his basic task of communicating his subject matter—not because he did not know mathematics, but because he could not be understood by his hearers.

In marked contrast, a college professor who must have been told in his youth to speak distinctly exaggerated his final consonants in such a way that his meaning was obscured by this mannerism, and he became a subject of mimicry and ridicule to all his students.

Articulation is poor both when it lacks clearness and accuracy and when it is overly precise and pedantic. Articulation is said to be good when the sounds are distinct, accurate, and harmoniously blended into one another. In discussing good articulation we must be concerned with the accurate formation of sounds, pronunciation, blending words into phrases, assimilation of sounds by their neighbors, and the effects of stress and accent on sound production.

Pronunciation

While articulation involves the proper manipulation of the articulators to form clear, recognizable sounds, pronunciation means something more. "Correct" or "proper" pronunciation means acceptable production of sounds and the proper accent of syllables in words. Usually, we determine these patterns of sounds and stress by reference to a dictionary.

The pronunciations given in carefully edited dictionaries are, for the most part, those of formal speech. Statesmen, leading public speakers, actors, radio and television personalities, scientists, businessmen, English professors, and other public figures are consulted. Their pronunciations of words are analyzed and compiled by the editors of the dictionary. Where conflicts occur, the most commonly used pronunciations are selected and recorded in the dictionary as "standard." This means that when more than one pronunciation is given for a word, no one of those given is "better" than another; more than one pronunciation is in "standard" usage. The dictionary is therefore an excellent guide to the pronunciation of words in isolation as used by the best educated men in formal speech.

In the long run, if you have a question about pronunciation, the dictionary should be considered as the final authority. Do not discount the pronunciation given in the dictionary because it does not agree with yours; it may be that yours is substandard or unacceptable. However, you must remember that the average dictionary does not discriminate between acceptable dialects used in different parts of the United States, although these differences are dealt with in the more detailed guides to pronunciation given in good dictionaries. Hence, in certain cases the dictionary pronunciation must be modified by acceptable regional standards. Also, the dictionary does not reflect many of the changes in the articulation pattern which occur in less formal speech situations, nor can it show adequately the changes in the pattern caused by the influence of adjoining words or by the relative importance of words in a sentence.

Blending

The sounds of speech should flow from the end of one word into the beginning of another within a phrase in almost exactly the same way that they join from one syllable to the next in a long word. There should be no cessation of the stream of speech sounds, no stop in the flow of movement of the speech mechanism, within a thought group. This process of joining sounds within a given thought group without a perceptible break between the words is called *blending*. Blending involves some modification of sounds as they are joined in the continuous flow of speech, a process called *assimilation* which we shall discuss later. We treat blending as a separate concept in order to emphasize the necessity of an uninterrupted flow of speech, except where the ideas dictate a pause.

The separation of words not only sounds pedantic without gaining in clarity, but also interferes with the communication of meaning. Frequently, speakers who normally blend words in conversation or public speaking fail to do so when they read aloud. Perhaps you have heard a radio or television interview read from script where there was a marked contrast in smoothness between the skillful reading of the professional announcer and the faltering word-by-word manner of the other participant, untrained in oral reading. His pattern of speech sounds may resemble that of a child who is just learning to read, and who makes each word stand out by itself so that the meaning of the whole passage is lost. Perhaps some differences in timing and melody contribute to the meaninglessness in these situations, but there are also inevitable differences in the skill with which words are blended into a phrase.

Assimilation

In the normal flow of speech, sounds modify the production of surrounding sounds. This modification, known as assimilation, may occur when the combination appears within words or in blending. Assimilation facilitates the movement of the articulatory mechanism in passing from the formation of one sound to that of the next, thus giving smoothness to speech. On the other hand, assimilation may be so extreme as to result in the elimination of individual sounds or even whole syllables which are necessary to easy understanding of speech by the hearer. The problems caused by faulty assimilation increase rapidly as the situation becomes more formal, or as the difficulty of hearing is accentuated by the size of the audience and the acoustic properties of the room in which you are speaking.

In our discussion of the sounds of American speech, we shall point out those changes which are normal and acceptable in assimilation, and shall also see some of the more common errors of assimilation which make speech indistinct and unacceptable.

Unstressed Forms

When the meaning of the phrase modifies the rhythm so that a word or syllable has less prominence than when it is pronounced in isolation, it is called an unstressed form. Within the sentence, monosyllabic articles, conjunctions, and prepositions—such as *and, but, of, for*—are nearly always unstressed. Similarly, auxiliary verbs and other words which serve a secondary function in carrying the meaning of the sentence are usually reduced in importance by pronouncing them in their unstressed forms. Dictionaries recognize some of these variants, but not all, partly because they are so dependent on the context and intent of the speaker that they can be examined only in relation to specific utterance. The same thing happens to the unaccented syllables of polysyllabic words. Here the dictionary is more helpful, if the reader understands the meaning of the markings, and for the most part reflects the pronunciation of unstressed syllables. In subsequent pages, as we examine the vowel sounds, we shall note what changes commonly occur in their articulation as they appear in unstressed positions, and shall point out when such changes are acceptable and when they are inappropriate.

You may note the combined effects of blending, assimilation, and stress by taking a short sentence and articulating it in different ways: "I was going because I had heard of his work." First read the sentence slowly, articulating each word independently and with a clear break between words. Then read the sentence at your normal rate, blending the words and stressing *going, heard,* and *work.* You probably had no break in the flow of sounds from the beginning to the end, and you undoubtedly materially changed the vowel sounds in *was, because, had,* and *of.* The chances are also good that you dropped the н in both *had* and *his.* These changes induced by blending, assimilation, and stress would for the most part be fully acceptable in informal speech, but some of them would interfere with clearness in formal platform, stage, or television presentation.

Listening

Careful listening is the first step in the development of good articulation. Unless you have noticeable structural deviations, your present habits of articulation are largely a product of your environment—your home, your associates, your school life. You speak as you have heard others speak. If you wish to improve, you must listen to speakers whose articulation is better than your own as well as to those on your own level or below. You must make comparisons between them to see what the differences are. You should analyze these differences on the basis of the use of the articulatory structures and try to duplicate the movements of the articulators in imitation of what you hear. You must develop sufficient precision to be understood in every situation without forced attention from the listener, but you must not adopt an articulation pattern that calls attention to itself rather than to the subject matter with which you are dealing. Through such analyses, you can make any changes you wish in your articulation.

HOW TO SELECT A STANDARD

With pronunciations varying so widely from region to region, from person to person, and from situation to situation, it is difficult to determine what is standard—what is the "correct" pronunciation for you to use in a given instance. The answer to this question is to be found in three factors: the area in which you live, your purpose in speaking, and the occasion on which you speak.

The Area in Which You Live

We have pointed out in Chapter 2, pages 17 to 19, how pronunciation differs in various parts of the English-speaking world and how, in the United States, there are at least three major dialects: Eastern, Southern, and General American. Let us remind you again that for your standard of articulation you should first concentrate on learning the pronunciation of the educated people in the broad dialect area in which you live.

Your Purpose in Speaking

In a few cases, special dialects are required for special purposes. If you plan to go on the stage, your flexibility as an actor will be to some extent dependent on your ability to adopt the dialect appropriate to the part you are playing. Although the practice is falling into disuse for plays with an American setting, actors still find that they are often called upon to use a modified form of south British dialect, known as stage diction, particularly in Shake-spearean, classic, or British plays. The cast of a play which is laid in Scotland would all have to use a Scottish dialect. In a television comedy depicting a Midwestern family it would be obviously inappropriate for one member of the family to speak General American, another Southern, and a third East-ern. All must speak the same dialect. An actor who cannot hear and readily analyze and adopt a dialect appropriate to his role will not go far.

Radio and television speech has been stabilized with the acceptance of General American dialect, modified somewhat, as the standard of network announcers. Motion pictures also now tend toward the use of modified Gen-eral American as the standard, after some experimentation with stage diction. Here, of course, as on the stage, special roles may require special dialects.

The Occasion on Which You Speak

Speaking occasions differ in formality. The basic dialect you use should not be affected by these differences, but the degree of precision in your articu-lation should change. What may be adequate articulation for a casual street-corner conversation, an argument with an umpire, or a bull session will not be precise enough for a formal social occasion or a business interview. Simi-larly, an even more exacting standard is required of you when you stand before an audience as speaker, reader, or actor. The larger the audience, the greater the number of distractions, the poorer the acoustics of the hall— the greater is the demand upon you for distinct sound production. The ad-vent of public-address systems has made pure lung power less necessary to effective speaking, but it has not reduced in any way the necessity for clear articulation. In some cases, it may actually increase the problem by accen-tuation of echoes or by mechanical distortion of the sounds produced.

On the other hand, overprecision may be quite annoying in informal speaking situations, and reading which separates each word from the next, instead of blending sounds in the normal manner of smooth communication, loses effectiveness. Moreover, as we have already noted, unblended speaking or reading aggravates the problem of glottal shock.

METHODS OF REPRESENTING PRONUNCIATION

Spelling

When written languages were first developed, the symbols used repre-sented sounds, and to some extent this original function of the alphabet has persisted. In some languages, alphabetical symbols come much closer to representing sounds than in English. The difficulty in English spelling arises from two chief sources: (1) the diverse origin of English words; (2) the failure of spelling reform to keep pace with changes in pronunciation. Modern English words are derived from virtually every language root, but the most common ones are Anglo-Saxon (of Germanic origin), Norman French, Latin, and Greek. The English spelling of words is generally a direct derivation from the original root, each of which has a somewhat different system of sound symbols. These divergencies have never been reconciled, nor has any systematic spelling reform ever been undertaken to bring them all into a common system.

The resulting inconsistencies are so apparent that it is hardly necessary to point them out. The word *fish* could be spelled GHUTI if we used the GH in *enough*, the U in *busy*, and the TI in *portion*. While it is true that GH and TI never have those sounds in the positions we have given them in our spelling of *fish*, the spelling GHUTI nevertheless points up the absurdity of using those symbols to represent those sounds in any position. We say that in English there are at most six vowels (A, E, I, O, U, and sometimes Y). But in actual use there are fifteen or more vowel sounds. How, then, shall we represent those for which we have no symbol? In normal English spelling, the letter A may represent at least seven different sounds as in: *at*, *ate*, *ask*, *car*, *many*, *ball*, and *intricate*. On the other hand, the so-called long E sound may be represented by a number of different letter symbols as in: *machine*, *receive*, *believe*, *even*, *sneak*, *lee*, and *Caesar*. The family of words which includes the letter grouping OUGH is another illustration of the inadequacy of our spelling; note the differing pronunciations in *dough*, *bough*, *enough*, *through*, *cough*, and *hiccough*. The OES ending in *does*, *shoes*, and *floes* is another example of the same difficulty. Moreover, some letters used in spelling do not represent any sound at all in speaking, as the K in *knee*, the B in *comb*, and the L in *calm*. You undoubtedly can list many other examples of the same kind.

Diacritical Marks

Dictionary editors have attempted to solve the problem of representing sounds by respelling words and supplementing the alphabetical symbols with a system of dots and lines known as *diacritical markings*. This is a decided improvement over English spelling as a manner of representing sounds, and for the pronunciation of words in isolation it is perhaps accurate enough for most uses. Diacritical systems, however, although they are similar, are not uniform. In order to interpret a dictionary pronunciation accurately, you must consult the guide to pronunciation for that particular dictionary.

Fig. 12. Phonetic Symbols and Diacritical Marks

	Phonetic Symbol	Key Word		Webster	Funk & Wagnalls	American College
1.	[i]	eat	[it]	ē	ī	ē
2.	[ɪ]	it	[ɪt]	ĭ	i	ĭ
3.	[e]	chaos	[keɒs]	â	—	ā
4.	[ɛ]	ever	[ɛvɚ]	ĕ	e	ĕ
5.	[æ]	at	[æt]	ă	a	ă
6.	[a]	ask	[ask]	a̍	ɐ	—
7.	[u]	moon	[mun]	o͞o	ū	o͞o
8.	[ʊ]	book	[bʊk]	o͝o	u	o͝o
9.	[o]	obey	[obeɪ]	ô	o̱	ō
10.	[ɔ]	all	[ɔl]	ô	ө̄	ô
11.	[ɒ]	often	[ɒfn]	ŏ	ө	ŏ
12.	[ɑ]	father	[fɑðɚ]	ä	ā̱	ä
13.	[ʌ]	up	[ʌp]	ŭ	U	ŭ
14.	[ə]	about	[əbaʊt]	a̍	ə	ə
15.	[ɝ]	bird	[bɝd]	ûr	U̅r	ûr
16.	[ɜ]	bird	[bɜd]	û	U̅	û
17.	[ɚ]	weather	[wɛðɚ]	ē	—	ər
18.	[ɑɪ]	time	[tɑɪm]	ī	ɑi	ī
19.	[ɔɪ]	boy	[bɔɪ]	ѳi	ѳi	oi
20.	[ɑʊ]	sound	[sɑʊnd]	ou	ɑu	ou
21.	[eɪ]	day	[deɪ]	ā	ē	ā
22.	[oʊ]	go	[goʊ]	ō	ō	ō
23.	[ɛɚ]	air	[ɛɚ]	âr	ār	âr
24.	[m]	may	[meɪ]	m	m	m
25.	[n]	no	[noʊ]	n	n	n
26.	[ŋ]	ring	[rɪŋ]	ng, ŋ	ŋ	ng
27.	[p]	pay	[peɪ]	p	p	p
28.	[b]	bay	[beɪ]	b	b	b
29.	[t]	time	[tɑɪm]	t	t	t
30.	[d]	dime	[dɑɪm]	d	d	d
31.	[k]	come	[kʌm]	k	k	k
32.	[g]	go	[go]	g	g	g
33.	[f]	feel	[fil]	f	f	f
34.	[v]	veal	[vil]	v	v	v
35.	[θ]	think	[θɪŋk]	th	t͡h	th
36.	[ð]	them	[ðɛm]	th	th	th
37.	[s]	soon	[sun]	s	s	s
38.	[z]	zoo	[zu]	z	z	z
39.	[ʃ]	ship	[ʃɪp]	sh	s͡h	sh
40.	[ʒ]	measure	[mɛʒɚ]	zh	ʒ	zh
41.	[h]	how	[hɑʊ]	h	h	h
42.	[w]	water	[wɑtɚ]	w	w	w
43.	[j]	yes	[jɛs]	y	y	y
44.	[r]	red	[rɛd]	r	r	r
45.	[l]	leap	[lip]	l	l	l
46.	[tʃ]	church	[tʃɝtʃ]	ch	c͡h	ch
47.	[dʒ]	judge	[dʒʌdʒ]	j	j	j

Webster's Collegiate Dictionary, for example, lists sixty-six symbols in the key to pronunciation, whereas the American College Dictionary lists only forty-eight, some of which are quite different from Webster's symbols. Note these differences in Figure 12.

In addition to this, diacritical markings do not distinguish among different dialects, in many cases. The symbol à as it is used in the Webster dictionaries is dependent on your pronunciation of the word *ask*. However, the pronunciation of this word varies from one part of the country to another— from the A in *father*, to the A in *bat*. The symbol à is thus accurate enough to give you the pronunciation of other words in your own dialect, but it is not exact enough to represent the sounds of speech as you hear others produce them. Since the symbol represents a broad range of usage, it cannot represent an exact sound. Precisely the same difficulty is encountered in words marked with the symbol ŏ, since varying interpretations render the symbol ambiguous.

Phonetics

In order to transcribe and study spoken language, scholars have devised a phonetic symbol for each sound. Often the alphabet letter can be used to represent a sound. For such sound units, however, as SH, TH, and NG, where there is no single letter to indicate the sounds, or for vowels where the alphabet letter stands for a variety of sounds, special symbols had to be created. All of these phonetic symbols are given in Figure 12.

By means of such symbols a written record can be made, for example, of the different ways in which men from the various regions in this country or from foreign countries may say the same word or phrase. Also, by means of phonetics the listener can record the changes which take place in sounds when they occur together and affect each other's production or when they are stressed or unstressed in the flow of speech.

The use of phonetics, then, permits accuracy in the transcription of speech. Also, the study of phonetics goes beyond this in providing a description of the formation of each sound.

PHONETICS AS A TOOL FOR IMPROVING ARTICULATION

Ear Training

We have chosen to use the phonetic system of representing sounds primarily because we believe it to be the best method by which to make an intensive study of articulation problems. In addition to its great accuracy in representing sounds, the phonetic method makes thorough and precise ear training possible. We have already pointed out that your present manner of speaking results from imitating the speech you have heard around you. Now that your speech habits are relatively fixed, however, you have stopped listening. You probably do not hear any but the extreme deviations from your own pattern. There is no possibility for you to improve your articulation until you begin to listen to your speech and compare it with what you want to achieve.

The first step in this process is to learn to recognize sounds in isolation. When you have familiarized yourself with all of the sounds which normally appear in American speech, you should listen to individual words as your instructor pronounces them to you. Some of these pronunciations will not be the ones you would expect from the spelling or even from the diacritical markings given for the word in the dictionary. Nevertheless, you should learn to recognize these deviations and to write them phonetically. When you can do this adequately, you are ready to write phrases, recording the assimilation pattern and changes in the pronunciation of unstressed syllables.

By the time you have mastered this technique, you should be hearing differences in the articulation pattern of people about you, and you should be conscious of the phonetic structure of your own speech. If you overassimilate, or if you make too great changes in unstressed vowels, you should begin to hear it in your own speech. If you can make a tape or phonographic recording of your speech, you will speed the process of self-analysis.

Modification of the Articulation Pattern

When you are able to hear your own speech and record it phonetically, you are ready to begin any reconstruction which may be needed. By analyzing the phonetic record of your speech, you can discover where clarity is lacking, where vowel or consonant sounds are distorted, and where greater (or in a few cases, less) precision would give it greater force or emphasis. Moreover, by comparing the way in which you produce connected sounds with the phonetic transcript of another voice whose articulation pattern is unmistakably better than your own, you can make a further study of your own problems.

A knowledge of phonetics may thus aid you to improve your speech in two ways. It will serve as a tool for training your ear to hear your own speech and that of people about you. It will furnish a method for objective study of your own speech in relation to the speech of others.

Specialized Uses of Phonetics

If you plan to go on the stage, you will find a knowledge of phonetics an invaluable tool in helping you to master special dialects you may wish to use. Moreover, your ear will be more acute; you will detect differences more readily, and know what adjustments must be made to produce the special sounds called for in the speech you seek to learn.

Teachers can use phonetics as a method of analyzing the sound deficiencies of school children, and in many cases can help students to make the modification they need. Those who make speech correction a career, of course, need a knowledge of phonetics more extensive than we present here.

METHODS OF CLASSIFYING SOUNDS

Several different methods may be used to classify speech sounds. The distinction most commonly made is between vowels and consonants. This is a somewhat arbitrary distinction, based on the relative importance of the tone and noise components of the sound. When the resonance passages are relatively open, so that the distinctive quality of the sound depends on the shape of the resonator, the sound is called a *vowel*. On the other hand, when the breath stream is stopped, narrowed, or diverted by the articulators, the sound is called a *consonant*. Consonants may combine tonal and noise elements, or they may consist of noise alone.

A second type of distinction which is often made is the positional one— the description of the position and movement of the articulatory organs in the formation of a sound. In this sense, vowel sounds may be distinguished from one another by describing the way in which changes in the position of the tongue, lips, and jaw modify the shape of the resonator and its opening, thus determining the quality of the vowel. Similarly, the consonants may be labeled in terms of the point of narrowing or contact between the articulators at which the distinctive characteristics of the sound are produced. Thus, a bilabial sound is one articulated by both lips; a linguadental sound is produced by bringing together the tongue and the teeth; and so on. We use this type of classification in the vowel and consonant charts in the two following chapters, and in the description of the individual sounds.

A third classification is the acoustic method. Consonants may be grouped according to the type of sound which the ear hears. While it is true that these effects are the result of a particular kind of articulatory position, it is convenient to describe them in terms of the acoustic effect alone. Thus, consonant sounds may be voiced or voiceless—that is, made with or without laryngeal tone. They may be nasals, plosives, fricatives, or glides. Since numerous articulation problems arise from both similarity in sound and similarity in position, these last two methods of classification may help you to understand your articulation problems.

THE MECHANISM FOR ARTICULATION

Like all other phases of the speech process, good articulation involves effective muscle control. Muscles regulate the articulators: the tongue, the lower jaw, the lips, the velum, and the walls of the pharynx, as shown in Figure 13. All of the movements of these articulators serve the primary purposes of chewing, sucking, and swallowing; but as an overlaid function we have learned to use them to form the sounds of our language.

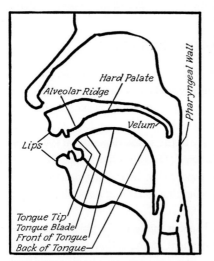

Fig. 13. Diagram showing the articulators in the oral cavity

By far the most active and flexible of these articulators is the tongue. Its complex system of muscles enables it to change its shape and position in the oral cavity in many ways; because of this, it is an influential factor in determining both vowel and consonant formation. In discussing its function in articulation, we shall refer to the flexible tip; to the blade, or broad, flat part immediately behind the tip; to the front, where the thickest part of the tongue begins; and to the back, where the surface of the tongue curves downward into the pharynx.

The muscles which change the position of the lower jaw and those which manipulate the lip opening are also important in determining the sound produced. The muscles in the walls of the pharynx and in the velum open and close the entrance into the nasal passage. Other structures involved in articulation are the teeth, the alveolar ridge, and the hard palate. Refer to the descriptions of the oral and pharyngeal cavities in Chapter 5 for more detailed information of these structures.

The articulators are moved in different ways so as to close off the nasal pharynx, to vary the size and shape of the oral and pharyngeal cavities and of the lip opening to produce the different vowels. In forming consonants, the lips may move toward or away from each other; they can protrude or extend horizontally; or the lower lip may touch the upper teeth. The tongue can approach or contact the teeth, the alveolar ridge, the palate, or the velum. The velum can be raised against the back wall of the pharynx or lowered to permit an opening into the nasal passage.

In your own mechanism, locate as many of the articulators as you can. Experiment with the varied movement of which each is capable. When their positions and movements are described in the analysis of a sound, you thus will be able to duplicate those positions and movements for yourself.

THE PHONETIC TRANSCRIPTION OF SOUNDS

We have said that a phonetic symbol represents a single sound articulated in a given way. This statement is not strictly accurate as no person ever produces a given sound twice in exactly the same way, nor do different persons ever produce the same sound exactly alike. Hence, a given phonetic symbol represents an actual family of sounds all of which sound alike to the ear. This concept is called the *phoneme theory*, which holds that so long as the ear reports a given sound, it *is* that sound, no matter what minor or major variations there are in the actual structure or manipulation of the organs of articulation. For example, one person may make an s with the tongue tip behind the lower teeth, while another makes it with the tongue tip on the alveolar ridge; both, however, sound alike. You will produce the κ in *keep* and that in *duke* in different places in the oral cavity because the muscle movements which occur before and after a sound affect the immediate formation of that sound.

If the sounds become too dissimilar to the main or most frequently heard members of the phoneme, they are recognized as the distortions heard in defective speech or as actual substitutions of sounds from another phoneme. The distinction between one phoneme and another is always made on this acoustic basis.

As you gain experience in listening to sounds, you will come to recognize slight variations which result from positional differences in the articulation of the sound. Some of the differences are so slight that even the trained ear fails to catch them. As long as the different sounds have the same acoustic properties—as long as they sound alike—we consider them to be the same sound and use one phonetic symbol to indicate the entire phoneme.

You will learn the phonetic system more quickly if you will divorce it completely from alphabetic or spelling symbols with which you are familiar. While many of the phonetic symbols are exactly the same as their alphabetic counterparts, they no longer stand for spelled letters but for sounds alone. Identify them not by giving their alphabetic name, but by pronouncing the sound which they represent. The symbol [u], for example, is not the letter which you pronounce *you*, but a sound. Remember, also, that there are no "silent letters" in phonetics, such as frequently occur in spelling. Finally, recall that a symbol stands for one sound and one sound only; it cannot, like a spelling symbol, represent different sounds in different words.

As you study each new symbol, complete a three-way association pattern. Learn the appearance of the symbol; listen as the sound is pronounced by the instructor; produce the sound yourself and observe the articulatory adjustments you make to form it. Now use the sound in connected speech and listen to it. Listen also to other members of your class and to your family and friends, and compare your production of the sound with theirs.

SUMMARY

Articulation is the process of forming meaningful sound symbols with the action of the articulators: the soft palate, the tongue, the lower jaw, and the lips. It involves problems in pronunciation, blending, assimilation, and stress. It should be clear and precise without being pedantic or exaggerated. While the dictionary is essential in determining your standard, you must temper its advice by listening to the speech of educated persons in the broad dialect area in which you live. You must also learn to modify your articulation to suit your purpose and the occasion.

Phonetic symbols are more accurate and useful than spelling or diacritical markings as methods of indicating pronunciation. Because of this, they are invaluable tools for improving your articulation. Their accuracy in representing speech sounds enables you to recognize sound differences in yourself and others, and to select those sounds which will be appropriate to your speech. When you are able to hear these differences, the process of improving your speech will be much more rapid.

Exercises

LISTENING AND SELF-ANALYSIS

1. Listen carefully to the members of your class. Do all of them speak the same dialect? What differences do you hear? Discover the sectional origin of those whose dialects differ from your own.

2. Do other members of the class speak distinctly at all times? Are some of their sounds omitted or so changed as to make the speech difficult to understand? Do any members of the class fail to blend words, particularly in reading aloud? What effect does this have on the meaning communicated?

3. Listen to the record which you made at the beginning of the course. Is your speech similar to that of other members of the class? Is your articulation clear and easy to understand? Is it overprecise? Do you separate words in reading where the meaning does not require it? Do you run some words or syllables together, slighting the unaccented parts?

EXERCISES IN THE USE OF THE DICTIONARY

1. Read the sections at the beginning of Webster's Collegiate Dictionary entitled "A Guide to Pronunciation." As you read Chapters 7 and 8 in this book, compare the Webster guide with the comments on phonetics given in the chapter. Raise questions with the instructor based on your observations.

2. Compare the pronunciation keys listed in Figure 12. What differences do you note?

7

The Vowel Sounds in Speech

Accent is the soul of language; it gives to it both feeling and truth.
—ROUSSEAU

A visiting lecturer in one of your classes speaks in a sharp, staccato, and monotonous voice. You can understand what he is saying, but his speech disturbs you. Each sound seems to be produced as though it were a bullet from a machine gun. The voice is strident, and the rhythm is so jerky that you are distracted in taking notes on his lecture. The thing which disturbs you in listening to this speaker is the way in which he produces the sounds of the language, especially the vowel sounds.

For all of the vowels, the tone flows relatively freely through the open mouth; hence, changes in duration, loudness, pitch, and quality are more apparent to the listener in the vowel sounds than on the consonants. For the most part, the consonants appear to stop and start the vowels. The vowels give the greatest evidence of your abilities in the use of the vocal skills. In this chapter, notice how the formation of the vowels depends upon the basic skills of voice production: breathing, phonation, and resonation. The exhaled breath stream provides the power. As all vowels are voiced, the vibrating vocal folds give the sound, and the manipulation of the size, shape, and surface condition of the oral resonator differentiates one vowel from another.

PRINCIPLES OF VOWEL PRODUCTION

In the establishment of standards for acceptable vowel production, you must remember that vowel sounds are unstable, both in their method of articulation and in their acoustic effect. You will be given a description of each vowel as it occurs in isolation. In spoken language, if the vowel is in an emphasized word or a stressed syllable, it will be similar in production to its description in isolation. However, if the vowel occurs in an unstressed word or syllable, it may be altered or a different vowel may be used for it. A detailed discussion of the effects of accent and stress on vowel sounds will follow the description of the vowels.

It is well to remember, also, as we noted in Chapter 6, that there is nothing static about the formation of sounds in connected speech. When you talk, your thoughts are formulated into word groups, or phrases. As each phrase is spoken, the articulatory mechanism moves continuously from the beginning of the phrase to the pause which precedes the next phrase. No sooner is the position for the vowel assumed than the lips, tongue, and lower jaw move into the position for the next sound. A static description of the vowel, therefore, tends to be misleading.

Any rules, then, which are set down for acceptable vowel production must be flexible. With this in mind, the following suggestions are offered.

The vowels must possess:

1. sufficient accuracy (the correct phoneme) to be readily understood and meaningful;

2. freedom from exaggerated (often incorrect), pedantic production;

3. open resonance passages based on proper balance of tension and relaxation of muscles;

4. sufficient duration, when the vowel is stressed, to allow the changes in pitch, loudness, and quality to be readily discerned;

5. enough unstressing or short production, when the vowel *should* be unstressed, to contribute to an acceptable rhythm pattern for speech.

The Formation of Vowels

In order to produce a vowel, the following five conditions must be present:

1. the vocal folds must be in vibration so that the sound is voiced;

2. the velum must be raised so that the opening into the nasal cavity is closed and the breath stream is directed through the oral cavity;

3. the mouth must be open, with the tongue tip behind the lower front teeth, so that there is a relatively open passageway from the level of the vocal folds through the lips;

4. the lower jaw, the tongue, and the lips must move to vary the size and shape of the oral cavity and of the lip opening to differentiate each sound;

5. the position of the articulators must be held momentarily (the time varying with the vowel) for stable production.

As you watch in a mirror, form the sound EE as in the word m*e*, then the oo in m*oo*n, and finally the AH in f*a*ther. Notice the differences in lip opening for each of the three sounds, as suggested in the diagrams in Figure

14. Try them again, and feel the differences in tongue and jaw positions as you move from sound to sound. The number of different jaw, lip, and tongue positions and combinations of positions for the production of the vowels is infinite. As the positions and tensions of these three parts vary, coupled with the movements of the walls of the pharynx, the variety of vowels which we have in General American speech is produced. Fifteen to seventeen of

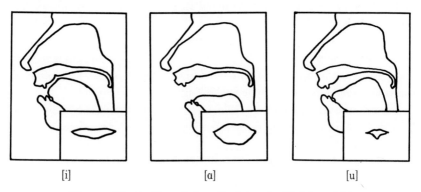

[i]   [ɑ]   [u]

Fig. 14. The position of the articulators for [i], [ɑ], *and* [u]

them are in common American usage. However, as vowels are influenced in production by the sounds which precede and follow them in connected speech, there is, in reality, an infinite series based on the slight differences in the positions of the structures.

The relative instability of the vowels makes it extremely difficult to classify them accurately into any systematic scheme. They can be distinguished by such differentiating features as the relative openness of the mouth passage, the roundness or spread of the lips, the general tension or laxness of the functioning muscles, and the relative duration of the sound. The most satisfactory scheme of classification for our purposes is that of relative tongue position in the production of the sound.

In this system, the high point of the tongue in the mouth is used to place the vowel in relation to the other vowels. Thus, if you will repeat the EE and AH sounds, and notice the position of the tongue for each, you will find that the tongue comes much closer to the hard palate for EE than it does for AH; EE, therefore, is a higher vowel than AH is. While this is a convenient classification into which all vowels can be fitted, it is only a relative one, with wide possible individual variation in tongue position for the production of any sound. It must be remembered that in the last analysis the ear is the judge of the accuracy of the sound, no matter how it is produced. If you find that you do not produce a vowel with the tongue in the exact position indicated on the chart, and yet the vowel sounds correct, then do not worry about the accuracy of your tongue placement. At best, the position on the chart is relative and indicates approximately the position for the production of the family of sounds, the phoneme, of that vowel.

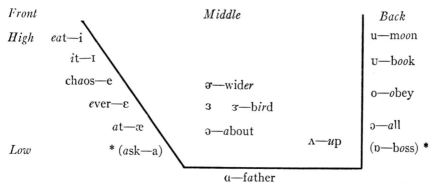

Fig. 15. *The vowel diagram*

* The sounds [a] and [ɒ] are relatively uncommon in General American speech. Many of you may have difficulty hearing and producing them. However, they are common enough to warrant inclusion in this chart and in the later descriptions.

In Figure 15, the commonly used American vowels are arranged according to the high point of the tongue. The left-hand side of the chart represents the front of the tongue and the right-hand side the back of it; the top of the chart represents the hard palate and the bottom the surface of the tongue held flat in the mouth. It is the front of the tongue, not the tip or blade, which rises for the front vowels, and the back for the back vowels. Refer to Figure 13, page 136, for the names of the parts of the tongue.

As has been suggested, the positions indicated are relative and not absolute ones. The variations in tongue position from one vowel to another are relatively slight; they are not actually so broad as they may seem to be on the diagram. The phonetic symbol and a key word are given for each sound.

Observation and Listening

Repeat the key word for each vowel several times, then isolate the vowel and repeat it a number of times until you are sure that you hear it accurately. Try to feel the adjustment of the tongue, jaw, and lips which you make for that sound. After you have tried each sound by itself, try the front vowels and the back vowels in series. As you repeat the front vowels from [i] through [a], notice how the front of the tongue drops as you descend from vowel to vowel; how the jaw moves down for each sound; how the opening for the breath stream becomes larger; and how the lips, as the jaw moves down, change from a horizontal spread to a relaxed, open position.

Say the back vowels beginning with [u] and moving down to [ɒ]. Note how the back of the tongue drops from sound to sound; how the jaw descends; how the mouth opening becomes larger; how the position of the lips changes from a close rounding to a wide-open position. Try the front vowel [i] and then move directly to the back one [u]. Note how the high point of the tongue moves from the front to the back as you say these sounds. If you have difficulty isolating any individual sound, run through the series from top to bottom; from the vowel next above the difficult one, drop the tongue slightly, drop the jaw a little, and increase the size of the mouth opening.

The middle vowels may be harder for you to duplicate accurately than those produced at the front and back, as the middle ones are less stable in terms of tongue position. Try each of them, and notice that if there is any upward movement of the tongue it is in the middle of the oral cavity. Start with the [ɑ] and move on up through the other sounds to feel this slight movement of the tongue. The [ə] is called the neutral vowel, as the tongue, jaw, and lips are in their most relaxed positions, with the middle of the tongue raised slightly. Try moving from a high front vowel to a middle one; feel how the tongue moves and where its high point is for each. The descriptions of the individual sounds will help you to fix the sound and produce it in various word combinations.

DESCRIPTION OF VOWELS

In the following sections each vowel is described in detail and examples are given for common combinations of the vowel in American speech. Study the description, produce the vowel in isolation, and notice your production of it in each of the examples. How does your production compare with that indicated? Listen to the sound as others produce it in the example words.

FRONT VOWELS

[i] as in *eat*

You raise the front of your tongue high, almost to the hard palate; your jaw is nearly closed, and your lips are spread in a narrow opening; the vocal folds vibrate, and the sound is emitted through the mouth. (Since the vocal folds vibrate and the sound is emitted through the mouth on all vowels, that feature of production will be omitted from future descriptions.) This sound is long, but length varies, depending upon the stress placed on the word or syllable in which it appears. You should avoid undue tension which will distort quality. Care should be used so that there is neither an on-glide nor an off-glide, with [mi] becoming [mɪi] or [miɪ]. Some persons with a Yiddish or south European language background may incorrectly substitute [ɪ] for [i] so that *heat* becomes *hit*.

we	re*a*p	rece*i*ve
feet	bel*ie*ve	mach*i*ne
pe*o*ple		monk*ey*

[ɪ] as in *it*

The front of your tongue is slightly lower and farther back and is more relaxed than it was for [i]; your jaw descends a little, and the lips are less spread. This is a short vowel. This sound is sometimes confused with [i], particularly by persons with a romance-language background, so that *hit* resembles *heat* and *lip* resembles *leap*. You should avoid any drawl which will tend to make the sound a diphthong and change it to [ɪə] as in [ɪət].

s*i*t	b*u*sy	w*o*men
symbol	v*i*llage	s*ie*ve
m*i*nute		*E*nglish

[e] as in ch*a*os

The front of your tongue is placed lower down and slightly farther back for this sound; your lips are more relaxed but still slightly spread, and the jaw is lower than for the previous sound. This sound is very short and usually occurs in unstressed syllables. You will probably associate this sound with the diphthong [eɪ], and when you try to produce [e] in isolation you will actually say [eɪ]. (See page 154 for the diphthong [eɪ].) Usage of [e] or [eɪ] varies with the stress on the syllable, its length, and the sounds which follow.

Repeat the words listed. Does your tongue remain stationary in sounding the vowel or does it move in a glide? If there is a slight gliding movement following [e], you are using the diphthong [eɪ] and not the vowel [e]. A fault in production may be nasalization and stridency, especially when there are close nasal consonants as in *same, main,* or *name*. With this production, there is excessive tension in the tongue and pharynx and the velum is partially lowered.

r*a*ke	b*ai*t	s*a*me
c*a*pe	d*a*te	f*a*tal

[ɛ] as in *ever*

The front of your tongue is considerably lower and slightly farther back than for [e]; your lower jaw has dropped, and the lip opening is less spread. This is a short vowel. It is a relatively unstable vowel, and in certain combinations there is a tendency for various other sounds to take its place. In some provincial and careless speech, [ɪ] is frequently substituted for it in *men, pen, many, them, yes, chest,* and *forget;* it becomes [e] in *egg, hair, head, leg, care,* and *bed;* or [ɝ] in *very, where, merry,* and *America.* These substitutions are substandard General American speech. If you drop the front of your tongue too far, [æ] may occur as in the dialect variation often spelled "yaas." It, too, can become nasalized, as in *men.* When it is drawled, a diphthong will result with the addition of [ɔ].

s*e*nd	g*e*t	st*ea*dy
m*a*ny	fri*e*nd	s*ays*
l*eo*pard	ag*ai*n	b*u*ry

[æ] as in *at*

You have a slight elevation in the front of the tongue with a little retraction of it; your jaw moves down a degree and the lips are slightly more open. This vowel is of medium length. There is a decided tendency to nasalize this sound into a flat and disagreeable one when the tongue is too tense and the velum is lowered; this is especially true when it is near a nasal sound, as in *man, hang, damp, map, rang,* or *pan;* or near a plosive sound, [p], [b], [t], [d], [k], or [g], as in *gavel, happy, cat,* and so on. [ɛ], [ʌ], or [ɪ] may be incorrectly substituted for [æ], as in *gather, rather,* or *can.* Here, too, you must use care not to diphthongize the sound into [æə] in words like *had, hand,* or *man.*

c*a*t	h*a*ng
m*a*n	g*a*s
pl*ai*d	

[a], the intermediate A

This is an unstable sound and may not occur in your speech. It is the sound frequently encountered in stage speech and in some forms of Eastern

Seaboard speech in such words as *ask, chance,* and *bath.* However, in General American speech, [æ] is commonly used. For the [a] the front of your tongue will drop down and back slightly from [æ] and your mouth will be more open. This sound is part way between [æ] and [ɑ]. In British and some American dialects, the [a] words are pronounced with [ɑ]. Contrariwise, in New England and some other sections of the country, the [a] is often substituted for [ɑ], as in *art, department, Harvard,* and *garden.*

dance	*class*	*after*
half	*aunt*	*path*

BACK VOWELS

[u] as in m*oo*n

The back of your tongue will be tensed and raised nearly to the velum; your lips are rounded and tensed into a small, pursed opening. [u] is a long vowel. The lips must be rounded for this sound, if proper resonance is to be achieved. If the sound is too relaxed, the incorrect [ʊ] may occur as in *room, roof, soon,* or *spoon.* Incorrect diphthongization can take place as [uə] in words like *school* and *pool.*

true	*food*	*shoe*
boot	*you*	*rule*
flew	*two*	*fruit*
group	*Sioux*	*move*

[ʊ] as in b*oo*k

You will relax the mechanism slightly from the position for [u] and drop the back of the tongue a bit; the jaw drops slightly, and your lip opening is larger, but still definitely rounded. This is a short vowel. Foreigners often confuse [u] with [ʊ] and use a sound resembling [u] in such words as *foot* and *would.* If you unround the lips and shift the tongue toward the middle position, the [ʌ] will occur in *took, look, book, put,* and *pulpit.*

foot	*could*	*good*
full	*butcher*	*put*

[o] as in *o*bey

This sound bears the same relation to [ʊ] as [e] did to [ɪ]. Your tongue will drop slightly and will be less tense than for [ʊ]; your jaw drops, and the lips unround a little. This sound usually occurs in unaccented syllables. If it is accented, after the production of [o] the lips, jaw, and tongue tend to move toward the position for [ʊ], and the diphthong [oʊ] is produced. Check your production of the sound in the words below to see whether it remains stable or is the diphthong. You must use care to keep the lips rounded for the sound. Some persons may relax this sound in the direction of [ʌ] or [ə].

h*o*tel	*o*mit	pr*o*trude
*o*pinion	*o*bedient	

[ɔ] as in *a*ll

For this sound, the back of the tongue is slightly lower than for [o]; your jaw drops a little, and the lips are less tense and are unrounded to an ellipse (they may also protrude). It is a long sound. Incorrectly, the off-glide [ɚ] is at times added to [ɔ] in words like *law, saw,* or *raw,* and [ə] may be added to [ɔ] in a word like *water.* (The intrusive R is discussed in detail on page 190.)

t*a*lk	b*ou*ght	l*au*d
cr*aw*l	c*a*ll	fr*au*ght
br*oa*d	g*o*ne	

[ɒ]

Like the [a], this is not in common use in General American speech. In British pronunciation, it is used consistently on o words, such as *fog, coffee, god, not, rob,* and *doctor.* For [ɒ], the back of your tongue is lower than for [ɔ]; the jaw drops slightly, and your lip opening becomes wider and less rounded. The [ɒ] sound is part way between [ɔ] and [ɑ]. American pronunciation of the o words is completely inconsistent; in a few areas the [ɒ] sound is used. In your pronunciation you will probably use [ɔ] or [ɑ]. For example, how do you pronounce the vowels in the phrase "hot dog"?

*o*ffer	l*au*rel	w*a*ter
l*o*ss	d*o*ll	B*o*ston

MIDDLE VOWELS

[ɑ] as in f*a*ther

Your tongue is held low and flat in the mouth, with little tension; the jaw is lowered slightly from the position of rest to its lowest position, and the lips are wide open. This is the most open vowel sound, and it is long in duration. The [ɑ] may sound very much like [ɔ] if the tongue is not dropped and relaxed from the [ɔ] position. This sound takes on an unpleasant quality if the tip of the tongue is raised. It is susceptible to nasalization when it is near a nasal sound, as in *calm* or *bomb*. It may also be drawled, with the addition of the off-glide [ə].

Many of the short o words like *not, bob,* and *doctor* are pronounced with this sound in General American speech. The most frequent use of [ɑ] is in the diphthong [ɑ] as in *car*. (See page 155.)

ps*a*lm	c*a*lm	sha*h*
p*a*lm	*a*men	sp*a*
*a*lms		

[ʌ] as in *u*p

The middle of your tongue, between the front and the back, is raised slightly from the position for [ɑ]; your jaw rises a little, and the lips remain about the same. This is a short vowel. *It infrequently occurs in an unaccented syllable.* There are many individual variations in tongue position within the phoneme from person to person.

*u*s	c*o*me	tr*ou*ble
w*o*n	d*oe*s	n*o*thing

[ə] as in *a*bout

In general, for this sound your tongue will be relaxed with the body very slightly raised toward the hard palate; the jaw will be in a relaxed position with the mouth slightly open. This vowel is the unaccented substitute for most other vowels and *can occur only in a wholly unaccented syllable or in an unstressed monosyllable.* It is extremely unstable in production, and while the high point of the tongue will be in the central area, the exact placement will vary widely depending upon the stressed vowel for which it is substituted and the sounds surrounding it. The [ə], known as the *schwa* vowel, is in reality a phoneme which contains a number of sounds, all varying slightly in position and sound from one another. The [ə], in most instances, is almost a vowel glide. Instead of stopping momentarily in the position for the [ə], as it does for the other vowels, the mechanism merely glides through it and on to the next sound.

In spelling, the sound can be represented by any vowel symbol, as it is the unstressed form of any vowel sound. When a vowel loses its stress, it may actually lose its identity. For instance, note the difference in the initial sounds in the two words, *able* and *ability*. Although the first sound in *ability* was once the same as that in *able*, the unstressing of the first syllable of *ability* gives an unaccented vowel which can no longer be identified as [eɪ]. If the sound is produced in isolation, it becomes [ʌ], because that happens to be the accented sound near the neutral position; however, the schwa is not merely the unstressed form of [ʌ]. The sound is always short.

It is difficult to give clear example words for this sound, as the stress patterns from section to section of the country and from person to person vary so greatly that the sound commonly may be stressed in one area or by one person and unstressed in another area or by another person. Try the following list of words aloud to see whether or not you use the [ə] for any of the vowels. Usage in these words varies widely.

telephone	cap*a*ble	comp*a*ny
sof*a*	fam*ou*s	rec*o*gnize
exc*e*llent	evidence	from here
*a*maze	the boy *a*nd girl	know *o*f him
ide*a*	sever*a*l	dist*a*nce
*a*wake	*a*ccount	progr*a*m
hous*e*s	breakf*a*st	diff*i*cult
garl*a*nd	welc*o*me	Apr*i*l
c*o*nnect	*a*lone	terr*i*ble
wanted	s*u*ppose	*a*ttention

[ɜ] as in b*ir*d

The front of your tongue will be higher than the back; the tip and blade will be raised from the front of the mouth and curled slightly backward toward the roof of the mouth, without actual contact of the tip with the palate (note that [ɜ] and its unstressed counterpart [ɚ] are exceptions to the general rule for vowels that the tip and blade of the tongue are behind the lower teeth); and the lips are open as for [ə], but there is slightly more tension than for the schwa. This is the vowel used by those persons who do not "drop their R's." The tongue takes the same general position as for the consonant R but, instead of gliding from that position to a vowel, holds it, as for all vowels, with the resulting "R-colored" vowel sound. *The sound is used only in stressed positions* and is the vocalized form of the spelling forms *-er, -ir, -ear, -our, -or, -ur,* and *-yr.* It varies greatly in position and sound with the section of the country and the speech habits of the individual. You must be careful not to curl the tongue excessively, nor to have too great tension, nor to prolong the [ɜ] unnecessarily. The example words for [ɜ] are listed under [ɜ], the following sound.

[ɜ]

This is the middle vowel used by those who do "drop their ʀ's." It is in common use in parts of New England, New York City, and the South, and in British speech, but not in General American speech. For the [ɜ], the tongue will be in the same general position as for [ɝ], but the tip is held behind the lower front teeth; the jaw and the lips are also in the same general position as for [ɝ]. [ɜ] *occurs only in an accented position and never before another vowel in the same syllable.* It represents the same spelling combinations as does the [ɝ]. If you have difficulty producing the [ɜ], say the sound [ɝ]; then repeat it, holding the tongue tip behind the lower front teeth; avoid excessive tension; the resulting sound will approximate [ɜ]. In an unstressed position, this sound becomes [ə]. In some dialects in the area in and around New York City, [ɜ] is diphthongized into [ɜɪ] or [ʊɪ]; these productions are unacceptable. The comic-strip version [ɔɪ] is sometimes heard, but less commonly than the other two diphthongized forms. Discover which of the two sounds, [ɝ] or [ɜ], you habitually use in the following words.

wo*r*d	*jour*ney	mu*r*der
hea*r*d	wo*r*ld	my*rrh*
gi*r*l	atto*r*ney	fu*r*
fe*r*n	co*lo*nel	

[ɚ] as in weath*er*

Your tongue, lips, and jaw are in the same general position as for [ɝ], but more relaxed; and the sound resulting is shorter and more relaxed. This is the unaccented version of [ɝ] and *occurs only in unaccented syllables and unstressed* monosyllables. As with [ə], it is frequently produced as a glide with the mechanism moving through the position rather than stopping in it. It is spelled with more than one letter but is a single sound. You must be careful to keep the sound unstressed and neither prolong it nor give it any prominence. Speakers who use the [ɜ] will substitute the [ə] for the [ɚ].

teach*er*	murd*er*	bu*r*lesque

FORMATION OF DIPHTHONGS

A diphthong is a very short, stable vowel followed directly by a glide to or through another vowel or series of vowel positions. The sound [oʊ], in the word *go*, is a combination of the sound [o] and a glide to [ʊ] blended together so that neither the [o] nor the [ʊ] is a distinct, separate sound. The tongue, jaw, and lips take the position for the [o], hold it momentarily, and then move rapidly to the position for the [ʊ] where the sound stops instantly or the mechanism moves on to the next sound. The result is a continuous, unbroken sound. The energy is greatest on the [o] and gradually diminishes as the glide continues to the end of the [ʊ]. Try the diphthong [oʊ] in *go*. Say it slowly, prolonging the sound. Feel the movement of the tongue and the lips as you go from the [o] position to that of [ʊ].

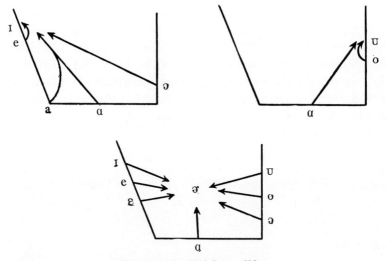

Fig. 16. The diphthong glides

Of the five alphabet letters which we have previously been taught to call the "five vowels," four are not pure vowels but diphthongs. Only for the E does the articulatory adjustment remain relatively stable during the production. For A, I, O, and U, the short initial vowel is immediately followed by a glide movement to another vowel position with no cessation of voice, and a diphthong results.

There are five main diphthongs. In addition, other combinations of various vowels with the unstressed [ɚ] or [ə] may be classified with the diphthongs, as they have a similar gliding movement in them. All of these are receding diphthongs, that is, combinations of two vowels in which the first sound is stressed and the second unstressed. Thus, the first vowel in each receives stress and is held slightly, and as the mechanism moves into or through the position for the second, that glide sound is much less loud and much less definite in formation.

Figure 16 shows the relationship of the elements in the various diphthongs. The beginning of the glide is indicated by the tail of the arrow; the head points to the final position.

Observation and Listening

Experiment with the production of each of the diphthongs as you did with each of the vowels. Try the sound in isolation; notice the movement as you go from one element to the other. Try the example words, listen for your production, and listen to the way your friends produce them. Descriptions are not given for the diphthongs, as they are made up of vowel sounds which have already been described in detail.

Full Diphthongs

The two vowel elements comprising the full diphthong are so blended together into the glide that both sounds are obscured and become a new sound, called a diphthong.

[aɪ] or [ɑɪ] as in *time*

Your tongue starts in the [a] or [ɑ] position, holds it momentarily, and then glides to the general area of the [ɪ] phoneme and the sound ends. The first element is sometimes heard as [ɒ] or [ɔ], but these productions are provincialisms to be avoided. When [aɪ] or [ɑɪ] is nasalized in words like *my*, *mine*, or *nine*, it is frequently drawled, with unpleasant results. Relative overstress on either of the elements will result in improper production. If there is too much stress on the first element, the second will disappear or become [ə]; this is common in rapid speech and is readily recognizable in Southern speech. Overstress on the second element will result in a syllable division between the elements in the sound, with [i] replacing the [ɪ].

fly	pie	eye
child	aisle	geyser
height	buy	

[ɔɪ] as in *boy*

You start this sound from the position for [ɔ] and glide to the [ɪ] phoneme. Dialect variations to be avoided include the substitution of [aɪ] or [ɝ] for [ɔɪ] in words like *boil* or *hoist* and *oil* or *joint*. The final element may occur as [i] when the glide goes beyond the [ɪ] phoneme.

hoist	oil	toy
loyal	noise	voice

[ɑʊ] as in s*ou*nd

Your organs of articulation begin this sound from the position for [ɑ] and glide into the [ʊ] phoneme. The first element may be properly produced as [a] and improperly given as [æ] or [ɛ]. The latter two substitutions are often nasalized when a nasal sound precedes or follows them. In some cases, a triphthongal production is heard in substandard speech, beginning with [ɛ] or even [ə]. There is a tendency for some speakers to substitute the tense [u] for the more lax [ʊ]. A distorted form of the diphthong heard occasionally uses [æ] and [u].

n*ow*	m*ou*th	l*ou*d
cr*ow*d	d*ou*bt	f*ou*nd

Partial Diphthongs

In partial diphthongs, the glide movement does not begin until a distinct vowel is first heard, followed by a more or less indistinct off-glide or finish. This contrasts with the less definite first element in the full diphthongs and their more distinct off-glide. Frequently, in American speech, these sounds are not diphthongs but vowels, using only the first element of the diphthong. You should analyze your own production of the example words for these two sounds to determine whether you use the diphthong or the vowel when you say them.

[eɪ] as in d*ay*

The front of your tongue starts in the [e] position and makes an off-glide toward the position for [ɪ]. As the last element of this sound is unstable, it varies greatly from person to person and for the same person from word to word; it may be entirely missing or become [i]. Notice the difference in the sound in the words *cake* and *play*.

gr*ay*	g*a*te	br*ea*k
v*ei*l	f*ai*l	*a*pron

[oʊ] as in g*o*

Your articulatory position is for the [o] and then assumes the off-glide [ʊ]. Although in General American speech in accented syllables the sound is rarely produced without some diphthongization, there are many instances where persons use the [o] alone. [u] is an occasional substitute for the final element.

kn*ow*	n*o*te	*oh*
b*oa*t	s*ew*	*goes*
d*ough*	b*eau*	

Centering Diphthongs

In American speech, there is a group of diphthongs which end in the central position; they are single sounds, although spelled with two letters. In parts of the East and South they end in [ə], and in General American speech in [ɚ]. The final off-glide is unstable, and the exact position of the articulatory organs for it is largely determined by the first part of the diphthong. These diphthongs can be made up of any vowel and a glide to the central [ɚ] or [ə]. They are given here in the General American form.

The most common of the centering diphthongs are:

[ɪɚ] as in *ear*

h*ere*	f*ear*	w*eir*d
d*eer*	f*ier*ce	t*ear*

[ɛɚ] as in *air*

b*ear*	p*air*	th*ere*
c*are*	w*ear*	h*eir*

[ɑɚ] as in st*ar*

s*er*geant	sm*ar*t	st*ar*ve

[ɔɚ] or [oɚ] as in *ore*

The use of [ɔɚ] or [oɚ] will depend upon the section of the country or the person speaking. Check your pronunciation of the words listed below to determine whether you use [ɔ] or [o].

d*oor*	c*oar*se	fl*oor*
c*ore*	t*ore*	*or*

[ʊɚ] as in p*oor*

s*ure*	t*our*	m*oor*

Centering Triphthongs

Centering triphthongs are sounds in which a noncentering diphthong ends in an off-glide, either on [ə] or on [ɚ]; in General American speech, the off-glide is [ɚ]. Care must be used in listening for these sounds to be sure that the three sounds occur in one syllable so that a triphthong results. In such words as *fire* and *flour*, the final [ɚ] sound is sometimes pronounced as a separate syllable, resulting in a diphthong plus a vowel, not a triphthong. Check your pronunciation of the example words.

hour	*sour*
hire	*mayor*

VOWELS IN CONNECTED SPEECH

Emphasis and Accent

As we saw in Chapter 6, when you wish to emphasize a word in logical explanation or in emotional expression you may produce it with greater force of utterance and make it longer in duration than the surrounding words. (Remember that this is only one aspect of emphasis; pitch and quality changes are also important.) At the same time, the less significant words are weakened; they are produced with less energy and shorter duration. In addition to such differences in stress for logical and emotional meaning, there are differences in stress among syllables in multisyllable words. The accented syllable is given greater energy and duration than the unaccented. These variations in syllable accent contribute to correct pronunciation and the complex rhythm pattern of each phrase. The vowel in the unstressed word or the unaccented syllable is frequently so weakened that it moves to a phoneme different from that used in the stressed or accented form even though the spelling is unchanged. If you fail to make such vowel changes, your speech will sound meaningless, awkward, stilted, or pedantic.

As an illustration of the effect of emphasis on vowels, in the following pairs of sentences read each statement with the emphasis on the italicized word. Transcribe the vowel you used in the first italicized word, and then the vowel in the same word in the paired sentence. For example, in "It *was* mine!" the vowel in *was* will be [ɑ] or [ɒ], or perhaps [ʌ]; in "It was *mine!*" the vowel in *was* usually becomes [ə]. Experiment with the other sentences changing meaningful emphasis in various ways and noting and transcribing the vowel changes.

1. It *was* mine.	It was *mine.*
2. She *is* annoyed.	*She* is annoyed.
3. It *has* happened.	It has *happened.*
4. They *have* gone.	They have *gone.*

5. I heard *of* him.   *I* heard of *him*.
6. He came *from* there.   *He* came from there.
7. Speak *to* him.   Speak to *him*.
8. I saw *her* house.   I *saw* her house.
9. Send it *for* him.   *Send* it for him.
10. He *had* no choice.   He had *no* choice.
11. It was *the* book.   It *was* the book.
12. I said, "*A* man."   *I said*, "A man."

The stressed words are called *strong* forms, as *the* with an [i]; the unstressed forms, *the* with [ə], are labeled *weak*. The strong forms tend to use definite vowels and the weak to migrate toward the indefinite central region. Notice in the weak forms how frequently short vowels such as [ɪ], [o], [e], [ʌ], [ɚ], and particularly [ə] occur. How far strong forms can be weakened in any given situation will depend upon your meaning, purpose, the situation, and the possibility of being misunderstood. If the vowel is so weakened that it is not understood or is actually omitted, such speech can be labeled *careless*. Here are some examples of how strong forms are weakened when they are unstressed in the flow of meaningful speech.

[hæz, həz, əz, z]   [hæv, həv, əv, v]
[kæn, kən, kn, kŋ]   [æz, əz, z]
[wɪl, wl, əl, l]   [ðæn, ðən, ðn]
[ʃʊd, ʃəd, ʃd]   [kʊd, kəd, kd]
[ðɛm, ðəm, ðm]   [ɑɚ, ɚ]

In a formal situation where you wish to make the articulation very distinct and easily understood, you may find it advisable not to weaken the forms beyond those presented in the second column. In casual conversation, however, you are likely to use the more extreme, weakened forms. As long as you are readily understood, such usage is not in error.

In the same way, vowels are weakened and actually change their phonemes in unaccented syllables. Notice what happens to the initial vowel in a word when the accent is moved from one syllable to another. In the word *o*bject, the vowel is [ɑ] or [ɒ], while in ob*ject* it becomes [ə]. Unless you make such changes your pronunciation will be incorrect and meaningless. Notice in the following pairs of words how the shift in accent changes the production of the italicized vowel.

*a*nalyze	*a*nalysis	c*o*nsultation	consult
*a*pplication	*a*pply	c*o*mpact	comp*a*ct

comparable	compare	cóntent	contént
decla*i*m	decla*m*ation	óbject	objéct
inst*a*ll	inst*a*llation	pérfect	perféct
dr*a*ma	dr*a*matic	réfuse	refúse

The prefixes *re-*, *be-*, *de-*, and *pre-* are pronounced [rɪ], [bɪ], [dɪ], and [prɪ] when the premium is placed upon clarity, and [rə], [bə], [də], and [prə] in casual conversation. The ending *-ed* is pronounced [ɪd] by some and [əd] by others in such words as *wanted* and *added*. Endings such as *-ment*, *-ence*, and *-tion* often use the schwa. Listen to the italicized words as the following phrases are spoken and note the vowels in the unaccented syllables.

1. I *receive* . . . .
2. He *believed* . . . .
3. We *preserved* . . . .
4. What *relation* . . . .
5. The *attempt* . . . .
6. *Pronounce* this . . . .
7. *Deliver* this . . . .
8. He *becomes* . . . .
9. The *interchange* . . . .
10. My *interpretation* . . . .
11. The *movement* . . . .
12. This *evidence* . . . .

If the single unaccented syllable is so far weakened that the sounds do not carry, or are actually omitted, the listener will have difficulty in understanding what is said. Such speech is called *careless*. When you speak with exceptional rapidity, whole syllables actually seem to be dropped; their energy of production is so weak that they do not carry.

As an experiment, try reading the first sentence of the following passage with equal accent on every syllable as though you were producing it in isolation. Note and transcribe the vowels which you use. Now read the sentence as meaningfully as possible. See how certain vowels are weakened as you unstress them for meaning and in the accent pattern. Try a similar experiment with the whole paragraph.

A little twist to an idea need not rely upon clever wording. We are not all geniuses of the mingled metaphor or the artful analogy. Consider the man who thoughtfully contemplates the lady at the social gathering and murmurs nostalgically, "She must have been beautiful in her younger days." I have a notion that his wife might turn that about in another way. If one dwells with some extra length on *younger*, or mouths over *beautiful*, or comes out with a little uncertainty on *must*, one can do wonders in adding flounces, bows, and ribbons to such a statement or in blending in a corroding acid that will work on the memory at a later date. Of course, the raised eyebrow helps too, but that takes practice.—E. H.

Either record the passage or have another student read it for you. Decide whether it is meaningful or not. Are the stressed words and accented syllables too pedantically exact; are the unstressed words and unaccented syllables so weakened that they are misunderstood; is there sufficient contrast between stressed and unstressed words for clear meaning?

Careless and Faulty Production

Careless and faulty articulation results from lack of effort, very rapid speech, or imitation of poor models, as well as from faulty physical structure, poor environment, troubled personal adjustment, and emotional upset in the immediate situation. Remember that the production of vowels by someone else may seem faulty to you if the speaker comes from another general dialect area in which his vowels are perfectly correct. In this chapter, after the description of each vowel we have indicated the major faults to be avoided.

Vowel sounds may be distorted, omitted, or added in words where they do not belong. In distortion, the sound may be made in an exaggerated way, as when a foreigner says the [i] in *seem*, producing a tense sound with the front of the tongue raised too close to the hard palate; or he may pronounce the [u] in *who* with excessive protrusion of the lips. Again, one vowel may be substituted for a similar one in another phoneme, as in the following examples.

[it iz tru] *for* [ɪt ɪz]   (It is true)
[aɪ sɔ ət] *for* [ɪt]   (I saw it)
[haʊ mɪnɪ mɪn] *for* [mɛnɪ mɛn]   (How many men?)
[dɪd i gɪt ɪt] *for* [gɛt ɪt]   (Did he get it?)
[hɛz i gɔn] *for* [hæz]   (Has he gone?)
[ɛsk ɪm] *for* [æsk]   (Ask him)
[maɪ kɔɚ] *for* [kɑɚ]   (My car)
[maɪ buk] *for* [bʊk]   (My book)

Vowels may be diphthongized when a person adds a schwa after a "pure" vowel, as in these examples.

[ə bɛəd] *for* [bɛd]   (A bed)
[ə mæən] *for* [mæn]   (A man)
[aɪ fiə wɛəl] *for* [fil wɛl]   (I feel well)
[maɪ haʊəs] *for* [haʊs]   (My house)
[gəoʊ] *for* [goʊ]   (Go)

The final half of the diphthong may be weakened, as is often true in Southern speech.

[haᵁfaᴵn] *for* [haʊ faɪn]   (How fine)
[ə laᵁd saᵁnd] *for* [laʊd saʊnd]   (A loud sound)
[ple] *for* [pleɪ]   (Play) *Not necessarily a fault.*

Vowels may be omitted when a "telescoped" version of a word is given, with one or more syllables slurred over.

[prɑbli] *for* [prɑbəbli]   (probably)
[kʌmpni] *for* [kʌmpəni]   (company)
[præps] *for* [pəhæps]   (perhaps)

A vowel may be added where it does not belong, as in the following words.

[æθəlɛtɪk] *for* [æθlɛtɪk]   (athletic)
[tuwɔɚd] *for* [tɔɚd]   (toward)
[ʌmbɚɛlə] *for* [ʌmbrɛlə]   (umbrella)

The distortion is, of course, the common fault. It is so common in casual conversation that it is scarcely noticed. If you carry slurred speech into a situation where your speech will be judged as uneducated or slovenly, then the careless speech can be damaging to your social and vocational future.

Listening and Analysis

If errors of carelessness are called to your attention, begin to list words and phrases in which they occur. Analyze what you do, the possible reasons for your errors, and begin to listen to and correct yourself in conversation. Practice the words in phrases with the correct vowel sounds; combine them into meaningful sentences. Listen to other speakers produce these sound combinations. Become a critical judge of others and of yourself.

The same suggestions hold true if you are of foreign-language background. Ask someone to criticize your production of single words, listen as he repeats them so that he may be a model for you, then reproduce what you have heard; use the words in meaningful contexts.

Exercises

1. Again make use of the recording of your voice. Listen to the way in which you produce the vowel and diphthong sounds. Are they all clear and correct and still blended into connected speech? Are there any faults present which have been discussed under the various vowel sounds? Transcribe the

first twenty-five vowel and diphthong sounds in the recording into phonetic symbols.

2. Read a news announcement—something dramatic, lively, and full of action. Check your reading for faulty vowels and diphthongs. Are they correctly produced in relation to patterns both of stress and of accent? Are there faults in pronunciation?

3. Prepare and read a selection from the Appendix. The following are suggested: Numbers 3, 4, 12, 20, 21, and 23. Use great care to produce the correct vowels and diphthongs, free from tension and articulation faults. At the same time be careful not to exaggerate production, and be careful to blend all sounds.

SUMMARY

Vowels give the greatest evidence of your use of the vocal skills involved in breathing, phonation, and resonation. Because they are unstable in their method of articulation and their acoustic effect, and because they are not static in formation, the rules for their production must be flexible. In spite of slight differences in formation, if a sound has the acoustic properties of a certain vowel, we consider it to be that vowel. The articulators with which we are concerned in vowel formation are the walls of the pharynx, the velum, the tongue, the lower jaw, and the lips.

When you produce a vowel, the following conditions must be present: (1) the vocal folds must vibrate, (2) the velum must be raised against the back wall of the pharynx, (3) there must be a relatively open passageway from the vocal folds through the lips, (4) the movements of the articulators must vary the size and shape of the oral cavity and its opening for each sound, and (5) the position of the articulators must be held momentarily. The vowels in General American speech may be divided roughly into front, middle, and back, according to the highest point which the tongue reaches in producing the sound.

A diphthong is a short vowel followed directly by a glide to or through another vowel or a series of vowel positions. There are five main diphthongs, three full and two partial, as well as a group of centering diphthongs ending in [ɚ] or [ə].

Although the vowels and diphthongs have been presented as if they were static units produced in isolation, in the flow of actual speech they vary greatly according to the stress given them. There are two major types of stress: emphasis for meaning and accent for pronunciation. When you stress a syllable, you give it greater energy of production and make it longer than the surrounding sound units. The unemphasized words and unaccented syllables are weakened, that is, they become short and somewhat indefinite in formation.

This stressing and unstressing of syllables contributes to the rhythm of your speech. But even more important, it allows you to point out, by means of your vocal changes, the words which carry the main ideas and to subordinate those which only connect the ideas.

In careless and faulty vowel production, the vowels may be distorted, diphthongized, omitted, or added where they do not belong. This distortion in casual conversation is often scarcely noticed. But if you wish to be clearly understood for professional or social reasons, you must produce the vowel sounds with clarity. You should be versatile enough to adjust your articulation to the demands of the immediate situation.

8

The Consonant Sounds in Speech

And the Gileadites took the passages of Jordan before the Ephraim-ites; and it was so, that when those Ephraimites which were escaped said, Let me go over; that the men of Gilead said unto him, Art thou an Ephraimite? If he said, Nay; Then said they unto him, Say now Shibboleth; and he said Sibboleth; for he could not frame to pronounce it right. Then they took him, and slew him at the passages of Jordan.—JUDGES 12

Frequently a student registers for a voice-training course because his speech has been criticized as difficult to understand. Someone has told him that he is slurring some of his sounds, particularly the consonants. The conclusion that poor consonant production is the major speech fault is often exaggerated by grade- and high-school teachers who belabor their pupils with pedantic drills and make learning dull by unnatural repetition of word lists.

Actually, such an approach separates a part from the whole. The faulty production of consonants must be examined as a dynamic aspect of the entire vocal process. If phonation and resonation are not effective, if muscle movements are cramped and awkward, if breathing cannot be controlled, improvement of articulation alone will not make you an acceptable speaker. Correct articulation is no more important than skilled timing, or interest-arousing melody, or pleasing quality. Yet while all of the aspects of speech share in producing the effect upon the listener, without accurate consonant production other skills may be wasted, for the speaker cannot be understood.

PRINCIPLES OF CONSONANT PRODUCTION

In describing vowels, we have shown that these sounds are characterized by varying and somewhat indefinite degrees of openness of the oral cavity.

To produce consonants, the breath stream is stopped momentarily at a particular place in the mouth, or made to flow through a narrow passageway, or diverted through the nose. The positions for the articulation of consonants are therefore much more definite than those for vowels.

However, this does not imply absolute uniformity of formation. Just as the vowels vary slightly from word to word and from person to person, the consonants, too, are influenced by neighboring sounds and by emphases in the running context of speech. There are, for instance, small differences in the way T is produced in *time, letter, sit, went,* and *just,* or in the unstressed word *to* and the emphasized *tell;* all of these, however, are recognizable as belonging to the T family, or phoneme.

Think of accuracy of production as a relative concept. Speech requires amazing agility in continuous muscle movement. Even as one sound is being produced, your mechanism is in the process of starting the next, so that the forward flow of sounds will not be broken. The articulation process involves dynamic movement rather than a series of static positions. The sounds must be clearly recognized by the listener, but pedantic accuracy must not interfere with a steady forward movement through the articulated phrase. Clarity, then, means accuracy in direction of muscle movement and in place of production, so that the consonant may be easily recognized. Smoothness of production of the whole meaningful phrase is achieved by the blending of these easily recognizable individual consonants and their accompanying vowels into a steadily moving pattern of sounds. Clarity and smoothness of articulation permit logical understanding of the language symbols.

Hence, consonants should have:

1. sufficient accuracy (the correct phoneme) to be readily understood and meaningful;

2. freedom from exaggerated (often incorrect), pedantic production;

3. smooth blending (without losing accuracy) into adjacent vowels and consonants;

4. freedom from misarticulation and distortion (a speech defect).

THE FORMATION OF CONSONANTS

In describing the formation of the vowels, five conditions were outlined for their production (see page 141). In a like manner, for the consonants the following conditions must be observed:

1. the vocal folds may or may not vibrate depending on whether the consonant is voiced or voiceless;

2. the velum must be raised, closing off the nasal passage, for all except the three nasal consonants;

3. the oral cavity must be blocked or narrowed for each sound;

4. the lower jaw, the tongue, and the lips must move to form the narrowing or block;

5. the articulators either hold the position for the consonant or glide through it depending upon the nature of the sound.

There are twenty-two consonant sounds in common usage in American English. They are formed by the articulators blocking or narrowing the breath stream in some way in the oral cavity, by the activity or nonactivity of the vocal folds, or by the diversion of the breath stream through the nasal passage. While the exact position of the articulators will vary slightly for any sound from individual to individual, and for one person as he produces different sound combinations or when he is in various different personal situations, yet for most consonants a relatively absolute description and classification can be made.

Fig. 17. Consonant Chart *

	Bilabial	Labio-dental	Lingua-dental	Lingua-alveolar	Lingua-palatal	Lingua-velar	Glottal
Nasals	m			n		ŋ	
Plosives	p b			t d		k g	
Fricatives		f v	θ ð	s z	ʃ ʒ		h
Glides (semivowels)	w			l	r j		

* Symbols at left of each column are voiceless; those at right are voiced.

Key Words

[m]	may	[k]	come, keep	[ʃ]	ship
[n]	no	[g]	go	[ʒ]	measure
[ŋ]	ring	[f]	feel	[h]	how
[p]	pay	[v]	veal	[w]	water
[b]	bay	[θ]	think	[l]	leap, school
[t]	time	[ð]	them	[r]	red
[d]	dime	[s]	soon	[j]	yes
		[z]	zoo		

In Figure 17, the consonants are arranged on the chart so as to classify them in at least three different ways. The vertical column may be thought of as an acoustic description; a *nasal* sounds to the ear as though it came through the nose. Also, roughly, this same classification may be thought of as indicating the way in which the general class of sounds is formed; a *plosive* is formed by a complete oral block, a building up of air pressure, and a sudden release and explosion. Each of these terms will be explained more fully as the group of sounds is discussed in detail.

The horizontal labels indicate the articulators which work to form the block or narrowing. For example, the first column, headed *bilabial*, indicates that those sounds are articulated by the two lips. The position of a symbol in a column indicates whether the sound is voiced or voiceless, whether the vocal folds vibrate or not. A symbol at the left of a column shows that the sound is voiceless; to the right, voiced. Certain variations on the positions indicated in the chart will be pointed out in the descriptions of the individual consonants.

Observation and Listening

Experiment with the production of various consonants. Observe how the five conditions for the production of a consonant apply. Discover the difference between those which are voiced and the voiceless ones; place your fingers on your larynx and sound [z] followed by [s]. Note the vibration on [z]; it is voiced. For [s] there is no vibration, and, hence, it is voiceless. Feel the movement of the velum as it shuts off the nasal passage by trying the nasal [m] followed by a nonnasal [v]. As you watch your articulators in a mirror, both see and feel how the lower jaw, lips, and tongue assume positions and move as you produce different sounds. Note how in every case the breath stream is blocked, narrowed, or diverted by the action of the articulators. Observe that for certain consonants the articulators remain relatively fixed while the sound is being produced, while for others they simply move through positions, or with still a third group there is a hold followed by movement.

Repeat the key word for each consonant several times; then try to isolate the sound and repeat it until you hear it accurately. You will discover that certain sounds, the voiced plosives and the glides, cannot be produced unless followed by a vowel. Try to feel the adjustment of the articulators for each sound. Experiment with the sound in the key word and in various combinations which you devise for yourself.

DESCRIPTION OF CONSONANTS

In the following sections each consonant is described in detail and examples are given for common combinations in American speech. Also, faults in assimilation are discussed for each general classification. Finally, there are observations on the problems of blending and careless and faulty production.

NASAL CONSONANTS

All except three sounds in American speech are resonated and articulated primarily in the oral cavity, and the presence of noticeable nasality is regarded as a vocal fault. Three sounds, however, are primarily dependent upon nasal resonance. In the production of each of these sounds, the exit through the oral cavity is completely blocked in some manner, the velum is lowered, and the vocalized breath stream passes into the nasal cavity and out through the nares. The distinction between the three nasals is dependent upon the size and shape of the oral cul-de-sac, not upon any difference in the nasal passage. All three sounds resemble vowels in that they are often given sustained tone and may stand alone as syllables without a vowel, as in *sudden* [sʌdn]. Aside from the position of the velum, the placement of the articulators for the three nasals [m], [n], and [ŋ] corresponds to the positions for the plosives [b], [d], and [g].

$$\left[\quad m \quad\right] \qquad \text{Voiced}$$

may
(Two lips)

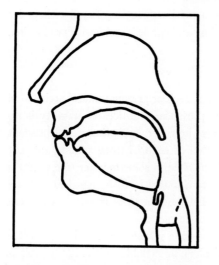

With the lips lightly closed allow the vocalized sound to come out through the nose. The teeth are slightly separated, and the tongue is in a relaxed position. Compare this position with that for [p] and [b] in the section dealing with plosives.

When the [m] appears in connected speech, the tongue assumes the position for the vowel which comes before or after it.

Faulty production: excessive pressure so that the flow of speech is interrupted; denasalization when the nasal passageway is blocked either temporarily or by some chronic condition (if this occurs, a [b] is substituted); insufficient duration.

Common Combinations

small
film, hump, farm

LINGUA-ALVEOLAR

(Tongue tip, gum ridge)

no

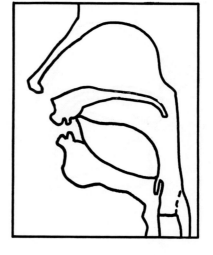

Raise the tip of the tongue to make contact with the alveolar ridge behind the upper front teeth; the sides of the tongue touch the inner edges of the teeth. This sound also may be made with the blade in contact with the alveolar ridge. Hold this oral closure and allow the vocalized sound to pass out the nose. Compare this position with that for [t] and [d] in the section on plosives.

This sound is longer in duration when combined with vowels or with continuant consonants than when it is combined with plosives: mi*n*ing, da*n*ce, as compared with re*n*t.

Final [n] is often syllabic: butt*on*, sudd*en*, oft*en*.

Faulty production: denasalization when the nasal passageway is blocked ([d] is substituted); weak production in final position; substitution of [m] when the [n] occurs before or after [p], [b], or [m], as in ha*pp*en, govern*m*ent.

Common Combinations

*sn*ow

re*n*t, la*n*d, tur*n*, o*n*ce, lu*n*ch

LINGUAVELAR   ri*ng*

(Tongue back, soft palate)

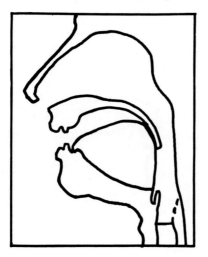

Raise the back part of the tongue so that a light contact is made with the soft palate; the air passageway through the mouth is thus closed. As you hold this closure, allow the vocalized breath to escape through the nose. The size of your mouth opening varies with the vowel which precedes the [ŋ]. Compare this position with that for [k] and [g] in the section on plosives.

When the suffixes -*ing* and -*er* are added to words ending in [ŋ], this sound usually maintains its identity and no [g] is added after it: si*ng*er, ri*ng*ing. (Stro*ng*er, lo*ng*er, and you*ng*er are typical exceptions to this rule.) Usage varies widely on other words in which NG, NK, or NC appear. Note the varying pronunciation on the following words: I*n*ca, i*n*come, a*ng*er, ba*n*k, to*ng*ue, ju*n*ction, li*ng*er, si*ng*le, ca*n*ker, co*n*crete, co*n*cord, co*ng*regation. In most words of this type, the [g] or [k] is pronounced following an [ŋ], but prefixes ending in N tend to maintain the identity of the [n], particularly if the syllable is stressed. No [g] or [k] should be inserted between words when the first word ends in [ŋ].

Faulty production: substitution of [n] in the -*ing* ending; denasalization when nasal passageway is blocked ([g] is substituted); insufficient duration; addition of [k] or [g], particularly if the sound which follows is a vowel: Lo*ng* Island [lɔŋg aɪlənd].

Common Combinations

stre*ngth*, belo*nged*, ra*nk*, a*ngle*

PLOSIVE CONSONANTS

As we have already noted, the articulatory positions for the production of plosive consonants correspond to those for the nasals, with the exception of the position of the soft palate. In the plosive group, the velum is raised and the entrance into the nasal cavity closed. Thus, instead of breath flowing continuously into the nasal cavity, pressure is built up behind the point of blockage at the lips, alveolar ridge, or velum. When the tongue is suddenly dropped, or the lips opened, the air pressure is released and a slight explosive sound is heard. This is most noticeable in the voiceless forms in the initial position of a stressed syllable. Here the explosion takes the form of a slight sound of escaping breath or aspiration before the succeeding vowel sound is heard.

*p*ay   BILABIAL   *b*ay
(Two lips)

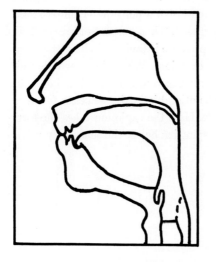

Hold the lips together lightly. For [p], allow the outgoing breath stream to build up pressure behind the block. Release the bilabial block and explode the air under pressure. Your lower jaw may move down when the release occurs. The same action is necessary for [b], except that the breath stream is voiced.

You can hear the slight aspirate explosion most readily when a vowel follows the initial [p] in a stressed syllable. The explosive phase is greatly modified or even eliminated when [p] is combined with another consonant, or in the final position. [b] is not ordinarily aspirated.

Faulty production: lower lip against edges of upper teeth; excessive pressure so that explosion calls attention to itself; pressure so light that a friction sound results.

Unvoicing in final position.

Common Combinations

*p*lace, *p*ride, *s*pend   *bl*ue, *br*ight
he*lp*, har*p*, gas*p*, prom*pt*, lum*p*   bu*lb*, he*rb*

Voiceless $\begin{bmatrix} t & and & d \end{bmatrix}$ Voiced

*t*ime   Lingua-alveolar   *d*ime
                    (Tongue tip, gum ridge)

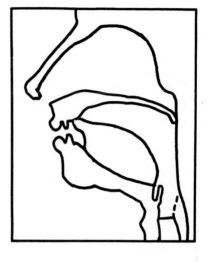

Place the tip of your tongue
against the alveolar ridge, behind
but not touching the upper front
teeth. The sides of the tongue make
contact with the inner edges of the
teeth. For [t], let the pressure of the
outgoing breath stream build up
behind the lingua-alveolar block;
release the contact and explode the
breath stream. You may move the
lower jaw down as the tongue contact is released. [d] is formed in the
same way except that the breath
stream is voiced. Both sounds may
also be made with the blade of the
tongue in contact with the alveolar
ridge. The explosive phase is most
obvious when the [t] or [d] is followed by a vowel. When a consonant follows
or when [t] or [d] is final, the explosion is modified or even eliminated.

Faulty production: tongue tip pressing against inner and lower edges of
the upper teeth (dental production); excessive pressure with too obvious
explosion; pressure too light for the sound to be identified; omission in final
position when in combination with other consonants: ju*s*t, ke*p*t, ol*d*, sen*d*.

Excessive explosion in medial position: en*t*er*t*ain, a*t*tribu*t*ed; substitution of [d]: liber*t*y [lɪbɚdɪ]; substitution of glottal stop in medial position: bo*tt*le, bu*tt*er.

Unvoicing in final position: rente*d*,
ol*d*.

Common Combinations

*t*ree, *t*wice, s*t*op
hea*r*t, we*p*t, wen*t*, wes*t*
bo*tt*le

*d*ry, *d*war*t*
lan*d*, ol*d*, yar*d*
la*d*le

$$\begin{bmatrix} \text{t} & \textit{and} & \text{d} \\ & \textit{continued} & \end{bmatrix}$$

In past tenses ending in *-ed,* the final sound is pronounced [t] if the sound before it is voiceless, [d] if the sound before it is voiced: ho*pp*ed, ro*bb*ed, wan*t*ed.

Voiceless $\qquad\qquad \begin{bmatrix} \text{k} & \textit{and} & \text{g} \end{bmatrix} \qquad\qquad$ Voiced

*c*ome $\qquad\qquad\qquad$ LINGUAVELAR $\qquad\qquad\qquad$ *go*
*k*eep $\qquad\qquad\qquad$ (Tongue back, soft palate)

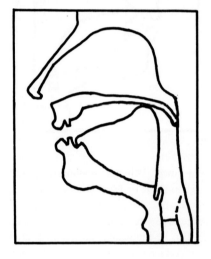

Raise the back of the tongue so that a light contact is made with the velum. Allow the breath stream to build up pressure behind the block, lower the back of the tongue, and the explosion for [k] results. For [g], the breath stream is voiced.

You hear the aspiration when the [k] occurs before a vowel. In the [g], the aspiration is greatly reduced or eliminated entirely. If the sounds are in final position, the tongue relaxes and little or no explosion occurs.

Faulty production: excessive pressure so that the explosion is obvious; pressure so light that friction results; guttural production.

Unvoicing in final position.

Common Combinations

*c*lass, *c*ream, *qu*een, s*ch*ool $\qquad$ *g*lass, *g*reen
mi*lk*, la*rk*, ta*sk*, fo*x*, pa*ct* $\qquad$ an*gl*e, bu*rg*
e*xc*use $\qquad$ e*x*act

Note that the letter x may be pronounced [ks] or [gz].

Assimilation Faults Involving Nasal and Plosive Consonants

We have noted in connection with each of the plosive and nasal consonants certain problems in faulty production. Some of these problems result directly from the similarity in tongue position between the plosive and its parallel nasal sound. When a number of sounds having a similar articulatory position are in close proximity to each other, you may have a tendency to telescope the sounds and even to omit entire syllables. This is particularly true of the alveolar sounds [t], [d], and [n]. The -*ted* and -*ded* syllables and the various NT combinations cause particular difficulty. In 1940, when Wendell Willkie was running for *President of the United States*, he continually reduced this nine-syllable phrase in his speeches to four or five syllables: [prɛz djunaɪdə steɪs]. You may hear his pronunciation of this phrase in the Columbia album *I Can Hear It Now*, Volume I.

The common addition of [g] to [ŋ] is, of course, a European heritage from language backgrounds such as Spanish, Hungarian, Italian, or Yiddish. However, the fact that [ŋ], [k], and [g] are made in the same articulatory position makes this error difficult to eradicate. In addition, speakers having this fault often rationalize it by pointing to the NG spelling of words in this category. Teachers sometimes give it additional support by urging their students who substitute [n] for [ŋ] not to drop their G's. This is a worthy aim, but an unphonetic way of expressing it, since [ŋ] is not two sounds, but one.

The substitution of one nasal for another is due to general similarity in the acoustic effect of the three sounds. Since it is somewhat easier to articulate [m] than [n], and [n] than [ŋ], speakers often take the path of least resistance, particularly in words where the articulators have previously been in the easier position. Corruptions of the words *something, happen, running,* and similar words are facilitated by these circumstances.

Exercises

1. Listen to a recording of your speech. Do you make any of the errors discussed in the description of the nasal and plosive sounds? Does your speech differ in the articulation of these sounds from that of your associates?

2. Listen to the following sentences as your instructor reads them to you. What articulation problems do you notice? Indicate errors by underlining them on the phonetic transcript. Do you make any of these errors?

a. [gʌvɚmən ʌv ðə pipl]
b. [junaɪd wi stæn//dɪvaɪd wi fɔl]
c. [hi wəz goɪŋg əweɪ wɪð ʌs]
d. [aɪ sɔ ə mæn lɛnθən ə roʊp]
e. [ɪts beʔɚ tu hæv lɪbɚdɪ ðn sleɪvɚrɪ]
f. [ɪts gʊnə hæpm mʌndɪ]

3. Read the following sentences for clear articulation of nasals and plosives, but do not fail to blend words within the phrase.

a. The accident dented the fender on my late-model car.
b. Today I'm going to get off at the Atlantic Avenue subway station.
c. The chairman of the subcommittee kept mentioning the October deadline.
d. The thug robbed the night club, but obtained only an empty bead purse.
e. At midnight the workmen witnessed the robbery.
f. He tiptoed through the dark night in the rain.
g. The six leaders exhorted the crowd to exert their maximum effort.
h. I saw him running away and looking up the street as he ran.
i. Seeing him coming toward me, I started singing a song to attract his attention.

4. Practice reading the following selections in the Appendix, paying particular attention to nasal and plosive sounds: Numbers 2, 3, 14, 27, and 29.

FRICATIVE CONSONANTS

There are nine generally recognized American fricative consonant sounds. These are [f], [v]; [θ], [ð]; [s], [z]; [ʃ], [ʒ]; and [h]. These sounds are formed by narrowing the mouth passageway at some point and in such a manner that the breath stream is partially obstructed. The air forced through this restricted opening produces a friction sound.

Voiceless $$\begin{bmatrix} f \quad and \quad v \end{bmatrix}$$ Voiced

*f*eel   LABIODENTAL   *v*eal
(Lower lip, upper teeth)

Raise your lower lip gently against the edges of your upper front teeth. Direct the breath stream between the lower lip and the upper teeth; the audible friction is the [f] sound. When, to this breath stream, you add the vibration of your vocal folds, the [v] sound is produced.

Faulty production: exaggerated position of lower lip, either protruding or drawn back too far; excessive pressure of the lip against the teeth so that the breath is almost or entirely stopped and a plosive sound is made; bilabial production occurring in some forms of foreign speech.

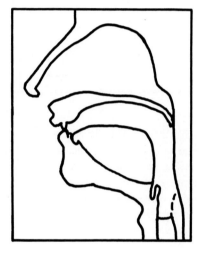

Common Combinations

*f*lower, *f*ree, *sph*ere   twe*lv*e, sta*rv*e
di*phth*eria, di*phth*ong
se*lf*, sur*f*, le*ft*, fi*fth*

Voiceless $\qquad$ [θ *and* ð] $\qquad$ Voiced

*th*ink $\qquad$ LINGUADENTAL $\qquad$ *th*em

(Tongue tip between teeth)

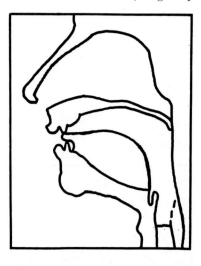

Protrude your flattened tongue tip slightly between your teeth so that the upper side makes very light contact with the cutting edges of the upper teeth. Direct the breath stream in a continuous flow over the center of your tongue and between it and the upper teeth. This will produce the [θ] sound. When vocal vibration is added, the voiced [ð] will result.

The TH sounds are the only ones which require the tongue to move forward in the mouth and touch the front teeth.

When the TH is encountered at the beginning of nouns, verbs, and adjectives, it usually represents the voiceless [θ] sound, as in *thimble, think,* and *thin.* However, the initial TH occurring in the article *the* and in pronouns, conjunctions, and adverbs, such as *they, than,* and *then,* generally represents the voiced sound. In the medial position, there is no consistent rule you can follow. In the final position, voiced [ð] is usually indicated by the addition of E to TH, as in *bathe.*

Faulty production: excessive protrusion; excessive pressure of the tongue against the edges or inside surfaces of the teeth so that a plosive sound results (dental [t] or [d]), often heard among speakers influenced by a foreign background; actual substitution of the [t] or [d] sound with the tongue tip on the alveolar ridge; substitution of the [s] or [z] sound, also traceable to foreign influence; use of the lower lip instead of the tongue tip between the teeth so that the [f] or [v] sound is substituted, as in infantile speech. [θ] and [ð] do not occur in most foreign languages.

Common Combinations

*th*ree, *thw*art
fi*fth*, wi*dth*
hea*lth*, stre*ngth*

mou*ths*, ba*thed*

Voiceless $$\begin{bmatrix} \text{s} \quad and \quad \text{z} \end{bmatrix}$$ Voiced

*s*oon   LINGUA-ALVEOLAR   *z*oo
(Tongue tip or blade, gum ridge)

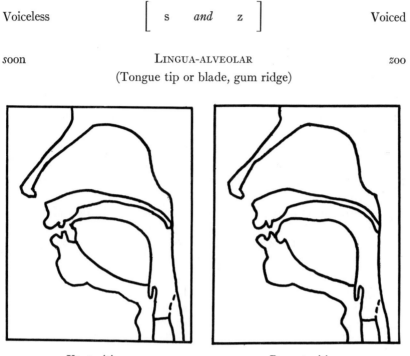

Up position   *Down position*

There are two main positions for the production of [s] and [z], both of which are satisfactory and which sound alike.

For either the up or the down position, your teeth are brought almost together in a natural bite. If the up position is habitual, you raise the tip of your tongue toward the alveolar ridge; the sides of the tongue touch the inner edges of your upper teeth while you maintain a narrow groove down the middle of your tongue. The breath stream is forced down this center groove and out through the small aperture formed by the grooved tongue tip held close to the alveolar ridge. The breath stream passing over the cutting edges of your front teeth makes the hissing, unvoiced [s] sound. When the vocal folds vibrate, the voiced [z] sound results.

For the down position, you place the tongue tip against the inner side of your lower front teeth. The blade moves up toward your alveolar ridge and is grooved in much the same manner as it was in the up position, and the breath stream is forced down the middle of this groove and out over the cutting edges of your front teeth.

The [s] and [z] are to be judged primarily by their acoustic quality. An individual with irregular teeth or an atypical occlusion may use a placement of the articulators different from yours, but if the acoustic result is good, he

179

$$\begin{bmatrix} \text{s} & and & \text{z} \\ & continued & \end{bmatrix}$$

has no articulatory defect. He has learned to adjust the position of his tongue to suit the particular structure of his mouth. Basically, if a fine stream of air is directed through a small opening between tongue and alveolar ridge, and comes over the cutting edges of the teeth at the front center of the mouth without undue pressure or prolongation, the [s] should be acceptable.

You can make a correct [s] or [z] whether you use the up or the down position. Probably chance factors or your particular oral structure originally started your present habits. In no case should you attempt to change your habits if your sounds are now acceptable. The effort to modify such small muscle movements merely to copy someone else's production will disturb the general coordination of your articulatory movements.

Some speakers use the up position when the tongue tip is to be raised immediately for alveolar consonants following [s]: *slow, snow, stay.* They may keep the tongue tip down for [s] when a vowel follows or precedes it: *say, sigh, ice.* This represents economy of action.

Since the [s] is one of the most frequent sounds in our language and is used in more consonant combinations even than [r] and [l], your production should be judged carefully by a skilled critic. Many speakers cannot hear their own [s] and [z] faults.

Faulty production: evident in any of the three general types of lisping. (1) Protrusion or central lisp, in which the tongue tip thrusts over the edges of the upper front teeth or presses against them in such a way that the [θ] sound is substituted for the [s]. This fault is generally encountered in the speech of young children, or it may have persisted in modified form into adulthood. If the lower jaw is allowed to swing forward out of normal bite position, the tongue will also be brought forward in the mouth and will probably contact the teeth when it is raised. (2) Lateral lisp, in which the tongue tip makes a closure at the center of the alveolar ridge or the upper front teeth and the breath is forced to escape over one or both lateral edges of the tongue; saliva between cheek and gum is then disturbed by the flow of air, and will contribute to the mushy sound of the lateral lisp. (3) Whistling or hissing [s], due to prolongation, extreme muscular tension in the tongue, or excessive air pressure.

The whistling or prolonged [s] is more common than the other two lisping faults. If you have been told that your speech is marked by this fault—a serious handicap in radio or stage work—use a mirror to study its production. Often the tongue tip or the blade is held too tensely against the alveolar ridge so that the opening through which your breath escapes is smaller than required. Also, the tongue may be raised toward a place on your palate farther back than necessary. With your raised tongue held in slightly different positions, listen carefully and judge the sounds produced. Experiment. Try greater relaxation of the muscles of the front of your tongue, with a larger opening between the tongue and your alveolar ridge, so that you produce a soft, somewhat slurred sound. Shorten the duration of this sound. Careful listening and trial-and-error practice will indicate the best position. Now use words with [s] in a final position; prolong the vowel sounds in these words, but shorten the final sibilant. Next, place these words within a phrase so that the final [s] is followed by a succeeding word, as in *glass of water, I will miss you.*

A fault encountered in the use of the [z] sound is unvoicing in the final position, so that such words as *was* become [wəs], as in [hi wəs əwei].

Foreign students should note that s is often used to designate the sound of [z] in English spelling. A final s is pronounced as [z] when the preceding sound is voiced, as in such words as *buds, dogs, plums, runs, graves, hills, cars,* and *brothers.* It is also pronounced as [z] in the final position when the schwa vowel sound [ə] comes between it and the preceding sounds with sibilant qualities, such as [s], [z], sh [ʃ], zh [ʒ], ch [tʃ], and j [dʒ], in such words as *passes, wishes, matches,* and *bridges.*

Common Combinations

*s*pool, *s*mile, *s*tay, *s*well, *s*phere, *s*nake, *s*kate, *s*leep, *s*plit, *s*pring, *s*treet, *s*cream
bo*x*, cla*sp*, la*st*, ta*sk*

In final position, the [z] combines with any voiced consonant except those with sibilant qualities noted above.

*sh*ip LINGUAPALATAL mea*s*ure

(Tongue tip or blade, behind alveolar ridge)

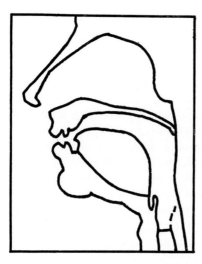 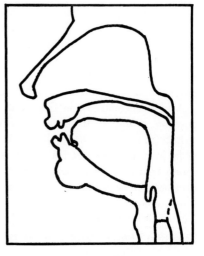

Up position *Down position*

The [s] is a narrow-breath-stream sound, whereas the [ʃ] and [ʒ] are broad-breath-stream sounds. With your tongue tip flattened in either the up or the down position, the sides of your tongue should touch the inner edges of your upper teeth. The teeth should be nearly closed. A fairly wide passage-way is thus formed down the mid-line of your tongue. The breath stream is directed through this passageway and out a wide but shallow opening made by the grooved tip or blade of your tongue raised toward the back of your alveolar ridge. Your lips usually are slightly rounded and protruded. The sound thus produced is the voiceless [ʃ]. When vocal-fold vibration is added, the voiced [ʒ] results. The latter sound may be spelled with s, z, or G, as in *measure, azure,* and *garage.*

These sounds differ from the narrow fricatives [s] and [z] in that the opening for the breath is wider and farther back on the hard palate and the lips are rounded. Note that [ʃ] and [ʒ] are not combinations of [s] or [z] with [h], but are single sound units.

Faulty production: protrusion lisp; lateral lisp; excessive tension, so that the sound is prolonged and accompanied by undue friction; substitutions of [s] or [z].

Voiceless $\left[\begin{array}{ccc} \int & and & 3 \\ & continued & \end{array}\right]$ Voiced

Unvoicing.

Common Combinations

*sh*rill
wi*shed*

Notice the use of these two sounds in the affricate combinations described on page 184.

Voiceless $\left[\begin{array}{c} h \end{array}\right]$

how GLOTTAL

To produce the [h], the glottis, or opening between the vocal folds, is partially closed, but not enough to produce vocal-fold vibration. Your articulatory mechanism assumes the position for the vowel sound which is to follow the [h], and the escaping breath produces a slight, breathy friction before the vowel is vocalized.

When [h] precedes the glides [j] or [w] as in [hjudʒ] or [hwɛn] the articulatory mechanism is in the position for the beginning of the glide and may actually be moving in the glide while [h] is being produced.

Faulty production: omission in foreign accent or in careless speech (however, when [h] is the initial sound in an unaccented word in the middle of a phrase, it may be slighted or even omitted without being considered faulty); velar friction in some types of foreign accent.

AFFRICATES

Any plosive combined directly with a succeeding fricative can be considered to be an affricate. However, usually only [tʃ] and [dʒ] are discussed in this category because in the combination [tʃ], for example, [t] and [ʃ] lose their individual characteristics and become a new sound. Most of the other common affricate combinations, such as [ts], [dz], or [kf], retain sufficient of the acoustic effects of the sounds in isolation to be readily recognizable even in these combinations.

Voiceless $\begin{bmatrix} t\int & and & d_3 \end{bmatrix}$ Voiced

*ch*urch   COMBINATION OF LINGUA-ALVEOLAR PLOSIVES AND   *j*udge
LINGUAPALATAL FRICATIVES

To produce the [tʃ], the approximate position and movements for the [t] are directly followed by those for [ʃ]. The tongue tip is held in contact with the alveolar ridge, the body of the tongue assumes the arched position for the [ʃ], the tongue tip releases suddenly, and the breath is exploded between tongue and palate in the opening characteristic of the [ʃ].

In producing [dʒ], the same action occurs, but since voice accompanies this activity, the [d] is quickly followed by [ʒ].

There is a tendency in these productions for the mechanism to assume a compromise position; the [t] block is moved slightly toward the [ʃ] position and the groove for the [ʃ] toward the [t] block.

Faulty production: substitution of [ʃ] and [ʒ]; exaggerated explosion or protrusion. If [ʃ] and [ʒ] are faulty in the individual's speech, these sounds will also be distorted. [dʒ] is commonly unvoiced.

Common Combinations

lu*nch*, bu*tch*er, mar*ch*ed   ra*nge*, bi*lge*, ju*dge*d

Articulation Faults Involving Fricative and Affricate Sounds

Many of the articulatory faults in the production of fricatives can be traced to the similarity in sound between some of these consonants. For instance, listen to another person produce [f], [s], [ʃ], and [θ] with his hand cupped over his mouth. When you cannot see the movements of the structures, the difference between the characteristic friction sounds may be difficult to hear. Children who do not watch the lips often say [fɪŋk] or [sɪŋk] for [θɪŋk]; [su] for [ʃu]; [sʌnɪ] for [fʌnɪ]; and so forth. Foreigners who do not have the TH in their language may substitute [s] and [z] for [θ] and [ð].

Other faults may be due to the similarity in position between two consonants. The tongue has only a little way to move from the [s] position to produce the protrusion lisp which sounds like [θ]: [si] changes to [θi]. A reverse tendency brings the tongue back from the position for [θ] and [ð] and the speaker substitutes the plosives [t] and [d]. In this substitution, the [t] and [d] are usually articulated with the tongue pressed against the upper teeth (dental production): [tɪŋk] for [θɪŋk] and [brʌdɚ] for [brʌðɚ].

The [s] combines with many consonants. Probably the most difficult blends for some people are those which require a very small movement from the position of [s] to the alveolar consonant following: [stim], [slip], [sniz]. It is especially hard to return to the position of the [s] and [z] again: [poʊsts], [goʊsts], [pɛnslz], [lɛsnz]. A well-known stumbling block is the word *statistics* [stətɪstɪks]. The addition of [s] or [z] to [θ] or [ð] may also be difficult: [bɝθs], [pæðz].

The voiced fricatives and the voiced affricate are frequently unvoiced by foreigners. In rapid, somewhat careless speech, this unvoicing is common. Make up conversational sentences for the following words to see if you unvoice the italicized consonants when you speak rapidly: glo*v*es, bro*th*er, doe*s*, gara*g*e, villa*g*e.

Often you hear a very noisy production of fricatives. Since there are so many of these sounds in our language, particularly [s] and [z], any extra pressure of breath as it escapes through the small passageways, or any prolongation of the friction sound, affects most of the words spoken. The characteristic sputtering and hissing of this type of speech is accentuated if the [t] and [d] sounds are produced in a dental position.

When these sounds are used in the running context of speech, you must guard against substitution of one fricative for another, faulty placement, unvoicing of normally voiced fricatives, and extreme tension in production.

Exercises

1. As you listen to a record of your own speech, do you discover any deviations from the average in your production of fricative and affricate sounds?

2. Listen to the following sentences as your instructor reads them to you. What differences in articulation do you notice?

a. [hæf ju ɛfɚ hɝt əf ɪm]

b. [aɪ tɪŋk dət i sɔ mi goʊ dɛɚ]

c. [zeɪ seɪ zɛɚ ɪs sʌmsɪŋ rɔŋ]

d. [dəs i noʊ ɪt wəs hɪs]

    e. [aɪ fɔt væt wəz maɪ mʌvɚ]

    f. [aɪ θɔ hɚ itɪn aɪθkwim]

    g. [i wəz rɒɪt ɪɚ]

    h. [ðə ʃɪkns ræn tə ðə ɛtʃ əf ðə roʊt]

    i. [pʊtʃɚ bægɪtʃ ɪnə gɚrɑtʃ]

    j. [aɪ kwɛsʃn ɪz sɛns ə jumɚ]

3. Read the following sentences for clear articulation of the fricatives and affricates. Be certain to blend words within the phrase.

    a. Diphthongs are combinations of vowel sounds spoken in a continuous glide.

    b. He severed his connection with the Western Insurance Company.

    c. The author faithfully presented the social conditions existing in both the Northern and Southern sections of this country.

    d. In spite of the excitement surging around him, he clasped his hands and gazed out at the distant sea.

    e. A pleasant voice and good speech are significant factors in successful business and social relationships.

    f. Quartz, otherwise known as silicon dioxide, is one of our commonest minerals.

    g. His unusual treasures were housed in a luxurious mansion.

    h. Though he lived in humble surroundings, he felt no humility.

    i. The true humorist views humanity with kindly and sympathetic amusement.

    j. True Christian virtue transcends church attendance.

    k. He righteously chose to ignore the question.

    l. The judge was subjected to savage jibes and jeers.

    m. Fifteen telephone posts were installed against the protests of the local residents.

    n. We hold these truths to be self-evident.

GLIDES

(Semivowels)

Four sounds, [w], [j], [r], and [l], are formed by the articulators as they move or glide through a series of positions rather than stopping in any one of them. Acoustically they are similar to vowels in that they are produced with the mouth in a relatively open position and, hence, possess strong resonance characteristics with a minimum of friction.

$$\left[\quad \text{w} \quad \right] \qquad \qquad \text{Voiced}$$

BILABIAL *water*

Round and protrude the lips and raise the back of the tongue as if you were going to produce the vowel [u]. As the tone begins, quickly move the lips and tongue into the position for the vowel which follows.

If the articulatory mechanism is held in the initial position, a sound similar to [u] results. The sound resulting from the glide into the succeeding vowel identifies the consonant [w]. Notice the movement of the lips and jaw in going from [w] to [ɔ] in the word *walk;* on the other hand, the glide is not strong between the words *you ought.*

Faulty production: exaggerated movement of the lips; substitution of [v] in foreign accent; overrelaxation of the lips so that the movement is not apparent.

Common Combinations

*tw*elve, *dw*ell, *thw*art, s*w*im, *qu*een, ang*u*ish

GLOTTAL FRICATIVE APPROACH TO [w]

[hw], probably used in American speech more extensively than a completely voiceless [w], sometimes symbolized by [ʍ], appears in such words as *why, when, where.* With the lips in the rounded position for [w], the friction sound of the [h] accompanies the glide movement of the lips. The blowing of the breath stream against the lips can easily be felt.

Faulty production: in rapid conversation or in careless speech [w] is often substituted for [hw]. When clear articulation is required, although the substitution is widely used, it is still considered better to say [hwɑt] than [wɑt], [hwɪtʃ] than [wɪtʃ], [hwaɪ] than [waɪ], and so forth.

$$\left[\quad \text{j} \quad \right] \qquad\qquad \text{Voiced}$$

LINGUAPALATAL   *yes*

Raise the tongue in a position close to that assumed for the vowel [i] and spread the lips slightly; as voice is produced, glide your tongue quickly into the position for the vowel following. If the initial position is held, [i] will result. Observe the movement on the initial sound in [jɛs].

In English spelling, when y appears at the beginning of a syllable it is pronounced [j]. The ı in conjunction with a vowel is pronounced [j], with the glide activity apparent: on*ion*, famil*iar*, sav*ior*.

The [j] occurs commonly with the long vowel [u] to form a combination which is similar to a diphthong. In its initial position, as in *use, union, uvula,* the glide movement is strong.

The use of the combination [ju] is not consistent in American speech. Following consonants which do not make use of the front of the tongue, the [j] is used. Examples: *pupil, beauty, cute, argue, few, view, music, human.* After consonants which do employ the front of the tongue, [ju] is used when a premium is placed upon exactness or "niceness" of articulation. In casual speech, its use will depend upon the early environment and education of the speaker. In some words a very short glide is used; some speakers use the [u] alone. Words like the following may be heard with [ju], [ɪu], or [u]: *student, tune, duty, assume, suit, resume, enthusiasm, new, lucid.*

Faulty production: pronounced friction noise.

GLOTTAL FRICATIVE APPROACH TO [j]

Like [hw], there can be a glottal fricative approach to [j], as in the word [hjumən]. With the articulatory mechanism in the position for the beginning of the glide [j], start the breath stream and the glide so that the first part of the glide is voiceless.

Faulty production: omission of the glottal fricative [h] as in [judʒ] or [jumɚ].

LINGUAPALATAL *red*

The vowel R's [ɝ] and [ɚ] have already been presented (see pages 150–151). The consonant differs from the vowel in two important ways—in the presence of greater friction and in the characteristic glide movement of the semivowel. For the vowels [ɝ] and [ɚ], there is no glide; the position is held as the sound is produced.

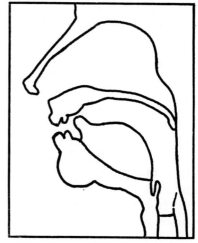

There are many variations in the formation of the consonant [r]. Most speakers will raise and slightly curl or retroflex the broadened tongue tip toward the palate just behind the alveolar ridge, start the vocalization for the sound, and then, with a gliding movement, change the position of the tongue and lips to that of the vowel which follows the [r]. Others will retract the tongue tip from the lower front teeth but elevate the tip very little. Some, as they start the sound, will curl the tip back toward the middle of the hard palate.

A slight friction often accompanies the production. This, plus the glide movement, makes the sound recognizable as a consonant. If the starting position were held, the vowel [ɝ] would be heard instead. The variations for the production of this vowel have already been discussed on page 150.

When the letter R occurs at the end of a word or before a final consonant, the consonantal glide is not present. The sound is either the accented [ɝ], as in [fɝ], [nɝs], or the unaccented [ɚ], as in [wɪntɚ]. In some localities where the R is not sounded in final position, these words will be pronounced without the R coloring: [fɜ], [wɪntə]. The letter R following a vowel is heard as the receding half of a centering diphthong: [fɪɚ], [kɛɚ], [mɔɚ], [kɑɚ], [pʊɚ] (see page 155).

Certain recognizable variations in the production of this consonant need description so that you may analyze what you hear in the speech of those around you.

The trilled R requires a tense tongue with the tip hitting the alveolar ridge repeatedly. It occurs in several foreign languages and in Scottish and

Irish dialects. To produce the British single-tapped ʀ, the tongue tip touches the ridge once, much as in the production of [d]. Listen to the British pronunciation of *sorry, cherish*. The extreme retroflex ʀ, such as is sometimes heard in pronounced Middle Western dialect, is made by curling the tongue tip back upon itself. This position muffles the sound by changing the resonance. Often the ʀ can be retroflex in position without sounding faulty. The back of the tongue may also be raised to produce a variety of ʀ. The German and Russian uvular ʀ is made with the back of the tongue raised toward the end of the soft palate, in such a way that the air stream causes the uvula to flutter. The Germans also use a back-tongue ʀ in which the passage is so narrowed that the sound is accompanied by strong friction noise.

The [r] is often used to link words together when the first word ends in the vowel [ɝ] or [ɚ] and the next word begins with a vowel: [fɝ r ɪz lɔŋ], [ðɛɚ r ɑɚ tu]. If the linking [r] is too strongly stressed, so that the second word sounds as if it started with an ʀ, the production is usually considered faulty. In certain sections of the country, where the final ʀ is pronounced [ɜ] as in *fur* [fɜ], [ə] as in *butter* [bʌtə], or omitted as in *far* [fɑ], the vowel is followed by a linking [r] to permit an easy transition to the vowel in the next word: [fɜ r ɪz lɔŋ], [ðɛ r ɑə].

An [r] is sometimes inserted between two words when the first ends with a vowel and the second begins with a vowel. The use of this intrusive [r] seems to facilitate movement from one vowel to the next. In Eastern Seaboard speech, such phrases as these may be heard: [ən aɪdɪə rəv hɪz], [əmɛrɪkə rɪz fri], [ðə sofə rɪz maɪn]. Notice, in producing these phrases, how the final schwa itself may be influenced, often becoming the [ɚ]. In General American speech, the intrusive [r] is considered a fault. In some cases, speakers use [ɚ] at the end of single words where it has no actual function: *law* [lɔɚ], *piano* [pɪænɚ].

Faulty production: substitution of [w] in lalling or infantile speech; excessive friction; muffled retroflex ʀ; foreign ʀ; insertion of [ə] or [ɚ] when [r] is combined with other consonants, as in *tree* [təri], *pray* [pəreɪ].

Common Combinations

*p*ride, *b*ring, *t*ry, *d*ream, *c*ry, *g*reen, *th*ree, *sh*rink, *s*pring, *st*reet, *f*ree

LINGUA-ALVEOLAR   *leap*, schoo*l*

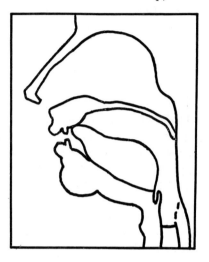

Hold the tip of the tongue lightly against the center of the alveolar ridge. The voiced breath flows out over the relaxed sides of the tongue, and immediately the mechanism glides into the position for the succeeding sound. The lips and back of the tongue assume the position of the vowel which follows or precedes [l].

The [l] sounds like a vowel because of its resonance. While the tongue tip remains on the ridge for the various sounds of [l], the body and back of the tongue take a vowel position. When [l] occurs in initial position or after an initial consonant, as in the words *lead, blue, play*, it is said to be *clear;* the position of the front of the tongue resembles that of [i]. When it occurs in final position or before a final consonant, as in *all, bulk, field*, it is called *dark;* the position of the back of the tongue is raised in a position resembling [u]. Occasionally a foreigner, when learning American speech, will use the clear or the dark [l] in all words.

Final [l], after a consonant, will be syllabic; that is, the [l] can form a syllable by itself without an accompanying vowel. In this instance, [l] is not a glide, but the position is held as for a vowel. Examples: *apple, bottle, able, uncle, little.*

Faulty production: substitution of [w] or [j] in baby talk; omission in final position; retroflex with tongue tip turned back on itself; dental [l], with the tongue pressed against the teeth as it occurs in some foreign languages; tip held against lower front teeth and sound produced with blade of tongue and accompanying friction noises and nasalization. When [l] is combined with an initial consonant, the schwa vowel should not be inserted: *blue* [bəlu], *place* [pəleɪs].

Common Combinations

*p*lace, *b*lue, *c*lean, *g*lass, *f*ly, *s*leep, fi*l*m, he*l*p, bu*l*b, me*l*t, he*l*d, si*l*k, she*lf*, twe*l*ve, hea*lth*, fa*l*se.

Articulation Faults Involving the Glide Sounds

The fact that the four semivowels are similar to vowels in acoustic effect and in position may account for some of the errors in their production. When we refer to the omission of final ʀ's, we mean that the schwa has been substituted for the final [ɚ], so that even the ʀ coloring of the vowel has disappeared. In rapid speech or baby talk, [l] is sometimes not completed; the tongue tip does not contact the alveolar ridge. We then hear substitutions of [ə] or even [ʊ] for the [l]: [pæs ðə sɔət], [aɪ fiə gʊd], [mɔə mɪʊk]. The [l] in final position is often omitted, so that the preceding vowel alone is heard: [kɔ] for [kɔl], [ɔ əv əm] for [ɔl əv ðəm].

Another error involving [l] is the insertion of the schwa before the final [l]: [fiəl], [puəl], [ʃeəl]. The articulatory mechanism does not move into the [l] position fast enough; since vocalization continues, we hear the [ə] as the movement takes place.

Since [r] and [l] both require complex muscle activity, children may substitute the easier semivowels which sound somewhat like [r] and [l]. Hence the child may say [wɛd dwɛs] or [aɪjaɪk ɪt], [jewoʊ] or [jeɪmboʊ]. If a person has used this lalling speech in childhood, he may still have little glide movement for these sounds and therefore give weak productions difficult to recognize. The tongue then needs to move more vigorously. The speaker may need the practice provided in actual speech correction.

Extreme tension of production for any of these four semivowels will result in excessive friction. With [r] and [l], the tongue may also be retracted so that the sounds have a muffled quality.

These consonants are strongly influenced by the speech models in the speaker's environment. You can easily recognize regional differences in their articulation. They can be said to be faulty only if they attract attention to themselves or if they interfere with communication.

Exercises

1. As you listen to a record of your own speech, can you recognize any deviation from the average in the production of your semivowels?

2. Listen to the following sentences as your instructor reads them. Do you hear faults in the production of the glides?

   a. [wɛn ɪz ðə wɛðɚ gʌnə wɔɚm ʌp]

   b. [jɛs ðə stjudənts wɪl əsjum əl rɪspɑnsɪbɪlɪtɪ]

   c. [si tʊk pwaɪd ɪn ɚ wɛd dwɛs]

   d. [aɪ riəlɪ fiəl bɛtɚ]

e. [waɪ dɪd i seɪ ɪt wz ɔ raɪt]

f. [pəliz gɪv mi ə bəlu wʌn]

g. [aɪ hæd noʊ aɪdɪɚ hi kəd pleɪ ðə pɪænɚ]

h. [ə lɪtə hɛəp wəd bi əpwɪʃɪetəd]

3. Read the following sentences for clear articulation of the semivowel sounds. Blend the sounds within the phrases.

a. Is he able to present a clean bill of health?

b. Twelve men reduced the castle to a pile of rubble.

c. He tried to follow his dream of building a great empire.

d. I feel that it is humanly impossible to complete the whole volume.

e. All right, I will file the will when he calls me.

f. I would rather read a railroad timetable than his erudite verse.

g. The long light shakes
Across the lakes,
And the wild cataract leaps in glory.
—TENNYSON

h. Helen, thy beauty is to me
Like those Nicaean barks of yore,
That gently, o'er the perfumed sea,
The weary, wayworn wanderer bore. . . .
—POE

THE BLENDING AND ASSIMILATION OF SOUNDS IN SPEECH

If you have always lived in the United States and do not have a serious speech defect, you will probably be able to produce all the consonants as they have been described. As the sounds are grouped into words and the words into communicative phrases, however, their production may change in the running oral context. In order that the words within the phrase may flow together smoothly, there must be a steady movement from one sound to the next, both within words and between words. You have heard people speak as if each word were a single dropped pebble. If you repeat the following sentence with short breaks between words, you may recognize this meaningless mannerism: "As they told Tom the news, they all watched his face."

After you have read the staccato production, read the first phrase as a unit. Notice the forward movement of the tongue from [z] to [ð] between the first two words, *as they;* the economy of one contact of tongue tip to gum ridge between *told* and *Tom;* the beginning of the [ð] even as the [m] is formed between the words *Tom the.* Observe further how the [w] starts while the tongue tip is up for [l] between the words *all watched;* [z] blends into [f] with continuing friction sound between *his* and *face.*

Thus the process of blending has made it possible for you to move steadily forward through a phrase. This smooth blending of sounds has a distinct value in communication. The phrase, as we have already said, is the unit of meaning. The continuous movement of the articulators through the phrase indicates this unity to the listener.

Read the following paragraph to yourself, deciding on the phrasing which is best suited to your purposes in communication. Repeat the passage aloud, maintaining the unity within each phrase with smooth, steady blending between the words.

In a few minutes more, there came over the scene another radical alteration. The general surface grew somewhat more smooth, and the whirlpools, one by one, disappeared, while prodigious streaks of foam became apparent where none had been seen before. These streaks, at length, spreading out to a greater distance and entering into combination, took unto themselves the gyratory motion of the subsided vortices, and seemed to form the germ of another more vast. Suddenly—very suddenly—this assumed a distinct and definite existence, in a circle of more than a mile in diameter. The edge of the whirl was represented by a broad belt of gleaming spray; but no particle of this slipped into the mouth of the terrific funnel, whose interior, as far as the eye could fathom it, was a smooth, shining, and jet-black wall of water, inclined to the horizon at an angle of some forty-five degrees, speeding dizzily round and round with a swaying and sweltering motion, and sending forth to the winds an appealing voice, half shriek, half roar, such as not even the mighty cataract of Niagara ever lifts up in its agony to Heaven.—POE

When you are convinced that you have developed the most effective reading of this passage from *A Descent into the Maelstrom,* read it aloud again, studying the articulatory movements which allow you to blend sounds skillfully. A recording of the selection will help you to make this analysis. Of course, you will experience no difficulty in blending vowel-consonant and consonant-vowel combinations, as in un<u>to</u> themselves, its<u> </u>agony. Notice that the following factors will bring about the blending.

1. If the neighboring consonants are similar in their place of production, the characteristic articulatory movements are made only once. For instance, the following word combinations in the selection make use of this rule: another radical, prodigious streaks, out to a greater distance, foam became, in diameter, and definite, but no.

2. If the sounds are alike in auditory character (fricatives, plosives, nasals, etc.), there is no break between them. In the passage above, these word combinations make use of the rule: whirl was represented, broad belt, jet-black (in these last combinations of plosives, the explosion of air takes place on the second plosive), as far, as the eye, half shriek, ever lifts.

3. If the sounds occur in different areas of the mouth, the articulatory mechanism gets ready for or even starts the production of the second sound while the first is still being produced. An important application of this rule arises when a plosive is exploded into the position of the succeeding consonant. Examples of such preparation for articulatory movements are: minutes more, surface grew, somewhat more, seen before, terrific funnel, could fathom, black wall, sending forth, half roar.

Some sounds do not blend together readily because they are too dissimilar in location and auditory character. In such cases, your speech mechanism will modify one or both sounds to make the combination easier to produce. This process is called *assimilation*. Some assimilation always takes place between sounds as they affect each other, but your discrimination may not be sharp enough to detect it.

Notice the examples of assimilation in the passage: themselves the, forth to, circle of more, of water, at length, even the. Check the variant tongue positions for the [l] in combination with different sounds, such as in gleaming, whirlpools, suddenly.

This tendency to modify the production of sounds for easy transition has long been apparent in the language.

Notice the assimilation of sounds which is acceptable in the pronunciation of the following words:

bank	[bæŋk]	picture	[pɪktʃɚ]	soldier	[soldʒɚ]
anger	[æŋgɚ]	nature	[neɪtʃɚ]	motion	[moʃən]

The ED and the s endings of words also show modification of the voicing for ease of combination. If you were born in this country, you learned the correct pronunciations through imitation. Foreigners often have difficulty in knowing when to voice and when to unvoice endings.

rubbed	stopped	[rʌbd]	[stɑpt]	marred	[mɑɚd]
tagged	cooked	[tægd]	[kʊkt]	called	[kɔld]
lived	laughed	[lɪvd]	[læft]	leaned	[lind]
gazed	guessed	[gezd]	[gɛst]	slammed	[slæmd]
edged	reached	[ɛdʒd]	[ritʃt]		

The final s in plurals, possessives, and present tenses is pronounced [z] after voiced sounds and [s] after unvoiced.

tubs	tops	[tʌbz]	[tɑps]	cars	[kɑɚz]
roads	hats	[roʊdz]	[hæts]	calls	[kɔlz]
dogs	kicks	[dɔgz]	[kɪks]	man's	[mænz]
lives	laughs	[lɪvz]	[læfs]	hams	[hæmz]
mouths	moths	[maʊðz]	[mɔθs]		

In listening for blending and assimilation, you should realize that two tendencies are at war in articulation: one, the inclination to give the easiest production of the sound with the least muscular effort; and the other, the attempt to achieve pedantic accuracy in the mistaken belief that it is necessary for clarity. For the most readily accepted speech, you should discover for yourself the middle way—enough assimilation and blending between words for smoothness in production, and sufficient clarity for immediate comprehension in the specific speech situation. With the nature of the speaking situation in mind, you can understand that some situations require an emphasis on clearness of production, and others, more casual in nature, permit more extensive assimilation of sounds.

CARELESS AND FAULTY PRODUCTION OF CONSONANTS

After each consonant, we have given specific examples of faulty production, and following each general classification, faults of articulation.

The same causes which contribute to the faulty production of vowels also affect consonants: little energy in production, rapid speech, or imitation of poor models. More basic reasons for indistinct articulation will lie in differences in physical structure, the environment, and the personality of the speaker.

Consonants may be distorted, omitted, or so weak that they are difficult to hear. One consonant may actually be substituted for another or be added to a word where it should not appear. Substitution and weak or slurred production are the most common faults in careless speech.

In extreme assimilation, any of these faults may be apparent. The same rules which operate to facilitate the blending of sounds are now so over-worked that one or more of the consonants lose their identity. Sometimes the extreme assimilation may occur on unaccented words within a phrase; if the words themselves are not necessary to meaning, the carelessness does not interfere with communication. But if the fault occurs on the stressed words, the poor articulation is then obvious and disturbing to the listener.

Phrases such as the following may be understood by someone who knows you well, but will not be understood with ease if you use them in speaking across a room or in talking to several people. Listeners who are strangers to you may also make unflattering judgments of your speech and education.

[aɪm gʌnə tɛl jə sʌmpm]	I'm going to tell you something.
[ɪ smaɪ prɑbm]	It's my problem.
[hɑ dʒə gɪt əweɪ]	How did you get away?
[don tʃə si]	Don't you see?
[waɪn tʃə tɛl əm]	Why didn't you tell them?
[hi dɪnt gɪmi ɪz bʊk]	He didn't give me his book.
[opm ðə dɔɚ wɛn naɪ nɑk]	Open the door when I knock.
[aɪ dɪnt rɛkənaɪz ðə kwɛʃn]	I didn't recognize the question.

Endings of words may be slurred or the final consonant omitted altogether.

[hi toʊl mi]	He told me.
[ðə wɝl ɪz rɑʊn]	The world is round.
[ðə gretəs mæn]	The greatest man.
[dʒɪs wʌn]	Just one.
[wi wɛn əweɪ]	We went away.
[aɪm gʌnə goʊ]	I'm going to go.
[gɪmi ə bʊk]	Give me a book.
[sɔɚtə bæd]	Sort of bad.
[kaɪnə naɪs]	Kind of nice.
[ɛnɪθɪn goʊz]	Anything goes.

Another common fault is the unvoicing of voiced consonants.

[maɪ bægɪtʃ]	My baggage.
[ðə dʒʌtʃ sɛt soʊ]	The judge said so.
[hi ɪs hɪɚ]	He is here.
[dəs hi noʊ]	Does he know?
[ɔɚgənaɪseɪʃn]	Organization.
[ðɪs dɔk kʌms hɪɚ]	This dog comes here.
[aɪ hæf tə goʊ hoʊm]	I have to go home.

The unvoiced consonants are sometimes mistakenly voiced.

[lɪbɝdi]	liberty	[lɛdʒɪsledʒɚ]	legislature
[rɛdʒɪzdɚ]	register	[mʌldɪplaɪ]	multiply

Some speakers will consistently substitute one consonant for another. Some of these are foreignisms.

[goʊɪn hoʊm]	Going home.
[wɑt dəz i min]	What does he mean?
[aɪ tɪŋk dæts maɪ bʊk]	I think that's my book.
[doʊz ɚ maɪn]	Those are mine.

Sometimes in careless speech, particularly when the second word starts with a vowel, the consonant at the end of the first word is omitted and used to start the second. Occasionally the result is ludicrous, if the words so joined receive great emphasis. This is a frequently used comedy device on radio and television.

[ɪt wə zɔfəl]	It was awful.
[aɪ hævə naɪdɪə fɚ ə nʌðɚ pleɪ]	I have an idea for another play.
[aɪm nɑ tɪntrəstəd ə tɔl]	I'm not interested at all.
[aɪ wʌnt sə maɪs]	I want some ice.
[wi wə leɪm tə pliz]	We will aim to please.
[hi ɪzn teɪbl tə goʊ]	He isn't able to go.
[aɪ nid sə mɛɚ]	I need some air.

You hear such phrases every day in the speech around you. As you begin to listen to faulty production, you will formulate your judgment as to when and where such speech is acceptable. There are times when careless speech will produce an unfavorable effect upon your listeners.

Specific classifications of errors are known as *articulatory defects*. For instance, any speaker who produces the sibilants [s], [z], [ʃ], and [ʒ] in an atypical way, so that the sounds call attention to themselves, is called a *lisper*. Those who cannot move the tongue tip with accuracy and agility in such sounds as [r], [l], and sometimes [t], [d], and [n], are said to have a *lalling* defect. The classification of *foreign accent* refers, of course, to distortions and substitutions of consonants and vowels, but also includes a rhythm pattern distinctly different from General American speech.

Some speakers will make all the plosives with great pressure and the fricatives with such small openings that the friction sound is obvious. For some personal reason, these tense speakers, with their staccato, barking speech, are overarticulating. You cannot listen to them with any feeling of ease. According to our definitions, this articulation is faulty, even though each sound is made "correctly."

If listeners have difficulty understanding you, you may have a habit of muffling your articulation. This is probably due to the muscular tension which results in inadequate movement of the oral articulators. This habit may have been brought about by extreme self-consciousness or a desire to hide some physical difference, such as protruding teeth or thick lips. Both articulation and voice quality are affected in muffled speech, since the tense lips and tight jaw distort sounds and the small mouth opening masks the tone. Practice for a larger mouth opening and a more relaxed jaw, coupled with resonance exercises, may help to break the habit.

Listening and Self-analysis

1. In listening to a public lecture or a speech on the radio or television, or in unobtrusive eavesdropping in a restaurant or bus, try to analyze the articulation of many varied speakers. Is their production of sounds careless, precise, muffled, or adequately clear? Can you analyze with some accuracy the ways in which these people combine sounds in meaningful speech? Write out some of their statements phonetically. How does their articulation differ from your own?

2. Listen to records made by actors and professional readers, and to recordings taken of political speakers. Note specific ways in which their articulation differs from yours.

3. Again listen to your original recording; check the accuracy of the consonants; note good or poor blending and assimilation; pick out any signs of carelessness.

4. After you have made your final recording, compare the clarity of articulation with that of the first record.

Exercises for Improvement

1. Read the following passage aloud to a classmate; record it if possible; listen while he reads it to you. Mark on the passage in phonetics the words which are pronounced inaccurately and which you and your classmate pronounce differently. Note, also, any sounds which are produced in a faulty manner, are slurred, or spoken with exaggerated precision. Check assimilation and blending.

Speak the speech, I pray you, as I pronounced it to you,—trippingly on the tongue; but if you mouth it, as many of your players do, I had as lief the town-crier spoke my lines. Nor do not saw the air too much with your hand, thus; but use all gently: for in the very torrent, tempest, and, as I may say, whirlwind of your passion, you must acquire and beget a temperance, that may give it smoothness. O! it offends me to the soul to hear a robustious periwig-pated fellow tear a passion to tatters, to very rags, to split the ears of the groundlings, who, for the most part, are capable of nothing but inexplicable dumb-shows and noise; I would have such a fellow whipped for o'er-doing Termagant; it out-Herods Herod; pray you, avoid it.

Be not too tame neither, but let your own discretion be your tutor: suit the action to the word, the word to the action; with this special observance, that you o'erstep not the modesty of nature; for anything so overdone is from the purpose of playing, whose end, both at the first and now, was and is, to hold, as 'twere, the mirror up to nature; to show virtue her own feature, scorn her own image, and the very age and body of the time his form and pressure. Now, this overdone, or come tardy off, though it make the unskilful laugh, cannot but make the judicious grieve; the censure of the which one must in your allowance o'erweigh a whole theater of others. O! there be players that I have seen play, and heard others praise, and that highly, not to speak it profanely, that, having neither the accent of Christians nor the gait of Christian, pagan, nor man, have so strutted and bellowed, that I have thought some of nature's journeymen had made men, and not made them well,—they imitated humanity so abominably.
—SHAKESPEARE

2. If you have specific articulatory faults, read again the material in Chapters 7 and 8 describing the sounds on which you have difficulty. Make lists of words and phrases containing these sounds in various combinations. Use them in conversational sentences in practice. Try also to introduce them into casual conversation with your friends.

3. Prepare a selection from the Appendix. Be sure that the sounds are accurate and correctly blended and assimilated. Do your classmates and the instructor think that your articulation has improved? The following selections are especially good for this exercise: Numbers 2, 8, 11, 19, and 29.

SUMMARY

A definition of good articulation must include reference to both accuracy of production of sounds and smooth blending of the consonants into a continuous flow of speech. The concept of uniformity of production of consonants, either in the speech of one person or from one speaker to another, is misleading. What is usually thought of as a single consonant will vary in its position, voicing, and duration under the influence of other consonants within the phrase, of the variations in stress, and, of course, with the different articulatory structures of different speakers. But if the consonant is readily recognizable and does not differ enough from the average to call attention to itself, it can be considered accurate.

Consonants differ from vowels in that the breath stream is blocked, narrowed, or diverted through the nose rather than flowing through the wide-open mouth. Also, all vowels are voiced, while consonants are both voiced and voiceless. All vowels are nonnasal, while three consonants exit through the nose. Finally, for several consonants the mechanism glides through a position, or blocks and moves rather than holding steady in it.

Consonants may be classified according to their acoustic quality and the method of formation. For nasals, the opening through the oral cavity is blocked, and the vocalized breath stream passes through the nose. A plosive is characterized by an oral block, the building up of air pressure behind the blockade, and the sudden and explosive release of the air. For fricatives, the breath stream is made to flow through a narrowed oral opening and friction sound results. Glides are characterized by movement through a position and, as semivowels, are similar to vowels in their openness and their resonance characteristics. The consonants can also be described in terms of the articulators used and their positions in the formation of the sound.

When sounds are combined into words in running oral context, each may affect the production of neighboring sounds. Thus the smooth, steady movement of the articulators can be maintained by simplifying the transition between sounds by means of blending and assimilation. If sounds occurring together are alike in their place of production, the movement for only one is made. If they are similar in acoustic effect, there is no break between the sounds. Often, while producing sounds made in different parts of the mouth, the mechanism starts the production of the second even as the first is being made. One sound can also change the production of another to make the two more similar. These processes aid smooth transition.

When assimilation or modification of sounds is extreme, so that consonants are omitted or slurred or one is substituted for another, careless and faulty articulation will tend to interfere with the speaker's communication. The goal in practicing to attain good articulation is not pedantic preciseness, but the use of sounds which can be easily understood and which fit smoothly into the pattern of communicative speech. Accuracy or clearness of articulation should be suited to the needs of the present speaking situation, and thus may vary. The immediate understanding of the language symbols by the listener is the basis of judgment of articulation.

9

Integrating the Vocal Skills

You will find poetry nowhere, unless you bring some with you.—
JOUBERT

For any activity, the whole is greater than the sum of its parts. Merely putting the parts together is not enough. There must also be an intent and desire to achieve, if the whole activity is to be successfully performed.

The novice pole vaulter is fortunate if his first attempt results in a nine- or ten-foot jump. No matter how hard he tries or how much he wants to go higher, his ceiling is ten feet. Then the track coach begins to analyze the vaulter's form. The coach shows him a better way to hold the pole, the proper distance at which to start his run, the best method to use in taking off from the ground, and the way to handle his body and thrust it over the bar. The vaulter practices and experiments with these vaulting skills and finally works them together so that he goes over the bar set at thirteen feet. The vaulter can achieve this height only if he has the drive to succeed. But this alone is not enough; he must integrate the separate skills into a coordinated whole as well. If he achieves near-perfect coordination, and has speed and strength as well, he may attain the select company of fifteen-foot vaulters.

In like manner, technical skills alone do not create a responsive voice. Only when the vocal skills are integrated and motivated by your intense desire to communicate and to infuse others with your emotions can you produce truly effective and communicative vocalization.

THE SKILLS

In previous chapters, you have learned about the skills which you have available for integration. They are the results of the purely physical activities of the vocal mechanism. In Chapter 3, two basic skills were discussed, those of loudness and of timing. The relationship between proper breathing and loudness was developed as well as the way in which breathing influences timing, including rate, duration, and pause. The basic concepts of pitch level involved in habitual pitch, optimum pitch, and key, and also the skills concerned with pitch variation for melody, including inflection and step, were presented in Chapter 4. In Chapter 5, with the consideration of resonance and quality, the skills in the establishment of acceptable quality and the change of quality to communicate meaning were explained. Finally, you have studied ways of articulating sounds accurately, clearly, and smoothly so that your intent may be easily understood by your listeners. These skills are the tools with which you must work to communicate ideas. If they are not clear to you, refer back to those sections of the book in which they are defined.

In discussing each of these skills, we have stressed the need for an alert and responsive body. We have noted that nothing of significance happens to the voice unless the various changes are based on controlled energy motivated by an earnest desire to communicate ideas to your listeners. To be sure, all vocal changes depend upon the muscular manipulation of the structures used in breathing, phonation, resonation, and articulation. Yet once you are using these structures skillfully, you achieve variations in timing, loudness, melody, quality, and articulation not so much by planning muscular movements as by responding emotionally and physically to the idea and feeling you wish to express. Under the stimulation of this response, *integration* of the vocal skills is achieved.

HOW MEANING IS ACHIEVED BY INTEGRATION

Complete integration occurs only on the level of automatic response. Yet the learner must pass through intermediate stages. So far you have been working with isolated skills: timing, melody, loudness, quality, and articulation. Your ultimate aim is to reach a level of competence at which you can forget the individual elements and concentrate on the idea to be communicated. Integration does not mean that these skills are no longer needed, but that you use them automatically to achieve your purpose in speaking. The primary skills are still the basic elements of vocal expression. They are to speaking what the primary colors are to painting. Even as the painter mixes and blends his colors to suit his expressive intention, just so must the speaker mix and blend—integrate—the various aspects of melody, timing, loudness, quality, and articulation to suit his expressive intention and to meet the intellectual and emotional demands of his material.

In order to achieve full integration, three requirements must be met:

1. You must know what the primary skills are, and have an alert and responsive body able to use them effectively. The cultivation of this first essential has occupied most of your attention so far in this course.

2. You must have a thorough understanding of the meaning and emotional values inherent in what you speak or read, and of the vocal changes most likely to express these values.

3. You must learn to make a fresh response to your material each time you speak or read, no matter how many times you may have been over it, so that your ultimate presentation is not a mechanical mixture of the expressive elements, but a new and vital experience you are sharing with your hearers. The attainment of the second and third of these requirements is the main concern of this chapter.

Analyzing Your Material

In order that you may work on the integration of the vocal skills and analyze your capabilities, the following section includes two types of analysis. The first provides for a thorough understanding of the ideas in the material to be read. The second provides for discovery of the ways in which you can use the skills to express those ideas. The selection which follows, from the Declaration of Independence, is excellent material for analysis. Read it through silently as many times as is necessary to understand the author's purpose, the central idea, the chain of reasoning, and the supporting arguments. Be sure that you know exactly what Jefferson is saying. Answers to the following questions may help you to understand.

1. When did he say it?
2. Why did he say it?
3. Under what circumstances did he say it?
4. To whom did he say it?
5. How was it received and what was its influence?

We hold these truths to be self-evident, that all men are created equal, that they are endowed by their Creator with certain unalienable Rights, that among these are Life, Liberty and the pursuit of Happiness. That to secure these rights, Governments are instituted among Men, deriving their just powers from the consent of the governed. That whenever any Form of Government becomes destructive of these ends, it is the Right

of the People to alter or to abolish it, and to institute new Government, laying its foundation on such principles and organizing its powers in such form, as to them shall seem most likely to effect their Safety and Happiness. Prudence, indeed, will dictate that Governments long established should not be changed for light and transient causes; and accordingly all experience hath shown, that mankind are more disposed to suffer, while evils are sufferable, than to right themselves by abolishing the forms to which they are accustomed. But when a long train of abuses and usurpations, pursuing invariably the same Object, evinces a design to reduce them under absolute Despotism, it is their right, it is their duty, to throw off such Government, and to provide new Guards for their future security.
—JEFFERSON

Your first problem in preparation for reading aloud is to determine the phrasing based on your analysis of meaning.
  1. Which words go together to form the meaning groups?
  2. Where shall the pauses come to separate those groups?
  3. Will the pauses all be of equal length, or will they differ?
Mark what you consider to be the proper phrasing. Then read the passage aloud. Does it sound right? Is the general meaning clear? Can it be read easily in terms of breathing, with loudness sufficient for the classroom audience? If your answer to any of these questions is "no," then restudy the phrasing.

You must determine the relative value of the various word groups in terms of the total idea. Answer these questions to assist you in this.
  1. Which phrases are the most important and must be pointed up if you are to transmit the idea?
  2. Which phrases are relatively unimportant?
  3. Which phrases relate most closely to which other phrases; stand parallel to them; are in contrast to them?
How are you going to show the values of the phrases and their relationships? You have all of the vocal tools for this purpose. Will you give emphasis to the most important phrases by increased loudness, greater energy, change in rate, the use of pause, pitch change, quality change, or combinations of these? Will you emphasize all of the important phrases in the same way? What skills will you use to show the relation of parallel or contrasting phrases?

Read the selection aloud again, using the phrasing you have determined, and try the skills on the various phrases to indicate the relative values and relationships. Are the values and relationships clear? Get someone else to listen to you and help judge this. If you are not communicating what you wish, try other ways of doing it. Do not be satisfied with the first pattern you hit upon, unless you are sure that it is the best one.

If each phrasal unit is to be clear, then the meaning and relation of the words in that phrase must be clear. Select a phrase such as, "that they are endowed by their Creator with certain unalienable Rights. . . ."

1. Which words communicate the major share of the meaning?

2. Which ones can be subordinated without losing meaning?

3. Which words connect most closely with others; contrast with them; echo them?

The same vocal tools you used for the phrases may now be employed to emphasize words and to show their relationships to each other. Put these skills to work in this phrase. Read it aloud. Are the meanings and relationships made clear by the methods used? Are there alternative methods? Try them, and select the most effective ones. Start at the beginning of the paragraph and do the same thing with each phrase. Finally, read the whole selection aloud and judge whether the phrasing is logical and whether phrase and word values and relationships are entirely clear.

Beyond these obvious elements of meaning, there are still more subtle ones for you to communicate.

1. What is the general emotional mood of the selection?

2. What emotional changes are there from word to word, from phrase to phrase?

You have probably worked out the denotative meanings of the words. Now, what associations do they have? What are their connotations? Does the word "equal" have merely the dictionary meaning of "exactly the same"? As it is used here, both in the phrase in which it occurs and as a part of the entire passage, does "equal" have connotations which are much broader than those of the dictionary definition? Many of the words in the selection will have very broad connotations if you stop to think about them. You must hold these broad meanings in mind as you read aloud, if there are to be quality and other changes in vocalization.

Even though you use all of the foregoing elements well, you may seriously impair the meaning and emotional impact of a passage by bad articulation. Suppose you read the last sentence of the passage from the Declaration of Independence this way:

[bət wɪn ə lɒŋ treɪn əv əbjusəz n juzɚˈpeɪʃnz/pɚsuən ənvɛɚəbɪ də seɪm
ɑbʒək/əvɪnsəz ə dəzaɪn tə rədus θm ʌndɚ æbslut dɛsptɪzm/ət ɪz ðɚ raɪt/ət

ɪz ðɚ dutɪ/tə θroʊ ɔf sɪtʃ gʌvmənt n tə prəvaɪd nu gɑɚdz fɚ ðɚ fjutʃɚ
səkjɝtɪ]

As you read this, note what effect your articulation has on the communication of meaning. Are you able to use elements of timing and melody as
effectively as when you articulate with greater accuracy and clearness?
What does weak articulation do to the quality of your tone? On the other
hand, if you read this passage with each word separated and no blending of
sounds, would you not also impair the meaning?

Integrating the Skills

Your task now is to convey to your listeners the ideas and feelings you
have discovered in your analysis. You need to respond not only to the bare
denotations of words and phrases, but to the mood, emotional changes, and
word connotations as well. All the skills contribute in various ways to this
end. When your analysis is complete, read the selection aloud, observing
your response to the idea. If possible, record the passage, using the skills
you have selected as being most appropriate. If on listening to the record
you feel your interpretation is inadequate, read the selection again with
vocal changes which seem to be more communicative. Repeat the process
until you are satisfied.

When you have completed a detailed analysis of this kind, you are likely
to have one of two problems to solve. Because your preparation has of necessity been somewhat mechanistic, you may find it difficult to read the selection to others without labored emphasis on the vocal changes you planned.
On the other hand, you may discover that you are unwilling or unable to
break old habit patterns in a public performance; instead of employing the
variations in melody, timing, or quality which you worked out in practice,
you may freeze up and revert to more familiar but less expressive methods
of speaking. At first glance these problems may appear to be diametrically
opposed to one another, but they have a common root—failure to respond
fully at the moment of utterance to the idea you are trying to communicate.
If what you say does not stimulate you, there is little likelihood that either
your habitual pattern or the one you worked out in practice will be convincing. Here are some suggestions which may help you make a fresh response to your material when you present it to your audience.

1. Before you begin to speak, assume the physical attitudes appropriate
to the general mood of the selection. For example, if you wish to read
Charles Sumner's "The Crime against Kansas" (Appendix, Number 19), you
need to assume the muscular tensions characteristic of angry denunciation.

This, of course, does not require flailing fists, but it does involve an alertness capable of such action, and facial expression suited to the mood. Similarly, to read "Life on the Mississippi" (Appendix, Number 22), you need the eager and friendly communicativeness of a small boy; to read the passage from "Two Years before the Mast" (Appendix, Number 21), you require calm, relaxed, and reflective attitudes; and so on. The degree to which you can assume the physical state which characterizes the dominant mood of your material is an index of your emotional responsiveness, and will have great influence on the freshness and vitality of your speaking.

2. Respond actively to sensory words as you say them. Use pauses to activate such responses, and duration to accentuate them. *Taste* Mark Twain's "mighty porterhouse steak" while you are saying the words (see page 51). *Hear* the pounding surf as you declare, "Roll on, thou deep and dark blue Ocean" (Appendix, Number 12). *See* the desolation you describe as you read "Ozymandias" (Appendix, Number 5). *Feel* the prickling discomfort of the insomniac in "The Night Has Been Long" (Appendix, Number 8). As you create these sensory impressions in yourself, you will find it much easier to use timing, melody, or quality effectively to convey your feelings to others. And as your skill grows, you will be able to respond to subtler meanings in the language you speak.

3. If you find it difficult to select the right pattern of time or melody for a particular idea, paraphrase the language. Instead of saying with Shakespeare (Appendix, Number 7), "When in disgrace with fortune and men's eyes/I all alone beweep my outcast state," say, "When people don't like me, I feel sorry for myself." Speak the informal words with earnest conviction. Listen to the melody and time pattern, and try to use a similar pattern for the more formal language. Try several such word changes until you can speak the author's words with conviction.

4. When you read or speak to others, show your interest in them. Consider it important that they share your ideas. Forget yourself and the strangeness of your position before a group and concentrate on securing a response from your listeners. The more genuine your wish to communicate with your audience, the easier it is to use your voice expressively.

PUTTING INTEGRATION TO WORK IN COMMUNICATION

Throughout the term, you have been analyzing and acquiring skills in the use of your voice. In this chapter we have suggested that effective communication demands the integration of these skills in response to ideas and feelings. We have seen how analysis of your material can be combined with emotional and physical responsiveness to make ideas meaningful as you voice them.

Before you begin the preparation of your final speaking assignment, we suggest that you review all of the self-analysis and listening suggestions made earlier in the book. How do you and your classmates measure up to the suggestions given in Chapter 3 for good breathing habits and effective use of rate, duration, pause, phrasing, and loudness? Are you relatively free from phonation faults described in Chapter 4? Do you use modifications in key, inflection, and step appropriately and effectively to express your meanings and moods? Do you resonate sounds through open passages, as recommended in Chapter 5, with a tone free from resonation faults such as nasality and stridency? Do your quality changes reflect your various attitudes and ideas? Have you learned to articulate clearly and accurately, but without pedantry, as outlined in Chapters 6, 7, and 8? In short, have you and your classmates mastered the elements of good voice usage?

But more important, can you now integrate these skills into a meaningful pattern of communication? Test yourself and your classmates in the exercises which follow.

Listening

1. Listen to the casual conversation of your friends. Are they communicating their ideas effectively? If so, what vocal skills are they using? Do they use and integrate all of the skills? What faults can you discover in the use of the individual skills and their integration?

2. Listen critically to the performances of your classmates. Does their vocalization suggest a complete grasp of the ideas they are speaking? Do you understand the total idea without difficulty? Is the phrasing clear? Are the meanings and the relation of phrases and of words made explicit? Are the emotional elements and connotative values brought out? Does the total effect concentrate your attention on the idea, or do the techniques employed draw undue attention to themselves?

Self-analysis

1. The analysis of the selection from the Declaration of Independence was, in reality, an exercise in self-analysis. Take another selection with a different type of idea, such as a story or a lyric poem, and follow through the same type of analysis. Answer the questions given in the original exercise.

2. Record the selection you use in the exercise above. Listen critically as you play it back. Is the meaning clear? If not, experiment with different ways of integrating the vocal skills and record again. Get a friend to listen and criticize.

3. Do you hear in your own voice the faults which your instructor and classmates report?

Exercises for Self-improvement

1. The following selections are to be analyzed and practiced in the same way as was the selection from the Declaration of Independence.

a. COLLEGE DORMITORIES

Students reside in fraternities, in sororities, in student cooperatives, in college-owned dormitories, in boardinghouses, in apartments and in homes with their own families. Of all these places of residence by far the most desirable is the college dormitory. . . . Like the houses of fraternities and sororities, it enables the student to live with other students, to eat with them, to discuss with them, to play with them. The solitary student is a pathetic figure; almost invariably, he has but the most meager resources. He lives in a room by himself, often prepares his own frugal breakfast, eats one meal—and that a cheap one—at some more than modest restaurant, cafeteria, or "beanery"; if there is a third meal, it may well consist of a cup of coffee and a piece of bread. He can't afford to participate in student activities or go to the theater or to concerts. He lives a most unfortunate life, often a most unhappy one. He lacks human contacts, may easily brood over some fancied injustice, and even decide that life is not worth living. If he survives at all, he will not by any means be equipped for human society; the chances are against his success as teacher, lawyer, or businessman. At the opposite pole the fraternity stresses that which to be sure is a part of college life; but it overstresses it. The social side comes first. . . .

The dormitory furnishes association with other students without making the social aspect of first importance. Its members constitute a cross section of the student body, and no discrimination should ever enter into a college-controlled dormitory. There is no "eternal" tie binding its members, but the group is large enough to permit each member to find kindred spirits and form lasting friendships. It promotes the democratic ideals which should animate the college. It places first things first—scholarship, for one—but does not neglect the social ties which are important to every human being.—DEUTSCH *

b. NATURE

As a fond mother, when the day is o'er
 Leads by the hand her little child to bed,
 Half willing, half reluctant to be led,
And leave his broken playthings on the floor,
Still gazing at them through the open door,
 Nor wholly reassured and comforted
 By promises of others in their stead,
Which, though more splendid, may not please him more;
So Nature deals with us, and takes away
 Our playthings one by one, and by the hand
  Leads us to rest so gently, that we go
Scarce knowing if we wish to go or stay,
 Being too full of sleep to understand
  How far the unknown transcends the what we know.
         —LONGFELLOW

c. LA GRANDE BRETÊCHE

On the banks of the Loire stands an old brown house, crowned with very high roofs, and so completely isolated that there is nothing near it, not even a fetid tannery or a squalid tavern, such as are commonly seen outside small towns. In front of this house is a garden down to the river, where the box shrubs, formerly clipped close to the walks, now straggle at their own will. A few willows, rooted in the stream, have grown up quickly like an enclosing fence, and half hide the house. The wild plants we call weeds have clothed the bank with their beautiful luxuriance. The fruit-trees, neglected for these ten years past, no longer bear a crop, and their suckers have formed a thicket. The paths, once gravelled, are overgrown with purslane; but, to be accurate, there is no trace of path.—BALZAC

* Monroe E. Deutsch, *The College from Within*, University of California Press, Berkeley, 1952, pp. 115–116. (By permission.)

d. SMELLS

Why is it that the poets tell
So little of the sense of smell?
These are the odors I love well:

The smell of coffee freshly ground;
Or rich plum pudding, holly crowned;
Or onions fried and deeply browned.

The fragrance of a fumy pipe;
The smell of apples, newly ripe;
And printers' ink on leaden type.

Woods by moonlight in September
Breathe most sweet; and I remember
Many a smoky camp-fire ember.

Camphor, turpentine, and tea
The balsam of a Christmas tree,
These are whiffs of gramarye . . .
A ship smells best of all to me.
      —MORLEY *

e. FAREWELL, A LONG FAREWELL

Farewell, a long farewell, to all my greatness!
This is the state of man: To-day he puts forth
The tender leaves of hope, to-morrow blossoms,
And bears his blushing honors thick upon him:
The third day comes a frost, a killing frost;
And—when he thinks, good easy man, full surely
His greatness is a ripening—nips his root;
And then he falls as I do. I have ventured,—
Like little wanton boys that swim on bladders,—
This many summers, in a sea of glory,
But far beyond my depth: my high-blown pride
At length broke under me, and now has left me
Weary and old with service, to the mercy
Of a rude stream that must forever hide me.
      —SHAKESPEARE

* Christopher Morley, *Chimney Smoke*, Doubleday, Doran & Company, Inc., New York, 1929, p. 71. (By permission.)

f. EDUCATION

By the "mud-sill" theory it is assumed that labor and education are incompatible, and any practical combination of them impossible. According to that theory, a blind horse upon a treadmill is a perfect illustration of what a laborer should be—all the better for being blind, that he may not kick understandingly. According to that theory, the education of laborers is not only useless but pernicious and dangerous. In fact, it is, in some sort, deemed a misfortune that laborers should have heads at all. Those same heads are regarded as explosive materials, only to be safely kept in damp places, as far as possible from that peculiar sort of fire which ignites them. A Yankee who could invent a strong-handed man without a head would receive the everlasting gratitude of the "mud-sill" advocates.

But free labor says, "No." Every head should be cultivated and improved by whatever will add to its capacity for performing its charge. In one word, free labor insists on universal education.—LINCOLN

g. WISDOM

But where shall wisdom be found? and where is the place of understanding?

Man knoweth not the price thereof; neither is it found in the land of the living.

The depth saith, It is not in me: and the sea saith, It is not with me.

It cannot be gotten for gold, neither shall silver be weighed for the price thereof.

It cannot be valued with the gold of Ophir, with the precious onyx, or the sapphire.

The gold and the crystal cannot equal it: and the exchange of it shall not be for jewels of fine gold.

No mention shall be made of coral, or of pearls: for the price of wisdom is above rubies.

The topaz of Ethiopia shall not equal it, neither shall it be valued with pure gold.

Whence then cometh wisdom? and where is the place of understanding?

—JOB 28: 12–20

2. When you started this course, you were instructed to make a recording of your voice. From time to time you have been asked to listen to this record

and to analyze it to determine what problems you have had and what skills you could use more effectively. You should now make a new recording, using the same reading materials and a similar informal talk or interview.

3. As a final test of your skill in using your voice for effective communication, prepare a seven- to ten-minute talk. Approximately one-half of this talk should be spoken extemporaneously, and the other half should be read. Your goal may be to entertain, to stimulate, to inform, or to persuade your hearers, but both speaking and reading portions must be interesting, lively, and communicative. Regardless of your subject or method of development, integrate your use of vocal skills by careful analysis of material and full emotional and physical responsiveness. Here are several plans for such a final speech.

a. Explain some of the factors in the life of an author which made him write as he did. Illustrate by reading selections from his works.
b. Discuss with the class your point of view on a public issue, or your philosophy of life. Read short, well-written passages from a number of writers illustrating this point of view.
c. Discuss a light, entertaining theme, and illustrate it with poetry or prose by good writers.
d. Make any other combination of extemporaneous speaking and reading which maintains unity throughout both sections of your speech.

4. You may find it helpful in listening to final speeches by your classmates to prepare a criticism chart based on the directions for listening and self-analysis throughout the book. Making such a chart will also serve as a review of the entire book. Record your reactions to each speech on the chart. Then make an over-all evaluation of the speaker's effectiveness. Has he improved? What does he still need to achieve? How well has he integrated the positive skills he possesses?

AFTER THIS CLASS

Even though you have made substantial progress in improving your speech during the past few months, you will not retain your new habits unless you really wish to. You will recall that in Chapter 2 we pointed out how environmental and emotional factors have influenced your habits of speech. Of course these influences did not stop when you enrolled in this course. Perhaps even while you have been trying to improve your voice some of these factors have been preventing or aiding you in developing skills.

At any rate, in the future you may be confronted by conditions which may tend to upset the new habits you have acquired. Perhaps you will face an emotional crisis which will disturb the quality of your voice. Or you may be thrown temporarily into an environment in which good articulation is of little value for social prestige. If you want to retain good speech habits, you must recognize these stumbling blocks and guard against them.

Your continued improvement is now *your* responsibility. The learning of new techniques under the stimulation of group work in a class may not ensure permanent improvement, even under favorable conditions. Since one semester is not sufficient time to fix new habits, we suggest that you continue to give conscious attention to your voice.

1. Listen frequently to the varied aspects of vocal production and articulation of your friends, your family, your professors, and the professional speakers whom you hear in the movies and on radio and television.

2. Listen to yourself in daily speaking situations in your classes. If you give oral reports, participate in discussion, or read aloud in other classes, these situations will present opportunities for you to judge the effectiveness of your speech.

3. Recall frequently the criticisms of your classmates and instructor. These once helped you to establish goals of improvement; do they continue to operate as motivating forces?

4. Read aloud to yourself occasionally. Do you sound interesting? Can you still vary timing, melody, and quality for fine shades in meaning?

5. Try consciously to bring in the new habits of vocal skills and clear articulation as you argue, discuss, question, and describe in daily conversation.

Eventually, the skills you have sought to establish will no longer have to be practiced consciously but will be used automatically.

Other courses will help you in your plans for continued improvement. Perhaps you will enroll in a class in public speaking, oral interpretation, radio speaking, or acting. The need for continued practice in vocal skill in any of these courses is obvious.

In psychology courses, consider the relationship between voice and personality. If you are training to become a teacher, study the influence of good and bad speech upon teaching procedures. When you read literature, notice how often stylistic devices are better understood when the passage is read aloud. In studying foreign languages, notice how your ability to reproduce alien sounds is aided by your understanding of the nature of the articulatory mechanism.

You will forget much of the technical material in this book. It was presented to you only to provide a sound basis for your improvement. What we hope you will not lose is your critical ability and your belief that speech skills are a strong personal asset to you, both socially and professionally.

Perhaps our objectives will be reached in a measure when someone says to you, "You talk a little differently than you used to. I think you sound more sure of yourself—as if you enjoyed speaking—as if you were confident that you're good at it. What have you been doing?" Then you will realize with some satisfaction that your endeavor to improve your speech is beginning to take effect.

APPENDIX

Selections for Practice

HOW TO USE READING SELECTIONS

The reading selections presented here are an integral part of the text. Although they are given apart from the main body of information and exercises, they are meaningful only if interpreted in terms of the concepts given earlier. For that reason, throughout the body of the book you have been referred to specific selections in this appendix to help you in learning particular skills. Of course, the authors of these selections did not intend to have them used in this way, and in reading them you cannot treat them as abstract exercises without any relationship to the context and original intent of the author. We have selected them for this book because we believe that without adequate control of the particular skills to which we have related them, you cannot give the selections the meaning and emotional expression which the authors intended. If you understand these skills and know how to use them, you can call them into play in support of the meanings and feelings which the authors had in mind. Yet, unless you react to those meanings and emotions, your manipulation of the mechanical elements will give a mechanical result.

Moreover, it is not the sole purpose of this course to train you as a good reader. You should also learn to transfer all of the skills of good voice usage to informal speech and to platform speaking. Particularly in the prose selections, therefore, you should identify yourself with the concepts and the type of motivation out of which the author derived his idea and language. You should create from your own experience a pattern of thought and feeling which will make his words vital to you. In this way you will hasten the transition to the informal and extempore speaking situations.

In order to help you correlate the intent of the author with the skills you wish to learn, each selection has been furnished with a brief introduction in which are noted the special meanings and feelings to be observed and the special skills of voice usage which can be practiced in bringing out these factors.

READING SELECTIONS

1. DOVER BEACH

The setting of this poem is the coast of England, at night, looking toward the French coast, but it might be anywhere—a pier on Chicago's north shore, Catalina Island, Long Island looking toward the Connecticut shore, the beach at Biloxi. You should visualize your own setting, and try to think the ageless philosophy and emotions which the author intended.

The mood of the poem is particularly well adapted to the use of a deliberate rate, with many long sounds, although one or two places suggest a definite change of pace. The last stanza needs a quality change to indicate the shift from the reflective concepts to the warmth of personal emotions. A modification of the resonance traits of the voice is needed to reflect this change.

> The sea is calm to-night.
> The tide is full, the moon lies fair
> Upon the straits;—on the French coast the light
> Gleams and is gone; the cliffs of England stand,
> Glimmering and vast, out in the tranquil bay.
> Come to the window, sweet is the night-air!
> Only, from the long line of spray
> Where the sea meets the moon-blanch'd sand,
> Listen! you hear the grating roar
> Of pebbles which the waves draw back, and fling,
> At their return, up the high strand,
> Begin, and cease; and then again begin,
> With tremulous cadence slow; and bring
> The eternal note of sadness in.
>
> Sophocles, long ago,
> Heard it on the Aegean, and it brought
> Into his mind the turbid ebb and flow
> Of human misery; we
> Find also in the sound a thought,
> Hearing it by this distant northern sea.

The Sea of Faith
Was once, too, at the full, and round earth's shore
Lay like the folds of a bright girdle furl'd;
But now I only hear
Its melancholy, long, withdrawing roar,
Retreating, to the breath
Of the night-wind, down the vast edges drear
And naked shingles of the world.

Ah, love, let us be true
To one another! for the world, which seems
To lie before us like a land of dreams,
So various, so beautiful, so new,
Hath really neither joy, nor love, nor light,
Nor certitude, nor peace, nor help for pain;
And we are here as on a darkling plain,
Swept with confused alarms of struggle and flight,
Where ignorant armies clash by night.

—MATTHEW ARNOLD

2. BEAT! BEAT! DRUMS!

This poem was written during the Civil War, but like any powerful piece of writing it applies equally to any war crisis of any people or nation. Ask your family and older friends how they felt on the afternoon of December 7, 1941, when they first knew the United States was at war. Can you re-create this feeling in the passionately ironic language of Whitman's poem?

You cannot read this selection with the interpretation it demands unless you feel a tremendous surge of energy in your body as you read. The articulation must be sharply defined—almost explosive. The breath stream must be under complete control and driven from strong actions of the abdominal muscles. The strong, vibrant tone needed to reflect the intense feelings of the poem can be secured in this way.

Beat! beat! drums!—blow! bugles! blow!
Through the windows—through the doors—burst like a ruthless force,
Into the solemn church, and scatter the congregation,
Into the school where the scholar is studying;
Leave not the bridegroom quiet—no happiness must he have now with
    his bride,
Nor the peaceful farmer any peace, plowing his field or gathering his grain,
So fierce you whirr and pound you drums—so shrill you bugles blow.

Beat! beat! drums!—blow! bugles! blow!
Over the traffic of the cities—over the rumble of the wheels in the streets;
Are beds prepared for sleepers at night in the houses? no sleepers must
    sleep in those beds,
No bargainers' bargains by day—no brokers or speculators—would they
    continue?
Would the talkers be talking? would the singer attempt to sing?
Would the lawyer rise in the court to state his case before the judge?
Then rattle quicker, heavier drums—you bugles wilder blow.

Beat! beat! drums!—blow! bugles! blow!
Make no parley—stop for no expostulation,
Mind not the timid—mind not the weeper or prayer,
Mind not the old man beseeching the young man,
Let not the child's voice be heard, nor the mother's entreaties,
Make even the trestles to shake the dead where they lie awaiting the hearses,
So strong you thump, O terrible drums—so loud you bugles blow.

                        —WALT WHITMAN

3. I HEAR AMERICA SINGING

    As the title suggests, this selection is buoyant and joyous in mood. The melody and time changes which it evokes should suggest, but not imitate, those of the songs described in the context.

I hear America singing, the varied carols I hear,
Those mechanics, each one singing his as it should be blithe and strong,
The carpenter singing his as he measures his plank or beam,
The mason singing his as he makes ready for work, or leaves off work,
The boatman singing what belongs to him in his boat, the deckhand singing
    on the steamboat deck,
The shoemaker singing as he sits on his bench, the hatter singing as he stands,
The wood-cutter's song, the playboy's on his way in the morning, or at noon
    intermission or at sundown,
The delicious singing of the mother, or of the young wife at work, or of the
    girl sewing or washing,
Each singing what belongs to him or her and to none else,
The day what belongs to the day—at night the party of young fellows,
    robust, friendly,
Singing with open mouths their strong melodious songs.

                        —WALT WHITMAN

4. THE PASSING OF ARTHUR

This selection records the solemn but hopeful approach to death by a believer in immortality. The rate is slow, with many long sounds. There are no abrupt melody changes, although the melody is not monotonous.

> And slowly answer'd Arthur from the barge:
> "The old order changeth, yielding place to new,
> And God fulfils Himself in many ways,
> Lest one good custom should corrupt the world.
> Comfort thyself: what comfort is in me?
> I have lived my life, and that which I have done
> May He within Himself make pure! but thou,
> If thou shouldst never see my face again,
> Pray for my soul. More things are wrought by prayer
> Than this world dreams of. Wherefore, let thy voice
> Rise like a fountain for me night and day.
> For what are men better than sheep or goats
> That nourish a blind life within the brain,
> If, knowing God, they lift not hands of prayer
> Both for themselves and those who call them friend?
> For so the whole round earth is every way
> Bound by gold chains about the feet of God.
> But now farewell. I am going a long way
> With these thou seest—if indeed I go—
> (For all my mind is clouded with a doubt)
> To the island-valley of Avilion;
> Where falls not hail, or rain, or any snow,
> Nor ever wind blows loudly; but it lies
> Deep-meadow'd, happy, fair with orchard-lawns
> And bowery hollows crown'd with summer sea,
> Where I will heal me of my grievous wound."
>
> —ALFRED TENNYSON

5. Ozymandias of Egypt

The picture suggested by this selection might be set in any of the ancient lands of the Middle East, or in any area where there is a dead and forgotten civilization. But its real message is a warning to contemporary rulers that their days are numbered and their works are soon to be forgotten.

As in most sonnets, a change in rate, melody, and quality is essential to show the change in mood midway in the poem. There are really three moods to interpret— descriptive, boasting, philosophical. Experiment with changes in timing, energy, and quality to bring out these shifts in mood. The entire selection, however, demands a full and resonant tone to convey the vastness of the desert and the scope of a great idea.

> I met a traveller from an antique land
> Who said: "Two vast and trunkless legs of stone
> Stand in the desert. Near them, on the sand,
> Half sunk, a shatter'd visage lies, whose frown,
> And wrinkled lip, and sneer of cold command,
> Tell that its sculptor well those passions read
> Which yet survive, stamp'd on these lifeless things,
> The hand that mock'd them and the heart that fed;
> And on the pedestal these words appear:
> 'My name is Ozymandias, king of kings:
> Look on my works, ye Mighty, and despair!'
> Nothing beside remains. Round the decay
> Of that colossal wreck, boundless and bare
> The lone and level sands stretch far away."
>
> —PERCY BYSSHE SHELLEY

6. Composed upon Westminster Bridge

Look out upon your own city in the early morning on a bright spring day. Get the feeling of peace and strength which Wordsworth reflects in this poem.

This selection adapts itself well to a moderate rate and a quiet strength which comes from firm but not loud tones. Keep the phrases moving; make adequate use of pause and duration to point the ideas. Feel the moods of the poem and reflect them through changes in the quality of your voice.

> Earth has not anything to show more fair:
> Dull would he be of soul who could pass by
> A sight so touching in its majesty:

This City now doth like a garment wear
The beauty of the morning; silent, bare,
Ships, towers, domes, theatres, and temples lie
Open unto the fields, and to the sky;
All bright and glittering in the smokeless air.
Never did sun more beautifully steep
In his first splendour valley, rock, or hill;
Ne'er saw I, never felt, a calm so deep!
The river glideth at his own sweet will:
Dear God! the very houses seem asleep;
And all that mighty heart is lying still!

—WILLIAM WORDSWORTH

7. Sonnet XXIX

As in other sonnets, the mood of this poem changes in the ninth line. Visualize these moods by thinking first of your blackest troubles and then of the satisfying and redeeming qualities of friendship and love.

These concepts may be reflected, in reading, by a change in the pattern of melody and timing in the two parts of the poem. In the first part, the rate may well be moderately slow, varying as the mood changes. In the second part, the rate may increase and the melody be more varied. A quality change may be introduced in the last two lines, along with a new rate and inflectional pattern. Experiment with these elements until you can produce the mood you feel.

When in disgrace with fortune and men's eyes
I all alone beweep my outcast state,
And trouble deaf heaven with my bootless cries,
And look upon myself, and curse my fate,
Wishing me like to one more rich in hope,
Featur'd like him, like him with friends possess'd,
Desiring this man's art, and that man's scope,
With what I most enjoy contented least;
Yet in these thoughts myself almost despising,
Haply I think on thee,—and then my state,
Like to the lark at break of day arising
From sullen earth, sings hymns at Heaven's gate;
For thy sweet love remember'd such wealth brings
That then I scorn to change my state with kings.

—WILLIAM SHAKESPEARE

8. The Night Has Been Long

If you have ever attended a Gilbert and Sullivan opera, you are aware of the fact that there is little depth in the lyrics. They tell a story, but the emotions are purposely shallow, and the music gets most of its interest from changes in tempo. Yet in spite of the fast rate at which many of the lyrics are sung, a good Gilbert and Sullivan singer can always be understood, and never gasps for breath in the wrong place. In this selection, the story is an amusing one, and you should enjoy it as you read, but you need not expect to evoke great emotional response.

The selection should be studied carefully for the most effective places to pause for breath. The rate should be quite fast, with some prolongation of picture words and an occasional slowing down of a phrase, without breaking its rhythm, where you think the humor can be heightened. The articulation must be very precise, but the movement of the phrase must not be broken.

When you're lying awake with a dismal headache, and repose is tabooed
    by anxiety,
I conceive you may use any language you choose to indulge in without
    impropriety,
For your brain is on fire—the bedclothes conspire of usual slumber to
    plunder you:
First your counterpane goes and uncovers your toes, and your sheet slips
    demurely from under you;
Then the blanketing tickles—you feel like mixed pickles, so terribly sharp
    is the pricking;
And you're hot and you're cross, and you tumble and toss till there's nothing
    'twixt you and the ticking;
Then your bedclothes all creep to the floor in a heap, and you pick 'em up
    all in a tangle;
Next your pillow resigns and politely declines to remain at its usual angle.
Well, you get some repose in the form of a doze, with hot eyeballs and
    head ever-aching;
But your slumber teems with such horrible dreams that you'd very much
    better be waking.
You're a regular wreck, with a crick in your neck
And no wonder you snore, for your head's on the door.
And you're needles and pins from your soles to your shins,
And your flesh is a-creep, for your left leg's asleep, . . .
And some fluff in your lung, and a feverish tongue,
And a thirst that's intense, and a general sense
That you haven't been sleeping in clover.

But the darkness has past, and it's daylight at last,
And the night has been long—ditto, ditto, my song—
And thank goodness, they're both of them over!

—W. S. GILBERT

9. ONCE BY THE PACIFIC *

Perhaps more than any other modern poet Robert Frost has written lines which are meant to be spoken. The writing is deceptively artless, retaining the flavor and movement of conversation, while at the same time the images are vivid and compelling. What he sought to achieve in his writing was "the speaking tone of voice somehow entangled in the words."

In this poem, Frost has made an angry ocean storm the symbol of the troubles brewing in the world. Recall the headlines you have read about world unrest, industrial strikes, interracial conflict, or juvenile delinquency. Recall also the last severe storm you have seen. Combine these images in the words of the poet, and respond to the emotions they invoke.

> The shattered water made a misty din.
> Great waves looked over others coming in,
> And thought of doing something to the shore
> That water never did to land before.
> The clouds were low and hairy in the skies,
> Like locks blown forward in the gleam of eyes.
> You could not tell, and yet it looked as if
> The shore was lucky in being backed by cliff,
> The cliff in being backed by continent;
> It looked as if a night of dark intent
> Was coming, and not only a night, an age.
> Someone had better be prepared for rage.
> There would be more than ocean-water broken
> Before God's last *put out the light* was spoken.

—ROBERT FROST

10. SHINE PERISHING REPUBLIC †

You are not likely to catch either the mood or the subtle meanings of this poem in a single reading. Study it carefully, paraphrase parts of it, or supplement its

* Robert Frost, *Complete Poems of Robert Frost*, Henry Holt and Company, Inc., New York, 1949. (By permission.)

† Robinson Jeffers, *Selected Poetry*, Random House, Inc., New York, 1937, p. 168. (By permission.)

generalizations with examples of your own choosing. When you are sure of the meaning, reflect the varying moods of the poem by changes in your time pattern, melody, and vocal quality. Ask your roommate to listen to your reading, and discover whether he understands the intent of the poem as you do. If not, perhaps you should change your method of reading; or perhaps his interpretation of the idea is more accurate than your own. When you are confident of your interpretation, read it to the class.

While this America settles in the mould of its vulgarity, heavily thickening
    to empire,
And protest, only a bubble in the molten mass, pops and sighs out, and the
    mass hardens,

I sadly smiling remember that the flower fades to make fruit, the fruit rots
    to make earth.
Out of the mother; and through the spring exultances, ripeness and deca-
    dence; and home to the mother.

You making haste haste on decay: not blameworthy; life is good, be it stub-
    bornly long or suddenly
A mortal splendor: meteors are not needed less than mountains: shine,
    perishing republic.

But for my children, I would have them keep their distance from the
    thickening center; corruption
Never has been compulsory, when the cities lie at the monster's feet there
    are left the mountains.

And boys, be in nothing so moderate as in the love of man, a clever servant,
    insufferable master.
There is the trap that catches noblest spirits, that caught—they say—God,
    when he walked on earth.

—ROBINSON JEFFERS

11. PSALMS

In these two selections, the psalmist deals with themes of great elevation of thought, drawing his inspiration from the grandeur of nature—the mountains and the stars. In each psalm, picture to yourself the natural setting which inspired the writer, and react as he did to the philosophical implications of the scene.

The primary tools for effective reading of these passages are sustained tone, limited range of melody, relatively slow rate, and frequent use of long duration to point up the important ideas. Careful phrasing for both breath control and meaning is essential.

a. Psalm 121

I will lift up mine eyes unto the hills, from whence cometh my help.
My help cometh from the Lord, which made heaven and earth.
He will not suffer thy foot to be moved: he that keepeth thee will not slumber.
Behold, he that keepeth Israel shall neither slumber nor sleep.
The Lord is thy keeper: the Lord is thy shade upon thy right hand.
The sun shall not smite thee by day, nor the moon by night.
The Lord shall preserve thee from all evil: he shall preserve thy soul.
The Lord shall preserve thy going out and thy coming in from this time forth,
    and even for evermore.

b. Psalm 8

When I consider thy heavens, the work of thy fingers, the moon and the
    stars, which thou hast ordained;
What is man, that thou art mindful of him? and the son of man, that thou
    visitest him?
For thou hast made him a little lower than the angels, and hast crowned
    him with glory and honour.

12. CHILDE HAROLD'S PILGRIMAGE

These four stanzas are selections from a long poem by Byron. The first two stanzas picture the ball given for the officers of the allied forces on the night before the Battle of Waterloo. Try to imagine a gay party where all of the dancers realize that a battle is about to be fought and are half-listening for the opening guns.

The last two stanzas are a rhapsody on nature. One must appreciate the grandeur of nature both on land and at sea to understand fully Byron's feelings in this section.

All four of the stanzas contain phrasing problems to which you must pay attention. The first two stanzas must have energy without excessive volume, and require much variety of melody to depict the scene. In the last line of the first stanza and in the last four lines of the second, there are changes which must be reflected vocally.

The last two stanzas, particularly the fourth, must be read at a slow rate, with much attention to duration. At the same time, you must achieve subdued and sustained power in both stanzas.

a. Canto III

XXI

There was a sound of revelry by night,
And Belgium's capital had gather'd then
Her Beauty and her Chivalry, and bright
The lamps shown o'er fair women and brave men;
A thousand hearts beat happily; and when
Music arose with its voluptuous swell,
Soft eyes look'd love to eyes which spake again,
And all went merry as a marriage bell;
But hush! hark! a deep sound strikes like a rising knell!

XXII

Did ye not hear it?—No; 'twas but the wind,
Or the car rattling o'er the stony street;
On with the dance! let joy be unconfined;
No sleep till morn, when Youth and Pleasure meet
To chase the glowing Hours with flying feet—
But hark!—that heavy sound breaks in once more,
As if the clouds its echo would repeat;
And nearer, clearer, deadlier than before!
Arm! Arm! it is—it is—the cannon's opening roar!

b. Canto IV

CLXXVIII

There is a pleasure in the pathless woods,
There is a rapture on the lonely shore,
There is society, where none intrudes,
By the deep Sea, and music in its roar:
I love not Man the less, but Nature more,
From these our interviews, in which I steal
From all I may be, or have been before,
To mingle with the Universe, and feel
What I can ne'er express, yet cannot all conceal.

CLXXIX

Roll on, thou deep and dark blue Ocean—roll!
Ten thousand fleets sweep over thee in vain;
Man marks the earth with ruin—his control
Stops with the shore; upon the watery plain
The wrecks are all thy deed, nor doth remain
A shadow of man's ravage, save his own,
When, for a moment, like a drop of rain,
He sinks into thy depths with bubbling groan,
Without a grave, unknell'd, uncoffin'd, and unknown.

—LORD BYRON

13. THE LUNATIC, THE LOVER, AND THE POET

In the following lines from Shakespeare's *A Midsummer Night's Dream*, the noble Duke Theseus talks about the powerful influence that imagination has upon our thoughts. With particular reference to the three types of men mentioned, he implies that many of us, carried away by our imaginations, may become the victims of our own fancies. Read the speech with these thoughts in mind.

You will find that this selection lends itself to the development of vocal quality. Try to suggest with your voice the qualities of the ideas and images expressed. Also, pay careful attention to phrasing, pauses, and the changes in melody necessary in order to communicate the intended meaning.

Lovers and madmen have such seething brains,
Such shaping fantasies, that apprehend
More than cool reason ever comprehends.
The lunatic, the lover, and the poet,
Are of imagination all compact:
One sees more devils than vast hell can hold,
That is, the madman; the lover, all as frantic,
Sees Helen's beauty in a brow of Egypt:
The poet's eye, in a fine frenzy rolling,
Doth glance from heaven to earth, from earth to heaven;
And, as imagination bodies forth
The forms of things unknown, the poet's pen
Turns them to shapes, and gives to airy nothing
A local habitation and a name.

Such tricks hath strong imagination,
That, if it would but apprehend some joy,
It comprehends some bringer of that joy;
Or in the night, imagining some fear,
How easy is a bush supposed a bear!

—WILLIAM SHAKESPEARE

14. Marching Along

This selection from Robert Browning's *Cavalier Tunes* is a swaggering marching song sung by loyal supporters of King Charles I. It praises the King and his Cavaliers while contemptuously deriding the Puritans and their leaders.

In reading this aloud, you will find that the swinging rhythm is conducive to freedom of tone. In practicing, be sure that you observe the phrasal pauses and see that you have ample breath support for sustained, resonant tones.

Kentish Sir Byng stood for his King,
Bidding the crop-headed Parliament swing;
And, pressing a troop unable to stoop
And see the rogues flourish and honest folk droop,
Marched them along, fifty-score strong,
Great-hearted gentlemen, singing this song.

God for King Charles! Pym and such carles
To the Devil that prompts 'em their treasonous parles!
Cavaliers, up! Lips from the cup,
Hands from the pasty, nor bite take nor sup
Till you're—

CHORUS—
Marching along, fifty-score strong,
Great-hearted gentlemen, singing this song.

Hampden to hell, and his obsequies' knell.
Serve Hazelrig, Fiennes, and young Harry as well!
England, good cheer! Rupert is near!
Kentish and loyalists, keep we not here,

CHORUS—
Marching along, fifty-score strong,
Great-hearted gentlemen, singing this song!

Then, God for King Charles! Pym and his snarls
To the Devil that pricks on such pestilent carles!
Hold by the right, you double your might;
So, onward to Nottingham, fresh for the fight,

Chorus—

March we along, fifty-score strong,
Great-hearted gentlemen, singing this song!

—ROBERT BROWNING

15. Once More unto the Breach, Dear Friends

In this speech from Shakespeare's *Henry V*, the King addresses his soldiers before attacking a French town. One cannot read this speech without being inspired by Henry's pride in his men and his country, and by his driving will to triumph over the French. Read it aloud with feelings of pride and challenge. Follow Shakespeare's own advice, beginning with the sixth line, "Then imitate the action of the tiger," and continuing to the middle of the seventeenth line. Shakespeare was of the opinion that physical states form the foundation of spiritual qualities. In a similar manner, by engaging your body in the physical tensions and relaxations corresponding to the emotional tensions and relaxations involved, appropriate vocal qualities will be aroused. Allow your emotions to color your voice.

In addition, this selection adapts itself to changes in rate, melody, and energy, as well as to projection and strength of tone.

Once more unto the breach, dear friends, once more;
Or close the wall up with our English dead!
In peace there's nothing so becomes a man
As modest stillness and humility:
But when the blast of war blows in our ears,
Then imitate the action of the tiger;
Stiffen the sinews, summon up the blood,
Disguise fair nature with hard-favored rage;
Then lend the eye a terrible aspect;
Let it pry through the portage of the head
Like the brass cannon, let the brow o'erwhelm it
As fearfully as doth a galled rock
O'erhang and jutty his confounded base,
Swill'd with the wild and wasteful ocean.
Now set the teeth and stretch the nostril wide,
Hold hard the breath, and bend up every spirit
To his full height! On, on, you noblest English,
Whose blood is fet from fathers of war-proof!

Fathers that, like so many Alexanders,
Have in these parts from morn till even fought,
And sheathed their swords for lack of argument.
Dishonour not your mothers; now attest
That those whom you call'd fathers did beget you.
Be copy now to men of grosser blood,
And teach them how to war. And you, good yeomen,
Whose limbs were made in England, show us here
The mettle of your pasture; let us swear
That you are worth your breeding; which I doubt not;
For there is none of you so mean and base
That hath not noble lustre in your eyes.
I see you stand like greyhounds in the slips,
Straining upon the start. The game's afoot:
Follow your spirit; and upon this charge
Cry 'God for Harry, England, and Saint George!'
—WILLIAM SHAKESPEARE

16. WHITE DARKNESS *

Although the phenomenon described here is peculiar to Antarctica, you may visualize it in part if you have ever walked some distance in a blizzard. At any rate, try to conceive of a landscape completely bathed in diffused white light. The author's report of the circumstances is colored by his emotional response to the eerie experience. Respond to this feeling as you read.

The third and fourth paragraphs build to a minor climax from a factual analysis of the explorer's experience to a generalization about the reaction of the human mind to a landscape devoid of detail. Increased intensity, without much greater loudness, is one way of emphasizing the gravity of the conclusion.

Antarctica is the land of White Darkness.

Day after day the landscape is veiled in a thick, downy whiteness in which visibility is at times non-existent. Strange things happen, such as the sudden disappearance before the eyes of moving objects.

Two men, dressed in white, may be walking across the snow side by side. They are in a world of complete whiteness. The air is white; earth and sky are white; the wind in the face is white with clouds of snow. Suddenly one man becomes conscious that the other no longer is walking beside him. He has disappeared, as though the thin, white air has dissolved him. Yet he

* Thomas R. Henry, *The White Continent*, William Sloane Associates, New York, 1950, pp. 36, 39–40. (By permission.)

continues to talk as if nothing has happened, unaware that he has become a substanceless phantom. His voice is unchanged; it seems to come from the same direction and the same distance. A moment later he reappears—perhaps floating in the air a few feet ahead and at about eye-level. Still he talks as if he were walking beside the other man. He has no awareness of his own preternatural levitation. . . .

In white darkness there are no shadows; these are seen only when the sun is high in a cloudless sky. As a result Antarctica most of the time is a shadowless land. On a cloudy day the illumination of the landscape is so diffuse that there is no perspective by which one can estimate the contours, size, or distance of white objects. The feet cannot find the snow underfoot. One staggers and stumbles like a drunken man. Walking becomes extremely difficult and tiresome. Sledge and tractor drivers cannot move for days at a time until shadows reappear by which they can detect the parallel ridges which indicate the presence of crevasses. Otherwise they might well stumble blindfolded into an area crisscrossed with thousand-foot-deep rifts in the ice which are the death traps of polar explorers.

Elsewhere, perhaps, shadows do not play an important part in life. But in the infinity of whiteness black images on the snow provide a pattern by which the human mind can function. Without them the difficulties of finding one's way are enormously multiplied. They may mean the difference between reason and utter confusion—in extreme cases between life and death. Where all reality is white it vanishes in whiteness, and the world is left empty of substance.—THOMAS R. HENRY

17. THE HUMANITY OF THE SLAVE

This excerpt is from a speech given by Lincoln in Peoria, Illinois, on October 16, 1854. He is addressing the citizens of the South, asking them to question the concept of slaves as property. Lincoln had a direct, conversational style of speaking which is evident in this selection. Try to picture the excitement of political debate and the burning issues involved in the slavery controversy before you try to read the selection.

You have a problem of energy and directness in reading this material. The questions are pointed and the statements positive and assertive. You must keep the underlying vocal energy all through the reading. See that the phrasing is clear and that there is a variety of melody. You will find that the ideas build toward a climax of energy and positiveness without unnecessary loudness.

You have among you a sneaking individual of the class of native tyrants known as the *slave-dealer*. He watches your necessities, and crawls up to buy

your slave at a speculating price. If you cannot help it, you sell to him; but
if you can help it, you drive him from your door. You despise him utterly;
you do not recognize him as a friend, or even as an honest man. . . . If you
are obliged to deal with him, you try to get through the job without so much
as touching him. . . . Now, why is this? You do not so treat the man who
deals in cotton, corn, or tobacco.

And yet again. There are in the United States and Territories . . . over
four hundred and thirty thousand free blacks. At five hundred dollars per
head, they are worth over two hundred millions of dollars. How comes this
vast amount of property to be running about without owners? We do not
see free horses or free cattle running at large. How is this? All these free
blacks are the descendants of slaves, or have been slaves themselves; and
they would be slaves now but for something that has operated on their
white owners, inducing them at vast pecuniary sacrifice to liberate them.
What is that something? Is there any mistaking it? In all these cases it is
your sense of justice and human sympathy continually telling you that the
poor negro has some natural right to himself,—that those who deny it and
make mere merchandise of him deserve kickings, contempt, and death.

And now why will you ask us to deny the humanity of the slave, and
estimate him as only the equal of the hog?—ABRAHAM LINCOLN

18. A House Divided

This selection is the introduction to the speech Lincoln gave on his nomination to
the Senate in 1858. The controversy between the North and the South over slavery
was acute. Lincoln basically was opposing the extension of slavery. His statement
here is a direct and straightforward analysis of the problem as he saw it.

You must be careful to work out the phrasing and the interrelationships of the
parts of the idea if you are to read this passage effectively. It requires energy and
proper emphasis on both words and phrases. You must be sure to get variety of all
of the vocal elements if the ideas are to be clear and the reading free from monotony.

If we could first know where we are, and whither we are tending, we could
better judge what to do, and how to do it. We are now far into the fifth year
since a policy was initiated with the avowed object and confident promise of
putting an end to slavery agitation. Under the operation of that policy, that
agitation has not only not ceased, but has constantly augmented. In my
opinion it will not cease until a crisis shall have been reached and passed.
"A house divided against itself cannot stand." I believe that this government
cannot endure permanently, half slave and half free. I do not expect the
Union to be dissolved,—I do not expect the house to fall; but I do expect it

will cease to be divided. It will become all one thing, or all the other. Either the opponents of slavery will arrest the further spread of it, and place it where the public mind shall rest in the belief that it is in the course of ultimate extinction; or its advocates will push it forward till it shall become alike lawful in all the States, old as well as new, North as well as South.—ABRAHAM LINCOLN

19. THE CRIME AGAINST KANSAS

Sumner was one of the earliest and most fiery Senatorial advocates of the abolition of slavery. This speech was against the extension of slavery into the Nebraska Territory, which included Kansas. Sumner was quick to use invective in his speaking. For the violent attacks on the South contained in this speech, he was severely cane whipped by Preston Brooks of South Carolina.

The basic problem in this selection is one of energy and force. Be sure that you are communicating the urgency and positiveness of the speaker. Analyze the excerpt, and see how it builds to a climax. Be sure that you vary the energy as is necessary. At the same time, there should be variety of rate and melody. See that your repeated reading of the word "swindle" does not become monotonous. Conjure up a slightly different pattern of indignation with each repetition of the word, and allow your feelings to color your vocal quality.

Sir, the Nebraska Bill was in every respect a swindle. It was a swindle of the North by the South. On the part of those who had already completely enjoyed their share of the Missouri Compromise, it was a swindle of those whose share was yet absolutely untouched; and the plea of unconstitutionality set up—like the plea of usury after the borrowed money has been enjoyed—did not make it less a swindle. Urged as a bill of peace, it was a swindle of the whole country. Urged as opening the doors to slave-masters with their slaves, it was a swindle of popular sovereignty in its asserted doctrine. Urged as sanctioning popular sovereignty, it was a swindle of slave-masters in their asserted rights. It was a swindle of a broad territory, thus cheated of protection against slavery. It was a swindle of a great cause, early espoused by Washington, Franklin, and Jefferson, surrounded by the best fathers of the Republic. Sir, it was a swindle of God-given, inalienable rights. Turn it over, look at it on all sides, and it is everywhere a swindle; and, if the word I now employ has not the authority of classical usage, it has, on this occasion, the indubitable authority of fitness. No other word will adequately express the mingled meanness and wickedness of the cheat.— CHARLES SUMNER

20. The Wind *

Before you begin to read, put yourself in the reflective and rather melancholy mood indicated by the passage. Then respond to the specific images of the selection within the emotional context of the whole.

Here is a selection which emphasizes the idea of monotony. As a result, it is best read with a rather narrow pitch range. The pitch changes you use should be smooth and gradual, rather than abrupt and startling. There are many long sounds in the language of the selection; these can profitably be given strength by added duration.

I don't know whether you know that long, sad wind that blows so steadily across the thousands of miles of Midwest flatlands in the summertime. If you don't it will be hard for you to understand the feeling I have about it. Even if you do know it, you may not understand.

To me the summer wind in the Midwest is one of the most melancholy things in all life. It comes from so far and blows so gently and yet so relentlessly; it rustles the leaves and the branches of the maple trees in a sort of symphony of sadness, and it doesn't pass on and leave them still. It just keeps coming, like the infinite flow of Old Man River. You could—and you do—wear out your lifetime on the dusty plains with that wind of futility blowing in your face. And when you are worn out and gone, the wind—still saying nothing, still so gentle and sad and timeless—is still blowing across the prairies, and will blow in the faces of the little men who follow you, forever.—ERNIE PYLE

21. Two Years before the Mast

In 1840, Dana made a voyage as a seaman from Boston to the west coast of North America. This description is a part of the record which young Dana made of the trip. Imagine that you are standing on the deck of an old sailing ship in the fog. Out of the fog come the sounds which the author describes to you.

You must pay particular attention to your time pattern, including rate, duration, and pause, in reading this selection. Phrasing may be a problem for you unless you analyze it carefully before you read. There must be some subtle changes in melody and quality to bring out the meaning.

Towards morning the wind went down, and during the whole forenoon we lay tossing about in a dead calm, and in the midst of a thick fog. . . .

The calm of the morning reminds me of a scene . . . which I remember from its being the first time that I had heard the near breathing of whales.

* Ernie Pyle, *Home Country*, William Sloane Associates, New York, 1947, p. 3. (By permission.)

It was on the night that we passed between the Faulkland Islands and Staten Land. We had the watch from twelve to four, and, coming upon the deck, found the little brig lying perfectly still, enclosed in a thick fog, and the sea as smooth as though oil had been poured upon it; yet now and then a long, low swell rolling under its surface, slightly lifting the vessel, but without breaking the glassy smoothness of the water. We were surrounded far and near by shoals of sluggish whales and grampuses, which the fog prevented our seeing, rising slowly to the surface, or perhaps lying out at length, heaving out those lazy, deep, and long-drawn breathings which give such an impression of supineness and strength. Some of the watch were asleep, and the others were quiet, so that there was nothing to break the illusion, and I stood leaning over the bulwarks, listening to the slow breathings of the mighty creatures,—now one breaking the water just alongside, whose black body I almost fancied that I could see through the fog; and again another, which I could just hear in the distance,—until the low and regular swell seemed like the heaving of the ocean's mighty bosom to the sound of its own heavy and long-drawn respirations.—RICHARD HENRY DANA

22. LIFE ON THE MISSISSIPPI

Mark Twain had a gift for telling interesting stories in a simple, direct manner. In these two excerpts from *Life on the Mississippi*, he has captured the flavor of life in a small Missouri town on the Mississippi in the middle of the nineteenth century. Try to visualize the two characters he is describing and to feel the author's attitudes toward them. Try to tell each of the stories as though you had observed the characters in them.

In both of these selections, you must strive to get variety of melody if you are to picture these two persons fully. The phrasing must be carefully worked out in both, to achieve the conversational quality of Twain's style. The second excerpt presents a problem in energy, especially in the quotation from the mate. Work for an easy, conversational directness in both selections.

a. By and by one of our boys went away. He was not heard of for a long time. At last he turned up as apprentice engineer or "striker" on a steamboat. This thing shook the bottom out of all my Sunday-school teachings. That boy had been notoriously worldly, and I just the reverse; yet he was exalted to this eminence, and I left in obscurity and misery. There was nothing generous about this fellow in his greatness. . . . Whenever his boat was laid up he would come home and swell around the town in his blackest and greasiest clothes, so that nobody could help remembering that he was a steamboatman; and he used all sorts of steamboat technicalities in his talk,

as if he were so used to them that he forgot common people could not understand them. . . . This fellow had money, too, and hair-oil. Also an ignorant
silver watch and a showy brass watch-chain. . . . If ever a youth was cor-
dially admired and hated by his comrades, this one was. . . . When his
boat blew up at last, it diffused a tranquil contentment among us such as we
had not known for months. But when he came home the next week, alive,
renowned, and appeared in church all battered up and bandaged, a shining
hero, stared at and wondered at by everybody, it seemed to us that the par-
tiality of Providence for an undeserving reptile had reached a point where
it was open to criticism.

b. I was sorry I hated the mate so, because it was not in (young) human
nature not to admire him. He was huge and muscular, his face was bearded
and whiskered all over; he had a red woman and a blue woman tattooed on
his right arm . . . ; and in the matter of profanity he was sublime. . . .
When he gave even the simplest order, he discharged it like a blast of lightning, and sent a long, reverberating peal of profanity thundering after it.
I could not help contrasting the way in which the average landsman would
give an order with the mate's way of doing it. If the landsman should wish
the gangplank moved a foot farther forward, he would probably say: "James,
or William, one of you push that plank forward, please"; but put the mate
in his place, and he would roar out: "Here, now start that gangplank
for'ard! Lively, now! *What*'re you about! Snatch it! *snatch* it! There! there!
Aft again! aft again! Don't you hear me? Dash it to dash! are you going to
sleep over it! *'Vast* heaving. 'Vast heaving, I tell you! Going to heave it
clear astern? WHERE're you going with that barrel! *for'ard* with it 'fore I
make you swallow it, you dash-dash-dash-*dashed* split between a tired mud-
turtle and a crippled hearse-horse!"
I wished I could talk like that.—MARK TWAIN

23. THE FALL OF THE HOUSE OF USHER

Poe is noted for the gloomy, melancholy moods which he created in his writing.
This selection is an excellent example of such a mood created by the description of
the landscape and the reactions it arouses. The story to which this is an introduction is a tale of horror such as only Poe could write. Try to picture a dark day in
winter as you read.
The over-all rate of this reading is slow. In it, you must pay particular attention
to duration and pause; if you allow the rate to be too fast you will not communicate the mood. Because of the slow rate, phrasing for breathing may present a
problem. See what you can do with quality to set the emotional mood which Poe
is trying to establish. Be sure that there is melody variety, as well.

During the whole of a dull, dark, and soundless day in the autumn of the year, when the clouds hung oppressively low in the heavens, I had been passing alone, on horseback, through a singularly dreary tract of country; and at length found myself, as the shades of the evening drew on, within view of the melancholy House of Usher. I know not how it was—but, with the first glimpse of the building, a sense of insufferable gloom pervaded my spirit. I say insufferable; for the feeling was unrelieved by any of that half-pleasurable, because poetic, sentiment with which the mind usually receives even the sternest natural images of the desolate or terrible. I looked upon the scene before me—upon the mere house, and the simple landscape features of the domain, upon the bleak walls, upon the vacant eye-like windows, upon a few rank sedges, and upon a few white trunks of decayed trees—with an utter depression of soul which I can compare to no earthly sensation more properly than to the after-dream of the reveller upon opium: the bitter lapse into everyday life, the hideous dropping off of the veil. There was an iciness, a sinking, a sickening of the heart, an unredeemed dreariness of thought which no goading of the imagination could torture into aught of the sublime. What was it—I paused to think—what was it that so unnerved me in the contemplation of the House of Usher?—EDGAR ALLAN POE

24. THE NEW SOUTH

Henry Grady came north from Georgia, in 1886, to deliver the speech from which this sample is taken. The speech was given before the New England Society of New York. Grady created a sensational effect in this effort to bring about understanding between North and South. Remember that he was giving the speech before a basically hostile audience in an era when the Civil War was still being fought in words. You must try to see the picture which he is painting for his audience before you try to read the selection aloud.

Since many of the sentences are long and complex, you will need to analyze the phrasing carefully. Use melody and time changes to convey the complexities of meaning. The second paragraph suggests a complete change of mood. A contrast in rate and melody pattern may reflect this shift in feeling.

Let me picture to you the footsore Confederate soldier, as, buttoning up in his faded gray jacket the parole which was to bear testimony to his children of his fidelity and faith, he turned his face southward from Appomattox in April, 1865. Think of him as—ragged, half-starved, heavy-hearted, enfeebled by want and wounds, having fought to exhaustion—he surrenders his gun, wrings the hands of his comrades in silence, and lifting his tear-stained and pallid face for the last time to the graves that dot the old Virginia hills, pulls his gray cap over his brow and begins the slow and painful journey. What does he find—let me ask you who went to your homes eager to find, in the welcome you had justly earned, full payment for four years' sacrifice—what does he find, when, having followed the battle-stained cross against overwhelming odds, dreading death not half so much as surrender, he reaches the home he left so prosperous and beautiful? He finds his house in ruins, his farm devastated, his slaves free, his stock killed, his barns empty, his trade destroyed, his money worthless; his social system, feudal in its magnificence, swept away; his people without law or legal status; his comrades slain, and the burdens of others heavy on his shoulders. Crushed by defeat, his very traditions gone; without money, credit, employment, material, or training; and besides all this, confronted with the gravest problem that ever met human intelligence—the establishment of a status for the vast body of his liberated slaves.

What does he do—this hero in gray . . . ? Does he sit down in sullenness and despair? Not for a day. Surely God, who had stripped him of his prosperity, inspired him in his adversity. As ruin was never before so overwhelming, never was restoration swifter. The soldier stepped from the trenches into the furrow; horses that had charged Federal guns marched before the plough; and the fields that ran red with human blood in April were green with the harvest in June.—HENRY W. GRADY

25. THE FIFTY-YARD DASH *

This whimsical selection offers you an opportunity to relive some of your own childhood experiences—your mental victories and actual defeats. Recapture them and project yourself into the language of the author.

The selection is particularly well adapted to changes in rate and melody and to the use of pause. Since the language is colloquial, some of the characteristic assimilations of informal speech may be used, but the articulation should be clear.

That spring Longfellow School announced that a track meet was to be held, one school to compete against another; *everybody* to participate.

Here, I believed, was my chance. In my opinion I would be first in every event.

Somehow or other, however, continuous meditation on the theme of athletics had the effect of growing into a fury of anticipation that continued all day and all night, so that before the day of the track meet I had run the

* William Saroyan, *My Name Is Aram*, Harcourt, Brace and Company, Inc., New York, 1940. (By permission.)

fifty-yard dash any number of hundreds of times, had jumped the running broad jump, the standing broad jump, and the high jump, and in each event had made my competitors look like weaklings.

This tremendous inner activity, which was strictly Yoga, changed on the day of the track meet into fever.

The time came at last for me and three other athletes . . . to go to our marks, get set, and go; and I did, in a blind rush of speed which I knew had never before occurred in the history of athletics.

It seemed to me that never before had any living man moved so swiftly. Within myself I ran the fifty yards fifty times before I so much as opened my eyes to find out how far back I had left the other runners. I was very much amazed at what I saw.

Three boys were four yards ahead of me and going away.

It was incredible. It was unbelievable, but it was obviously the truth. There ought to be some mistake, but there wasn't. There they were, ahead of me, going away.

Well, it simply meant that I would have to overtake them, with my eyes open, and win the race. This I proceeded to do. They continued, incredibly, however, to go away, in spite of my intention. I became irritated and decided to put them in their places for the impertinence, and began releasing all the mysterious vital forces within myself that I had. Somehow or other, however, not even this seemed to bring me any closer to them and I felt that in some strange way I was being betrayed. If so, I decided, I would shame my betrayer by winning the race in spite of the betrayal, and once again I threw fresh life and energy into my running. There wasn't a great distance still to do, but I knew I would be able to do it.

Then I knew I wouldn't.

The race was over.

I was last, by ten yards.

—WILLIAM SAROYAN

26. AARON BURR

In reading this selection, try to visualize the person whom you know who most resembles Clark's portrait of Burr. React in your own way to each of the qualities, good or bad, portrayed in the successive phrases of the second paragraph. Try to reflect your feelings in your voice.

This selection needs careful phrasing and the use of pause. Both the individual short phrases and the selection as a whole need to be read in such a way as to produce a cumulative effect. Experiment with changes in pitch and rate to contribute to this effect.

To fill a long felt want, the lawyers have invented the phrase "moral insanity"; the incurable defect in Burr's make-up was "moral idiocy," so to speak: that is to say he was constitutionally and utterly void of moral principles and wholly incapable of discerning or appreciating it in others. Morally, he was totally color-blind.

Whether outstripping all his fellows at Princeton; deliberately scouting the religion of his fathers; fighting valiantly as a soldier of the Revolution; making love to all women, bewitching many and marrying a widow older than himself; standing proudly at the head of the New York Bar; filling the great offices of Attorney-General, Senator of the United States, and Vice-President; remaining silent and motionless when a word or motion would have made him President; killing Alexander Hamilton in a duel; fleeing in disguise a fugitive from justice; dreaming of an empire, himself the emperor; plotting the ruin and dismemberment of his country; on trial for his life on a charge of high treason; a vagabond in Europe, to-day dancing with ladies of the blood royal, to-morrow starving in a garret; stealing back muffled incognito to his native land; cut by his old acquaintances, repulsed by his quondam friends; at the age of nearly fourscore wedding Madame Jumel against her will; carrying for forty years a load of obloquy sufficient to have damned half the world; at last on the banks of the River Styx cracking jokes with the grim Ferryman himself;—anywhere, everywhere, in all places, at all times, and under all circumstances, he is the same: bland, bold, brilliant, amiable, seductive, plausible . . . ; and utterly without trace of conscience.
—CHAMP CLARK

27. THE VALUE OF DISSENSION

Someone has said that a dictatorship is like a fine steamer. It rides the waves easily and the passengers are comfortable in their staterooms; but when it strikes the rocks, it goes down and all are lost. Democracy, on the other hand, is like a raft. All of the passengers continually have wet feet, but it stays afloat. In the following selection, written in 1817 as a speech in defense of a man charged with sedition, Lord Jeffrey deals with a problem as contemporary as tomorrow morning. Since the issue is perennial, each of us must meet it for himself. Remember the criticisms of Congressional wranglings you have heard or read, and reply to them in the words of Jeffrey.

This selection provides an excellent opportunity for using changes in rate and pitch, coupled with proper use of pause, to put phrases in meaningful relationship to each other. The logical structure of the speech is clear, but subordination of some phrases and forceful emphasis of others are needed to carry the ideas to the listener. The type of analysis suggested in Chapter 9 will help you to decide how to read this selection.

There is a dissension known to this country, and known to all free countries, and to them only, which, however terrible it may appear to the sons of habitual slavery, or the minions of arbitrary power, or the contented and envied possessors of present influence, is of that wholesome nature that on it the life and health of the Constitution ultimately depend. It is not a frightful commotion, but a healthful exercise, not an exhausting fever, but a natural movement indicating and maintaining that vigour unimpaired. In a free country, where the principles of Government are well understood, and the laws well administered, parties will ever be found opposed to parties. . . . This dissension is the life and heart and spirit of our Constitution; and true policy should promote discussion on those great points on which discussion must always be keen, and, in some degree, stormy and violent, because it is on them that the liberty, the prosperity, and happiness of the nation depend, and to them that all men of spirit, ingenuity, and talents have devoted their whole lives. . . . If this dissension were prevented, liberty would be extinguished. That very hostility which appears to excite so much apprehension is the parent of public prosperity, and of all the advantages in a free state for which it is worth while to contend.—LORD FRANCIS JEFFREY

28. UNCLE STEVE COLE AND THE BEAR *

The colloquial quality of the language of this selection makes it particularly well adapted to the rhythm and melody of conversational speech. Pyle does not pretend to pass judgment on Uncle Steve's veracity. He simply tells the story as he heard it. As you read, you should adopt the same approach. Respond to the excitement of the battle with the bear, but do not overplay it, or laugh at it, or in any way indicate you think it is anything but the unvarnished truth.

Use the contractions and sound substitutions indicated in Pyle's spelling, but do not attempt to create a Tennessee mountain dialect unless you are thoroughly familiar with it. Melody and time changes can be used to good effect to point up the excitement of the fight and the contrasting mood of the description which follows.

Uncle Steve Cole lived in the Great Smokies National Park in Tennessee. He was a typical mountain man of the old school. I dropped in one afternoon to talk to him. He lit a fire, and sat down beside it and began spitting into the fireplace. He wasn't chewing tobacco, but he spit into the fireplace. He wasn't chewing tobacco, but he spit into the fireplace all the time anyhow.

Uncle Steve had killed more bears than any other man in those mountains. He hadn't the remotest idea how many, but he had killed them with muzzle-

* Ernie Pyle, *Home Country*, William Sloane Associates, New York, 1947, pp. 103–104. (By permission.)

loaders, modern rifles, deadfalls, clubs, and axes, and he even choked one to death with his bare hands. I got him to tell me that story.

He and a neighbor went out one night. The dogs treed a bear. Uncle Steve's story of it took half an hour to tell, but the gist of it is that they built a fire and the bear finally came down the tree. Uncle Steve stood there until the bear's body was pressing on the muzzle of the gun and then he pulled the trigger. "I figured I couldn't miss that way," Uncle Steve said. He didn't miss, but the shot didn't kill the bear. It ran fifty yards or so, and then the dogs were on it. And the first thing Uncle Steve knew, the bear had clenched his great jaws right down on a dog's snout and was crushing it to pieces.

Now, Uncle Steve's gun was an old-fashioned, sawed-off, muzzle-loading hog rifle, and he didn't have time to reload it. So, to save the dog, he rushed up to the bear from behind, put his legs around it, and started prying the dog's snout out of the bear's mouth. "And before I knew what happened," said Uncle Steve, "the bear let go of the dog and got my right hand in his mouth, and began a-crunchin' and a-growlin' and a-eatin' on my hand. One long tooth went right through the palm of my hand and another went through the back of my hand. There wasn't nothin' for me to do but reach round with my left hand for the bear's throat. I got him by the goozle and started clampin' down. Pretty soon he let go. Then I just choked him till he was deader'n four o'clock." Uncle Steve spit into the fireplace.

Mrs. Cole was sitting on the bed, listening. Nobody said anything for a minute. Then Mrs. Cole chuckled and said, "Four o'clock ain't dead." Uncle Steve didn't dignify her quibble with an answer. He just spit into the fireplace again.—ERNIE PYLE

29. THE FORCE OF CONVERSATION

Dr. Holmes has caught, in this selection from *The Autocrat of the Breakfast Table*, a factor in our thinking and writing which all of us have experienced. What is the value of a conference with your instructor? Why do you like to study with others? What happens to your thinking in a bull session? Let Dr. Holmes speak for you as you re-create these experiences.

The selection is particularly well adapted to the use of pause and variations in duration, melody, and quality. Try to reflect changes in meaning and imagery by the use of these vocal factors.

Besides, there is another thing about this talking, which you forget. It shapes our thoughts for us;—the waves of conversation roll them as the surf rolls the pebbles on the shore. Let me modify the image a little. I rough out my thoughts in talk as an artist models in clay. Spoken language is so plastic,—you can pat and coax, and spread and shave, and rub out, and fill up, and stick on so easily, when you work that soft material, that there is nothing like it for modelling. Out of it come the shapes which you turn into marble or bronze in your immortal books, if you happen to write such. Or, to use another illustration, writing or printing is like shooting with a rifle; you may hit your reader's mind, or miss it;—but talking is like playing at a mark with the pipe of an engine; if it is within reach, and you have time enough, you can't help hitting it.—OLIVER WENDELL HOLMES

Index